A NEW COVENANT

The Book of Mormon

Like potato chips—I couldn't consume just one chapter at a time. But more than that, I felt honored to read this book. After establishing an insightful foundation about covenants, it begins to soar into lofty spiritual concepts of eternal value. I often stopped to savor some of either Rich's thought-provoking sentences and scriptures, or those from his treasure trove of other writers. Although his effort is obvious, it is evident that this book came not from him, but through him. The readers will appreciate the expansive purpose of the Book of Mormon, be blessed considering the unbounded love of God, and gain a feeling of overwhelming self-worth. If taken to heart, they will respond in a life-changing way and a desire to assist in fulfilling our Father's precious covenants.
— Faye Shaw

Rich done an amazing job, and I liken it to taking a diamond in the rough and then cutting and polishing facets on it. His book is like looking at the jewel, a facet at a time, each chapter, or story, or illustration allows one to see the subject from a different perspective but never diminishes the jewel. **— Neil Simmons**

As I read the draft of Richard's new book on the covenants as illuminated by the Book of Mormon I quickly realized that it was the most important work he has written. For those who have made little study of the covenants, and even for many who have, it will be like opening the eyes of the blind. Scattered through the scriptures like the pieces of a puzzle are references to the covenants which Richard has prayerfully fitted together to reveal an awesome vision. A vast panorama that brings into clear focus God's loving, eternal plan which includes each one of us. A grand perspective from which we see beyond the adversities of life, to the meaning and purpose in all things. Here we find God actively working through His covenants to establish us eternally in His presence where there is fullness of joy unspeakable and full of glory. Little understood today, covenants are the most sacred, binding, and protective of all agreements. The covenants of God have directed the course of history, and are working out His purposes in these closing days. Take the time to enter into the words of this book, allow them to quicken your thinking. They have the potential to remove roadblocks in the way of our spiritual growth and preparation.

—John Moody

A NEW COVENANT

The Book of Mormon

(with Study Guide)

By

Richard E. Rupe

First Edition

ISBN: 9781091643512

Acronyms and Quotations

There are many groups that trace their roots to Joseph Smith Jr. and the founding of the church on April 6, 1830. The largest, most well-known group is The Church of Jesus Christ of Latter-day Saints **(LDS)** headquartered in Salt Lake City, Utah. This group was formed by those who, following the assassination of the prophet Joseph Smith Jr., chose to align themselves with Brigham Young and the greater part of the then existing quorum of twelve apostles. While the term "Mormon" is used in a general sense to apply to all who believe in the Book of Mormon, it is a term now most often used to describe a member of The Church of Jesus Christ of Latter-day Saints commonly called the Mormon Church.

The second largest branch of Mormonism, headquartered in Independence, Missouri, has since its inception been known as the Reorganized Church of Jesus Christ of Latter Day Saints **(RLDS).** That is, until 2001 when it changed its name to the Community of Christ. This group formed from those who refused to follow Brigham Young and subsequently united under the leadership of Joseph Smith III, son of the martyred prophet.

Another branch of Mormonism mentioned in this writing is the Church of Christ (Temple Lot) headquartered in Independence, Missouri. This branch evolved from five branches in Illinois and Indiana that, in the 1860s found themselves unaffiliated with any of the existing groups. Subsequently, they united under the leadership of Granville Hedrick and currently occupy the "Temple Lot" in Independence, Missouri; the space believed designated by Joseph Smith Jr. to be the site for the temple of the New Jerusalem.

Although the term "Restorationists" is not used in this particular writing, it should be noted that it is a term often employed to refer to any and all groups tracing their heritage to Joseph Smith Jr. and the restoration of the church on April 6, 1830; but, also at times to refer specifically to independent Restoration branches that have disassociated themselves from the then RLDS Church and believe that the church is in an unorganized state because no legitimate higher quorums are in existence. Capitalized terms such as "Restored Church," "Restoration," and "Restoration Movement" also are references to the original church as formed on April 6, 1830.

Unless otherwise specified, Bible references will be from the King James Version. Book of Mormon references will refer to the RLDS 1908 Authorized Edition with corresponding LDS references following separated by a "/" (i.e. RLDS/LDS). Likewise, Doctrine and Covenants references will be RLDS followed by LDS.

RLDS reference/ LDS reference

IV	Inspired Version of the Bible (Joseph Smith Translation)
DC	Doctrine and Covenants
NIV	New International Version
NLT	New Living Translation
BC	Time before the estimated birth of Christ
AD	Time after the estimated birth of Christ

Use of Wikipedia

While recognizing scholarly limitations inherent in its use, I nevertheless have chosen to use Wikipedia as a resource, very selectively, for informational purposes only, where greater clarity seems to be provided.

Footnote/Endnote/Selected Bibliography Explanation

Footnotes, appearing on the bottom of a page, are often used to provide further clarification or identification of a person or subject-matter. Endnotes appear following the last page of regular text grouped by chapter providing source note references. Source Note references are usually succinct entries (author, title and page references) that can then be used to point to the Selected Bibliography entry which contains more comprehensive information about a particular source.

Dedication

First, I dedicate this work to our Heavenly Father and His Only Begotten Son, Jesus Christ, who together determined, before the annals of time, that in the New Covenant they would do for mankind what we cannot do for ourselves. I humbly acknowledge that in reality this book is God's more than it is mine. Without the grace of God this book would not have been possible.

Secondly, I would like to dedicate this book to Ray Treat and Tom Nunn, and at the same time acknowledge their passing. Their collective covenantal works have served as a blessing not only to myself, but to so many others.

In Appreciation

I want to express my appreciation to John Moody for being my friend and mentor, always being willing to assist with the vast store of knowledge that is his. My thanks and appreciation go to others who have reviewed this work, namely: Neil Simmons, Gary Whiting, Nancy Short, and Daniel Muhlenkamp. Their helpful comments and honest feedback has served to give me confidence that I will not be unduly embarrassed by what I have written.

A special thanks goes to Faye Shaw. Faye is not only a subject-matter expert, but also one who knows grammar. Faye would say exciting things to me such as: "You can never have only one comma between a subject and a verb." Faye's invaluable editing skills and suggestions have made this book much more professional and readable that it otherwise would have been.

Lastly, I am indebted to several groups who have in one form or another been subjected to presentations of this material as it was in the process of development: namely: the First People Community of Christ Congregation; the Marysville Michigan Reorganized Church of Jesus Christ of Latter Day Saints; and, the Monetville Community of Christ Congregation of Ontario Canada.

For that same spirit which doth possess your bodies at the time that ye go out of this life, that same spirit will have power to possess your body in that eternal world.

\- Alma 16:232/34:34

Contents

PREFACE

As we begin our study of the New Covenant, I want to do so with this bit of explanation. Our God is a covenant-keeping God. Our three books of scripture reveal His covenants, His footsteps, where He has been and where He is going. The Book of Mormon is viewed as the New Covenant with the purpose of fulfilling all those covenants God has made with the houses of Israel and Judah.

This then was to be a book about covenant - which it is. However, I found myself being captivated by this from Hebrews:

> For this is the covenant that I will make with the house of Israel after those days, saith the Lord; I will put my laws into their mind, and write them in their hearts: and I will be to them a God, and they shall be to me a people:
>
> And they shall not teach every man his neighbour, and every man his brother, saying, Know the Lord: for all shall know me, from the least to the greatest (Heb. 8:10-11).

I found myself trying to imagine what this type of life would be like: to have such a relationship with God that we would no longer need anyone to teach us about Him. In attempting to follow this train of thought, I ended up in a place entirely unexpected - the grace, mercy and love of God. I believe this is the place where God wanted me, and this book itself, to end up. I found these thoughts to be literally life-changing. The heart of this book then has unexpectedly turned out to be about this anticipated relationship with God which typifies the New Covenant.

Traditionally, in the Restoration, I don't believe a whole lot has been written about God's grace. Perhaps another way to say this is that I don't believe it has been a primary emphasis. Does my focusing on God's grace mean that I have now tossed aside doctrine; that I have tossed aside the principles of the gospel which include repentance, faith, baptisms, the laying on of hands, the resurrection of the dead and eternal judgment (see Heb. 6:1-2)? Does that mean that I now deny the justice of God? No, and no. Merely because I do not always list all the steps involved in coming to Christ does not mean I am denying the doctrine of Christ.

Let us use as an example the gospel of John. It is somewhat striking to realize that in his entire book he never, even once, mentions the word "repent." "Believe" is the word used most often, with about fifty or more occurrences of believe, but not one of repent.

> But these are written that you may believe that Jesus is the Christ, the Son of God, and that by believing you may have life in his name (John 20:31).

Another example, the Book of Mormon, would include the phrases: "Come unto Christ," "Come unto him," and "Come unto me." Many times these covenant-meaning phrases by ancient writers would be accompanied by words of repentance and baptism, but just as often they would be used alone or with other expressions such as "believe in him," "offer your whole souls," "lay hold upon every good gift," or "be perfected in him."

When we fail to respond to Christ's invitation to "come unto him" he continues to strive with us until that day when it becomes apparent that we have no desire to respond, ever. Then the only alternative left to God is one of judgment.

> "There is only one real law – the law of the universe," said Dorothy Sayers. "It may be fulfilled either by way of judgment or by way of grace, but it must be fulfilled one way or the other."[1]

Grace would be meaningless without God's justice and judgment. I believe that a true relationship with Christ presupposes obedience to the gospel ordinances. I believe that the function of the Holy Spirit is to purge the dross from our lives. I believe that the closer we are to God the more aware we become of sin in our lives and the necessity of repentance. I believe that grace is a more powerful motivator to repent than judgment. It was John Newton who wrote in Amazing Grace; "'twas grace that taught my heart to fear."

PREFACE

My point in writing is not to deny doctrine but to make the larger point so well expressed by Arthur Oakman:

> The call of our day is the call of love…The real purpose of life can be understood only in the love of God. No human life is adequately nor intelligently motivated until it responds in the aura of this grace.

My inspiration for writing this book came in the form of a testimony given at a "Book of Mormon in Zion Conference" in Independence, Missouri, in 2015, where the Book of Mormon was identified as the New Covenant (see the opening chapter). At the time I was busily involved in getting ready to publish my second book, ***The Book of Mormon: God's Plan of Salvation***. However, as the "pain" of writing that book wore off, I found myself not being able to put this testimony aside. God began the process of pointing out to me the possibilities of, and the vital importance, of writing a book on the New Covenant.

I realize as I attempt to write on this covenant topic, that I am following in the footsteps of many giants such as Ray Treat, Tom Nunn and others who have had an impact on my life. I am extremely grateful to these stalwarts of the faith and all those throughout time who have searched for a city "whose builder and maker is God."

However, as never before, I am convinced of the timeliness of this topic. The conditions on earth are such that the world is on the brink of not only disintegration and chaos; but, also of unbelievable blessings and opportunities for redemption inherit in the New Covenant.

I have found that over the past three years as I have studied and contemplated the New Covenant, it has changed my life. It has given me not only a greater understanding and knowledge of God's Plan of Salvation, but also such a deep sense of joy and gratitude that I can scarcely restrain.

A NEW COVENANT

The New Covenant is a corporate as well as an individual covenant. A corporate covenant made with the houses of Israel and Judah; and, an individual covenant where He writes His laws upon our hearts and minds (see Hebrews 8:8, 10-11). The New Covenant life is a unique and God-centered way of life, birthed in one individual at a time that captures the essence of what it means to be created in the image of God.

As we begin our study, I searched for one scripture that could best capture what God has in mind for us.

> In the year that king Uzziah died I saw also the Lord sitting upon a throne, high and lifted up, and his train filled the temple.
> Above it stood the seraphims: each one had six wings; with twain he covered his face, and with twain he covered his feet, and with twain he did fly.
> And one cried unto another, and said, Holy, holy, holy, is the Lord of hosts: the whole earth is full of his glory.
> And the posts of the door moved at the voice of him that cried, and the house was filled with smoke.
> Then said I, Woe is me! for I am undone; because I am a man of unclean lips, and I dwell in the midst of a people of unclean lips: for mine eyes have seen the King, the Lord of hosts.
> Then flew one of the seraphims unto me, having a live coal in his hand, which he had taken with the tongs from off the altar:
> And he laid it upon my mouth, and said, Lo, this hath touched thy lips; and thine iniquity is taken away, and thy sin purged (Is. 6:1-7).

Isaiah in his own way, has just described for us the New Covenant. It's about having a live coal taken with tongs from the altar of God, and having it laid upon our mouths and touching our lips; therefore, it's about having our iniquity taken away and our sins purged. It's about beholding the fullness of God's glory, and dwelling in His presence forever and ever. It's about having a fullness of joy. It's about having a peace that surpasses all understanding. It's about being one with creation, one with God.

In 1872, when the Oglala Sioux medicine man, Black Elk, was only nine years old, he was suddenly taken ill and left prone and unresponsive for several days. During that time he had a great vision:

> Then I was standing on the highest mountain of them all, and round about beneath me was the whole hoop of the world. And while I stood there I saw more than I can tell and I understood more than I saw; for I was seeing in a sacred manner the shapes of all things in the spirit, and the shape of all shapes as they must live together like one being. And I saw that the sacred hoop of my people was one of many hoops that made one circle, wide as the daylight and as starlight, and in the center grew one mighty flowering tree to shelter all the children of one mother and one father. And I saw that it was holy[2] – Black Elk, 1872.

Black Elk saw more than he could tell and understood more than he saw. Black Elk was telling us that words were inadequate to describe his experience. That's the New Covenant. As I have struggled to adequately express in written word God's intention for us in the New Covenant, I have come to realize that while indeed we can teach the basics of the New Covenant, that in the final analysis it is a concept that must be spiritually revealed; hence, as you the reader study this topic, it should be with a prayer on your heart that God will do as the New Covenant says, "write these words on your heart."

To catch the New Covenant vision is to follow in the footsteps of mystics such as Black Elk, Isaiah, Ezekiel, John on the Isle of Patmos, the Apostle Paul, and all the Saints who have held communion with the general assembly and Church of the First Born. I believe that we will never encounter any topic more important in our spiritual lives than that of the New Covenant.

PART I:

THE OLD AND THE NEW

The Old Covenant attains its object only as it brings men to a sense of their utter sinfulness and their hopeless impotence to deliver themselves. As long as they have not learned this, no offer of the New Covenant life can lay hold of them.

\- Andrew Murray

CHAPTER 1

Making a New Covenant

I will put my law within them, and I will write it on their hearts. And I will be their God, and they shall be my people (Jer. 31:33).

The genesis of inspiration for writing this book came a few years back upon hearing a testimony recited by Ron Smith of Lamoni, Iowa, at a Book of Mormon Conference in Independence, Missouri. The following testimony related by Smith is the testimony of Tom Nyawere, an African from the nation of Kenya. It has spurred my study of the New Covenant to determine how it fits into God's overall plan of salvation.

The Testimony

> When I (Tom Nyawere) first heard about the Book of Mormon I had a question. My question was, "Does God have any book that is inspired for scripture besides the Holy Bible?" I did not have anybody to teach me so I asked the Holy Spirit.
>
> After a few days I had a dream. In my dream I saw a beautiful thing that was built. It had lots of water on top. The water was not in any container but it was not falling off. So I had to go closer to find out what was happening. As I got closer I heard a voice coming out of the water and I knew I should ask my question. So I asked. "Does God have any book inspired for scripture besides the Holy Bible?"
>
> The voice out of the water said, "What is that book in your hand?" I held it up, "It's a Bible." The voice said "Read Hebrews 8:8." I opened the Bible and read,
>
>> "Behold the days come saith the Lord when **I will** make a new covenant with the house of Israel and with the house of Judah."

> And the voice said, "What do you think the New Covenant is?" I said, "It's the New Testament." The voice said, "But it's written in the New Testament. What is that other book that you have?" I held it up and said, "It's a Book of Mormon." The voice said, "That is the New Covenant."

Reading a little further in Hebrews 8 we find this New Covenant explanation:

> For this *is* the covenant that I will make with the house of Israel after those days, saith the Lord; I will put my laws into their mind, and write them in their hearts: and I will be to them a God, and they shall be to me a people:
> And they shall **not** teach every man his neighbour, and every man his brother, saying, Know the Lord: ***for all shall know me,*** from the least to the greatest (Heb. 8:10-11).

For those familiar with Restoration scripture, it comes as no surprise that the Book of Mormon is known as the New Covenant. However, for me, it was exciting to hear this testimony from someone with no previous knowledge of the Book of Mormon that confirms the following words of Section 83/84[a], that the Book of Mormon is indeed the New Covenant:

> Your minds in times past have been darkened because of unbelief, and because you have treated lightly the things you have received, which vanity and unbelief hath brought the whole church under condemnation.
> And this condemnation resteth upon the children of Zion, even all; and they shall remain under this condemnation until they repent and remember **the new covenant, even the Book of Mormon** … (DC 83:8a,b/84:54-57).

The Old and the New

From Tom Nyawere's testimony, an important point to note is that his reply to the angelic messenger was entirely understandable and technically correct. In Greek (the original New Testament

[a] Note: this is not a reference to two separate sources but Section 83 from the RLDS and Section 84 from the LDS Doctrine and Covenants.

language), the word for covenant (***diathéké)*** has been translated as both "covenant" and "testament." Thus, these two words are regarded as basically the same. The term "New Covenant" then is synonymous with the collection of books in the Bible that we know as the New Testament, hence Tom Nyawere's reply. However, the angelic being was referring to a future event, a specific instance of the New Covenant that God **WILL MAKE** with the house of Israel and the house of Judah; a time long prophesied.

While biblical scholars would trace the existence of the New Covenant to the incarnation of Christ and "the New Covenant in his blood" (Matt. 26:28), the Inspired Version (Gen. 6:7, 24, 70-71/ Moses 6:7, 23, 67-68) and the letters of John (1 John 2:7-8) would say that the New Covenant is not new, but the old commandment from the beginning.

> Brethren, I write no new commandment unto you, but an old commandment which ye had from the beginning. The old commandment is the word which ye have heard from the beginning.
> Again, a new commandment I write unto you, which thing is true in him and in you: because the darkness is past, and the true light now shineth (1 John 2:7-8).

John is saying that the "newness" of the New Covenant is that the light is now shining brighter than before - that the true intent or purpose of the Law of Moses has been revealed.

While this will be discussed in more detail later on (see "The Horeb Covenant"), we can blame or credit the golden calf incident at Mt. Sinai (Ex. 32) for the designations we have today of old and new covenants. After their exodus from Egypt, God first offered Israel what we would call today the New Covenant; the New Covenant being where God would write His laws into our hearts and minds instead of on tablets of stone. With this covenant Israel would have become a special treasure to the Lord above all people; a kingdom of priests and a holy nation; mediators between God and the nations of the world.

While Moses was upon the mount for an exceedingly long time receiving instructions from God, the people prevailed upon Aaron to make the golden calf. This violated their covenant with God and brought Israel under a sentence of death. After Moses compelled the people to repent, executing those who would not repent, he appealed to the Lord to restore the covenant which He subsequently agreed to do. This time however, the covenant was different. This second covenant became known as the Law of Moses; the name assigned to the whole collection of written laws given through Moses to the house of Israel, as a replacement for the higher law that they failed to obey.

This Law of Moses, containing all its ceremonies, rituals and symbols, would be the higher law in shadow form; serving as a pointer to the time in which the New Covenant, or actual higher law, would once again be offered to Israel in the person of Christ. By the time Jeremiah and Ezekiel would write of this coming New Covenant, the Law of Moses had been in effect for centuries and thus was known as the "old covenant."

The Higher Law and the Higher Priesthood

In this study we shall find the New Covenant has existed whenever and wherever an authorized high priesthood (that of Melchizedek) has existed since the fall of Adam. Israel, by rejecting the higher law, in reality was rejecting the very presence of God; and thus the higher priesthood. With the death of Moses, the high priesthood was removed from Israel until the time of Christ.

We are told (DC 83:3b-c/84:19-22) that the Melchizedek priesthood "holds the key of the mysteries of the kingdom, even the key of the knowledge of God"; and that without this priesthood "the power of godliness is not manifest unto men in the flesh; for without this, no man can see the face of God, even the Father, and live."

> **Now this same priesthood which was in the beginning, shall be in the end of the world also....** And they were preachers of righteousness, and spake and prophesied, and called upon all men everywhere to repent. And faith was

> taught unto the children of men.... **And thou** [Adam] **art after the order of him who was without beginning of days or end of years, from all eternity to all eternity**.
> Behold, thou art one in me, a son of God; and thus may all become my sons. Amen (Gen. 6:7; 24; 70-71 IV/Moses 6:7; 23; 67-68).

The Book of Mormon is a New Covenant book in every way. While that population was faithful in their practice of the Law of Moses, it was also with a continual looking forward to the coming of Christ. While they kept the law, the people knew full well the reason for the law - that it was not an end in itself. While the presence of the Melchizedek priesthood is somewhat murky in the New Testament, it is crystal clear in the Book of Mormon. By definition, to be considered the New Covenant, the Book of Mormon must include the strong presence of the Melchizedek priesthood, which it does. Dwight Burford comments:

> Because the Book of Mormon is the New Covenant, it includes little information about Moses, the covenant he mediated, the law he gave, or the Levitical priesthood who administered the ordinances of the Law of Moses. Rather, it speaks of Jesus Christ, the covenant he mediates, and the ordinances of his priesthood, i.e. those of the Melchizedek order.[3]

Perhaps, as Tom Nunn comments, it should not be surprising that the Book of Mormon is a New Covenant book because, in the time of Lehi, Jeremiah was the primary prophet of Judah. One of the most important things in Jeremiah's ministry was the prophecy concerning the New Covenant. Anyone who took him seriously could not have helped being greatly provoked in thought by this word of God.[4]

A New Covenant Overview

This coming New Covenant era, this "writing of God's laws in the tables of our hearts rather than on tables of stone"; is a time envisioned by God since the very beginning. It is foretold (as shown below) in many Old Testament scriptures including Isaiah, Deuteronomy, Proverbs, Jeremiah and Ezekiel; plus in numerous New Testament references either explicitly or implied.

> And the Lord thy God will circumcise thine heart, and the heart of thy seed, to love the Lord thy God with all thine heart, and with all thy soul, that thou mayest live (Deut. 30:6).
>
> Let not mercy and truth forsake thee: bind them about thy neck; write them upon the table of thine heart… (Prov. 3:3).
>
> Hearken unto me, ye that know righteousness, the people in whose heart *is* my law… (Is. 51:7).
>
> As for me, this is my covenant with them, saith the Lord; My spirit that is upon thee, and my words which I have put in thy mouth, shall not depart out of thy mouth, nor out of the mouth of thy seed, nor out of the mouth of thy seed's seed, saith the Lord, from henceforth and for ever (Is. 59:21).
>
> And I will give them one heart, and one way, that they may fear me for ever, for the good of them, and of their children after them: And I will make an everlasting covenant with them, that I will not turn away from them, to do them good; but I will put my fear in their hearts, that they shall not depart from me (Jer. 32:39-40).
>
> Then will I sprinkle clean water upon you, and ye shall be clean: from all your filthiness, and from all your idols, will I cleanse you.
> A new heart also will I give you, and a new spirit will I put within you: and I will take away the stony heart out of your flesh, and I will give you an heart of flesh.
> **And I will put my spirit within you**, and cause you to walk in my statutes, and ye shall keep my judgments, and do them…. and ye shall be my people, and I will be your God (Ezek. 36:25-28).
>
> Forasmuch as ye are manifestly declared to be the epistle of Christ ministered by us, written not with ink, but with the

> Spirit of the living God; not in tables of stone, but in fleshy tables of the heart (2 Cor. 3:3).

NEW COVENANT PURPOSE

The purpose of the New Covenant is to literally fulfill all the covenants that God has made with the children of men since the beginning of time - the grand climax of all that has gone on before. It is the transitioning from the kingdoms of men to the kingdom of God.

The New Covenant [i.e. the Book of Mormon] is not something that comes out of the blue; it is ultimately related to the covenants that went before it. Nevertheless, there are new elements that stand in contrast to those of the previous covenants, yet all of these earlier covenants look beyond themselves to the future consummation of the promises that are contained within them. All those promises are fulfilled under the terms of the New Covenant... It is the covenant of completion, the covenant of consummation, which all of the other covenants point toward.[5]

I believe that all the other unfulfilled covenants of God have built within them pointers to the last days when God will make His covenant with Israel. In addition, we know from DC 83/84 and from Tom Nyawere's testimony; that since the Lord has equated the Book of Mormon to "the New Covenant," that all covenants of God point to the Book of Mormon for their fulfillment.

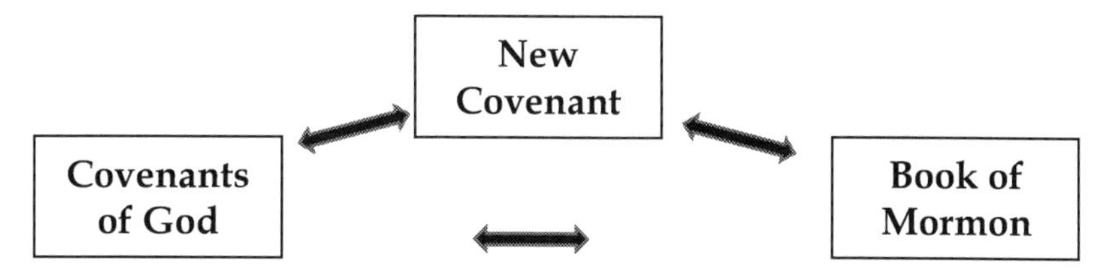

Essentially the goals of the old and new covenants are the same - to change the heart. However, the New Covenant that God will make with the house of Israel and Judah comes with power to do just that, power the old covenant lacked. Tom Nunn, in his book ***Covenants of the Lord: Bonded in Blood,*** looked at four chapters each in Jeremiah (30-33) and Ezekiel (34-37) and listed over seventy New Covenant promises to Israel.[6] While Jeremiah and Ezekiel preached messages of judgment they also included promises of God, messages of hope. These promises include a new heart and a new spirit with God's laws written within; forgiveness and pardon; promises of good; a delivery from captivity and a gathering; punishment for their enemies; the uniting of Israel and Judah under one head; and, finally, God's presence among them - "I will be their God and they shall be My people" (Ezek. 37:27).

It will be a time when the "arm of the Lord" will be revealed in great power causing a division among the people – literally the full maturation of the wheat and the tares. A time in which the scriptures say that "… kings shall shut their mouths; for that which had not been told them shall they see; and that which they had not heard shall they consider" (3 Ne. 9:94/21:8). A time in which the choice between good and evil will be a stark and clear choice, that all might be without excuse; when God will act to judge the wicked and preserve the righteous.

Dream Dreams and See Visions

It's about the time in which the gifts of the spirit will be revealed as never before. Our sons and daughters shall prophesy, our old men shall dream dreams and our young men shall see visions. And upon God's servants and handmaids, he will pour out His spirit as never before (see Joel 2:28-29).

It will come in a time of great despair, when all seems lost. A prophet like Ezekiel will come forth and be commanded of God to prophesy over the dead bones of Israel, and they will live once again. A time in which God will then move to more fully "establish" His Church and it will come forth out of obscurity. A "righteous remnant" consisting of Native Americans and repentant Gentiles will build a city, a New Jerusalem; that will be a beacon of light and hope to the nations of the world (see 3 Ne. 10:1-4/21:22-26).

And finally, the catalyst for all of this will be the lowly, maligned Book of Mormon, which is in itself called "the New Covenant." Joseph Smith, Jr., once called the Book of Mormon "the keystone of our religion."[7] It is that and more; I believe it to be "the keystone of God's Plan of Salvation." I believe it to be a tool that God has chosen to "gather together in one all things in Christ" (Eph. 1:9-10).

The First Shall Be Last

When will this New Covenant be enacted that God will offer to the house of Israel and the house of Judah? The New Testament gives us several clues as to the relative timeframe while the Book of Mormon is more explicit.

Paul, in Romans 11, begins that chapter by asking: Has God cast away His people Israel? Then he emphatically answers his own question: "God forbid, no, no, no!" Paul explains that the Jews have been only temporarily set aside by God that the Gentiles might be blessed (see Rom. 11:1, 11-12).

Paul goes on to compare the Jews to a natural olive tree and the Gentiles to a wild. He then issues a warning to the Gentiles saying that if God did not spare the natural branches, He certainly would not hesitate to cast aside the wild. That if He was able to graft in them, the wild branches, how much easier it would be to graft back the natural branches.

> For I would not, brethren, that ye should be ignorant of this mystery, lest ye should be wise in your own conceits; that blindness in part is happened to Israel, until the fullness of the Gentiles be come in. **And so all Israel shall be saved...For this is my covenant unto them, when I shall take away their sins** (Rom. 11:25-27).

Here Paul is alluding to the New Covenant, that in the last days, will be made with the house of Israel and the house of Judah; when "all Israel" will be saved, when He will "take away their sins." Verses 31 and 32 are also clues as to what God has in mind.

31 Even so have these [the Jews] also now not believed, that through your mercy they also may obtain mercy.
32 For God hath concluded them all in unbelief, that he might have mercy upon all.

Verse 31 is saying, that at a latter day, the Gentiles will play an important role in bringing the Jews, or all the house of Israel, from unbelief to belief; that blindness in part has happened to Israel until the "fullness of the Gentiles" comes in.

Verse 32 then alludes to something remarkable about the New Covenant that we will explore in greater depth; that is, concerning the grace of God, that we might all be convicted of sin, that none of us can boast in the presence of God. God's Plan of Salvation then in its entirety, is an act of charity, which is the pure love of God.

Concerning the promise made by God of making a new covenant with Israel and Judah (Heb. 8:8), we should keep in mind when Hebrews was written and what had happened to the house of Israel. You might remember it was around 722 BC that Assyria captured and then dispersed the Northern Kingdom of Israel. These northern ten tribes then had already become the "lost ten tribes of Israel." So, this is looking forward to a restoration of the house of Israel which will be no small feat. That event, this dispersal, had happened approximately 800 years before; so, with the advent of Jesus, he endeavored to make a new covenant with the house of Judah. But of course, by around 65 AD when it was thought the Book of Hebrews was written, the author, inspired by the Holy Spirit, prophesies that the time will come when God will make a new covenant with all twelve tribes. The Jews, for the most part, had rejected Jesus and his ministry and the gospel had already turned to the Gentiles. This is confirmed in the Book of Acts as Paul and Barnabas spoke out boldly and declared:

It was necessary that we first preach the word of God to you Jews. **But since you have rejected it** and judged yourselves

> unworthy of eternal life, we will offer it to the Gentiles (Acts 13:46 NLT).

The consensus is that the Book of Acts was also written in the mid to late 60s AD, although some think in the 80s or 90s. What's significant about this verse from Acts is that, while many Jews had believed, that overall the gospel had turned or was in the process of turning from the Jews to the Gentiles.

In Matthew 20 Jesus tells the parable of workers in the vineyard. You remember that the landowner hires workers at the beginning of the day and agrees on an amount to pay them. Then at the eleventh hour of the day, he finds other idle workers and then hires them. At the end of the day, he gives a penny to those he hired last. Then finally, he also pays those first workers in the vineyard a penny because that was the agreed upon price when they were hired. Of course they were disgruntled because they worked eleven more hours than those later workers and got paid exactly the same.

Those Jews who were the first workers, were paid last. The Gentiles, who were the eleventh hour workers and were hired last, they were paid first. So, then in verse 16 of Matthew 20, Jesus sums it up with a chiastic[b] saying: "So the last shall be first, and the first last."

The Jews (circa 33 AD)
    The Gentiles (circa 70 AD and thereafter)
    The Gentiles (1830 AD)
The house of Israel and Judah (pending)

To summarize, Jesus brought the New Covenant to the Jews first. It was a minority of Jews who became the first Christians and partook of the New Covenant while the Jews as a whole would have to wait. Then, we read in Acts 13:46 that the gospel turned to the Gentiles.

---

[b] A chiasmus is a literary device primarily used in the ancient world that presents a series of ideas and then repeats them in reverse order. Prophets often used this form of writing to emphasize the deeper meaning of texts.

Then in 1830, the fullness of the gospel, the New Covenant was given to the Gentiles - those who were last, those workers who were hired at the eleventh hour, became first to receive the fullness of the gospel. In Jesus' parable, they were paid first.

The Book of Mormon then tells us that the time will come (and indeed has come) when the Gentiles will reject the fullness of the gospel and then, for the very last time, the gospel will return to those original workers in the vineyard (see 3 Ne. 7:34-36/16:10-11). The gospel will, fulfilling the words of Hebrews 8:8, return to the house of Israel and the house of Judah. However, the Gentiles, despite rejecting the fullness of the gospel as a whole, will, through a faithful remnant, ultimately fulfill their God-given roles of taking the gospel for the final time to the house of Israel. In the words of Paul in Romans 11:31, that "through the mercy of the Gentiles, the house of Israel will obtain mercy." This occurs just as the Jews originally had mercy on the Gentiles and took the gospel to them.

The Book of Mormon more explicitly says it this way:

> And the time cometh that he shall manifest himself unto all nations, both unto the Jews, and also unto the Gentiles;
> And after he has manifested himself unto the Jews and also unto the Gentiles; then he shall manifest himself unto the Gentiles, and also unto the Jews,
> And the last shall be first, and the first shall be last (1 Ne. 3:198-200/13:42).

As the gospel was in the transition time of initially turning from the Jews to the Gentiles; this was a very stressful time for Paul as it must have been for the entire church. Paul was so sorrowful and felt such love for the house of Israel that he would have willingly sacrificed his own soul for their redemption:

> I say the truth in Christ, I lie not, my conscience also bearing me witness in the Holy Ghost, That I have great heaviness and continual sorrow in my heart. For I could wish that myself were accursed from Christ for my brethren, my kinsmen according to the flesh (Rom. 9:1-3).

As in the time of Paul, we are experiencing a similar transition, a passing of the torch back to the house of Israel. Our hearts are heavy because we have gained a glimpse of what could have been; and we sorrow for those opportunities lost. We are sad because of division in the church and mourn for those who no longer walk in our midst. Nephi saw our time, he saw that in the last days the dominion of the church, who were the saints of God, was very small because of the wickedness of the abominable church (1 Ne. 3:227-228/14:12). And yet, when we consider God's word and the glorious promises of a New Covenant that He is going to make with the house of Israel and the house of Judah, we rejoice that this time is near. If Zion is to be, this final turning must take place.

Study Guide

1. In reference to Hebrews 8:8, explain why Tom Nyawere was both correct and incorrect in describing the New Covenant as "The New Testament."

2. Explain how the Old Covenant is not old and the New Covenant is not new.

3. What is the purpose of the New Covenant?

4. What relationship does the New Covenant have with the Melchizedek Priesthood?

5. What would you say is the main difference between the old and new covenants?

6. Discuss the statement of Jesus (Matt. 20:16) when he says "So the last shall be first, and the first last."

The Two Covenants

During my research I discovered a book by Andrew Murray[c], written in 1898, entitled: ***The Two Covenants and the Second Blessing***. I was just amazed at Murray's insights into what the New Covenant is all about. Here we will examine quoted excerpts from his first four chapters and ultimately much more to come because we are blessed to have other books of scripture not available to Murray. Murray's writing provides a wonderful introduction to our topic of the New Covenant. He said things in a way that could only have been inspired by the Holy Spirit. I have cited references from the Library of Congress archive, however this material is available on the web from various sources.

In places I have added emphasis by bolding or underlining. All of what follows are Murray quoted excerpts with a brief commentary at chapter's end. At times Murray's scriptural quotes, while capturing the essence, may not be exact word-for-word quotes of the King James Bible.

It should be noted that Murray refers to the Law of Moses as the Old Covenant, a covenant of preparation for the New Covenant, which it is. However this covenant was given by God because Israel had refused the higher law (the New Covenant that had existed from the beginning) at Mt. Sinai (see "The Higher and Lesser Laws" and "The Horeb Covenant" chapters).

Chapter I: Covenant God

"Know therefore that the Lord thy God, He is God, the faithful God, which keepeth covenant and mercy with them that love Him and keep His commandments" (Deut. 7:9).

---

[c]Andrew Murray (1828-1917) was a South African writer, teacher, missionary and Christian pastor.

When God created man in His image and likeness, it was that he might have a life as like His own as it was possible for a creature to live. This was to be by God Himself living and working all in man. For this man was to yield himself in loving dependence to the wonderful glory of being the recipient, the bearer, the manifestation of a Divine life...

The one secret of man's happiness was to be a trustful surrender of his whole being to the willing and the working of God. When sin entered, this relation to God was destroyed; when man had disobeyed, he feared God and fled from Him. He no longer knew, or loved, or trusted God.

Man could not save himself from the power of sin. If his redemption was to be effected, God must do it all. And if God was to do it in harmony with the law of man's nature, **man must be brought to desire it**, to yield his willing consent, and entrust himself to God...

—

All that God wanted man to do was, to believe in Him. What a man believes, moves and rules his whole being, enters into him, and becomes part of his very life. Salvation could only be by faith: God restoring the life man had lost; man in faith yielding himself to God's work and will...

The first great work of God with man was to get him to believe. This work cost God more care and time and patience than we can easily conceive. **All the dealings with individual men, and with the people of Israel, had just this one object, to teach men to trust Him. Where He** [God] **found faith He could do anything.**

Nothing dishonored and grieved Him so much as unbelief. Unbelief was the root of disobedience and every sin; it made it impossible for God to do His work. **The one thing God sought to waken in men by promise and threatening, by mercy and judgment, was faith.**[8]

—

When we listen to God's Word which calls us to know, and worship, and trust our covenant-keeping God; it may be we shall find what we have been looking for: the deeper, the full experience of all God's grace can do in us. In our text Moses says: **"*Know therefore* that the Lord thy God, He is God, *the faithful God, which keepeth covenant* with them that love Him."** ...

Hear what God says in Isaiah: **"The mountains shall depart, and the hills be removed; but My kindness shall not depart from thee, *neither shall My covenant of peace be removed*, saith the Lord that hath mercy on thee."** ...

More sure than any mountain is the fulfillment of every covenant promise. Of the New Covenant, in Jeremiah, God speaks: "***I will make an everlasting covenant with them, that I will not turn away from them***, to do them good; but I will put My fear in their hearts, that they shall not depart from Me." **The Covenant secures alike that God will not turn from us, nor we depart from Him: He undertakes both for Himself and us.**[9]

—

The great lack of our religion is - we need more of God. **We accept salvation as His gift, and we do not know that the only object of salvation, its chief blessing, is to fit us for, and bring us back to, *that close intercourse with God* for which we were created, and in which our glory in eternity will be found.** All that God has ever done for His people in making a covenant was always to bring them to Himself as their chief, their only good, to teach them to trust in Him, to delight in Him, to be one with Him.[10]

In entering into covenant with us, God's one object is to draw us to Himself, to render us entirely dependent upon Himself, and so to bring us into the right position and disposition in which He can fill us with Himself, His love, and His blessedness.

Let us undertake our study of the New Covenant, in which, if we are believers, God is at this moment living and walking with us, with the honest purpose and surrender, at any price, to know what

God wishes to be to us, to do in us, and to have us be and do to Him. **The New Covenant may become to us one of the windows of heaven through which we see into the face, into the very heart, of God.**[11]

Chapter II: The Two Covenants: Their Relation

THERE are two covenants, one called the Old, the other the New. God speaks of this very distinctly in Jeremiah, where He says ***"The days come, that I will make a new covenant with the house of Israel, not after the covenant I made with their fathers"*** (Jer. 31:31). Our Lord spoke Himself of the New Covenant in His blood. In His dealings with His people, in His working out His great redemption, it has pleased God that there should be two covenants.[12]

They [the two covenants] indicate two stages in God's dealing with man; two ways of serving God, **a lower or elementary one of preparation and promise, a higher or more advanced one of fulfillment and possession.** As that in which the true excellency of the second consists is opened up to us, we can spiritually enter into what God has prepared for us. Let us try and understand why there should have been two [covenants], neither less nor more.

The reason is to be found in the fact that, in religion, in all intercourse between God and man, **there are two parties, and that each of these must have the opportunity to prove what their part is in the Covenant**. In the Old Covenant man had the opportunity given him to prove what he could do, with the aid of all the means of grace God could bestow. That Covenant ended in man proving his own unfaithfulness and failure…

In the New Covenant, God is to prove what He can do with man, all unfaithful and feeble as he is, when He is allowed and trusted ***to do all the work***. The Old Covenant was one dependent on man's obedience, one which he could break, and did break (Jer. 31:32). The New Covenant was one which God has engaged shall never be broken; ***He Himself keeps it and ensures our keeping it: so He makes it an Everlasting Covenant.***

This relation of God to fallen man in covenant is the same as it was to unfallen man [in the beginning]. **And what was that relation? God proposed to make a man in His own image and likeness.**[13]

—

Man was to be a creature made by God, and yet he was to be, as far as a creature could be, like God, self-made. In all God's treatment of man these two factors were ever to be taken into account. God was ever to take the initiative, and be to man the source of life. Man was ever to be the recipient, and yet at the same time the disposer of the life God bestowed. When man had fallen through sin, and God entered into a covenant of salvation, these two sides of the relationship had still to be maintained intact…

God was ever to be the first, and man the second. And yet man, as made in God's image, was ever, as second, to have full time and opportunity to appropriate or reject what God gave, to prove how far he could help himself, and indeed be self-made. His absolute dependence upon God was not to be forced upon him; …

…if it was really to be a thing of moral worth and true blessedness, it must be his deliberate and voluntary choice. And this now is the reason why there was a first and a second covenant, that in the first, man's desires and efforts might be fully awakened, and time given for him to make full proof of what his human nature, with the aid of outward instruction and miracles and means of grace, could accomplish…

When his utter impotence, his hopeless captivity under the power of sin had been discovered [through the Old Covenant], there came the New Covenant, in which God was to reveal how man's true liberty from sin and self and the creature, his true nobility and God-likeness, was to be found in the most entire and absolute dependence, ***in God's being and doing all within him.***

The two covenants represent two stages of God's education of man and of man's seeking after God. The progress and transition

from the one to the other is not merely chronological or historical; it is organic and spiritual. In greater or lesser degree it is seen in every member of the body, as well as in the body as a whole...[14]

This truth of there being two stages in our service of God, two degrees of nearness in our worship, is typified in many things in the Old Covenant worship; perhaps nowhere more clearly than in the difference between the Holy Place and the Most Holy Place in the temple, with the veil separating them...

Into the former (the Holy Place) the priests might always enter to draw near to God. And yet they might not come too near; the veil kept them at a distance. **To enter within that, was death. Once a year the High Priest might enter, as a promise of the time when the veil should be taken away and the full access to dwell in God's presence be given to His people. In Christ's death the veil of the temple was rent ...**

... and His blood gives us boldness and power to enter into the Holiest of all and live there day by day in the immediate presence of God. It is by the Holy Spirit, who issued forth from that Holiest of all, where Christ had entered, to bring its life to us, and make us one with it, that we can have the power to live and walk always with the consciousness of God's presence in us.[15]

—

Not only among the Galatians, but everywhere throughout the Church, there are to be found two classes of Christians. Some are content with the mingled life, half flesh and half spirit, half self-effort and half grace. Others are not content with this, but are seeking with their whole heart to know to the full what the deliverance from sin and what the abiding full power for a walk in God's presence is, **which the New Covenant has brought and can give. God help us all to be satisfied with nothing less.**[16]

Chapter III: The First Covenant

"Now therefore, if ye will *obey My voice, and keep My covenant,* ye shall be a peculiar treasure unto Me" (Ex. 19:5).

"*If ye keep* these judgments...*the Lord thy God shall keep* unto thee the covenant..." (Deut. 7:12).

Note now the terms of this first Covenant. "***If ye*** will obey My voice and keep My covenant, ye shall be unto Me a holy nation." Obedience everywhere, especially in the Book of Deuteronomy, appears as the condition of blessing. "A blessing if ye obey" (Deut. 11:27).

Some may ask how God could make a covenant of which He knew that man could not keep. The answer opens up to us the whole nature and object of the Covenant.

The law took men into its training, and sought, if I may use the expression, to make the very best that could be made of them by external instruction.[17]

—

The law had promised life; but it could not give it (Deut. 4:1; Gal. 3:21). "By the law is ***the knowledge of sin***: that ***every mouth*** may be stopped, and ***the whole world*** may become guilty before God."

"The law ***worketh wrath***." "The law entered, that ***the offence might abound***" [Rom. 4:15; 5:20].

The great work of the law was to discover what sin was: its hatefulness as accursed of God; its misery, working temporal and eternal ruin; its power, binding man down in hopeless slavery; and the need of a Divine interposition - as the only hope of deliverance.[18]

—

The Old Covenant is absolutely indispensable for the preparation work it had to do; utterly insufficient to work for us a true or a full redemption.

The two great lessons God would teach us by it are very simple. The one is the lesson of SIN, the other the lesson of HOLINESS. **The Old Covenant attains its object only as it brings men to a sense of their utter sinfulness and their hopeless impotence to deliver themselves. As long as they have not learned this, no offer of the New Covenant life can lay hold of them**...[19]

The practical lesson taught us by the fact that there was a first Covenant; that **its one special work was to convince of sin, and that without it the New Covenant could not come**, is just what many Christians need. And until they have learned this, they cannot possibly enter fully into the blessing of the New Covenant.[20]

Chapter IV: The New Covenant

The central demand of the Old Covenant, "***Obey My voice, and I will be your God***" [Jer. 7:23] has now been met. With the law written in the heart, He can be our God, and we shall be His people. Perfect harmony with God's will, holiness in heart and life, is the only thing that can satisfy God's heart or ours...

And it is this the New Covenant gives in Divine power, "...**I** ***will give them an heart*** **to know Me...** and I will be their God, and they shall be My people; for they shall turn to me ***with their whole heart***" [Jer. 24:7]. **It is on the state of the heart, it is on the new heart, as *given by God* that the New Covenant life hinges.**[21]

—

But why, if all this is meant to be literally and exactly true of God's people, why do we see so little of this life, experience so little in ourselves? There is but one answer: Because of UNBELIEF. We have spoken of the relation of God and man in creation as what the New Covenant is meant to make possible and real. **But the law cannot be repealed that God will not compel. He can only fulfil His purpose as the heart is willing and accepts His offer...**

In the New Covenant all is of faith. Let us turn away from what human wisdom and human experience may say, and ask God

Himself to teach us what His Covenant means. If we persevere in this prayer in a humble and teachable spirit, we can count most certainly on its promise: **"They shall no more every man teach his neighbour: Know the Lord, for they shall all know Me."** *The teaching of God Himself, by the Holy Spirit, to make us understand what He says to us in His Word, is our Covenant right.*[22]

Comment

Others may have their Murray favorite, but mine is this: **"God wants us to have a life like His own as it is possible for a creature to live."** I cannot imagine a life such as this but I would think that it is encompassed in the meaning of "being created in the image of God." Also, I love the statement that **the New Covenant may become to us one of the windows of heaven through which we see into the face, into the very heart of God.**

Murray asks the question as to why we see so little of this New Covenant life, both in others and in ourselves. He said that the one answer is: **unbelief**. However, I believe also that a major reason is that most are not even aware that a life like this is possible. Indeed, the purpose of this book is to describe the glorious opportunities that this generation has, unique in the annals of time, to be the agents of creation and bring to fulfillment in us the very purpose of creation.

Study Guide

1. According to Murray, why did God create man in His image and likeness?

2. In his Chapter II, what reason did Murray give for there being two covenants?

3. Why is the Old Covenant considered to be indispensable?

4. What are the terms of the Old Covenant?

5. How does God intend to meet those Old Covenant requirements?

CHAPTER 3

The Higher and Lesser Laws

And now ye have said that salvation cometh by the Law of Moses... And moreover, I say unto you, that salvation doth not come by the law alone; and were it not for the atonement which God himself shall make for the sins and iniquities of his people, that they must unavoidably perish, notwithstanding the law of Moses (Mosiah 8:3,5/13:27-28).

LDS scholar John Tvedtnes has written an essay entitled "The Higher and Lesser Laws."[23] This essay complements our study of the New Covenant as it provides excellent background and historical information. Whereas Andrew Murray's writing referenced "The Two Covenants," Tvedtnes refers to the same as the "The Higher and Lesser Laws." I've selected a few highlights for us to consider. In this article he examines the two sets of laws, the two sets of stone tablets that God gave to Moses on Mount Sinai. You may recall that the two sets of tablets revolve around the golden calf incident (see Ex. 32). In this book, the first set, pre-golden calf, we will refer to as the Horeb Covenant (see "The Horeb Covenant" chapter); while Tvedtnes uses the term "higher law." After the Israelites persuaded Aaron to make the golden calf idol, Moses, coming down from the mountain, smashed the first set into pieces. After punishing those responsible, Moses again ascended the mountain where he subsequently brought down the second set of stone tablets containing the Law of Moses, which Tvedtnes refers to as the "lesser law."

In his opening paragraph he says:

Rejecting God's Presence

> God originally intended to make the higher or Melchizedek Priesthood available to all Israel but instead gave a lesser priesthood to the tribe of Levi; this resulted from the unwillingness of the Israelites to accept one of the responsibilities of the higher priesthood, **which was to stand in the presence of God**.

Tvedtnes notes that the KJV of the Bible says nothing about Israel's rejection of the higher priesthood and the fact that the two sets of tablets differed in content. He points out that the Inspired Version (Joseph Smith Translation) of the Bible gives us a wealth of information about those events and that early Jewish and Christian traditions support Joseph Smith's teachings about these matters.

Concerning early Jewish traditions, one of the sources Tvedtnes quotes is from a mystical book, or set of books called the ***Zohar***.

> Composed in Spain in the 13th century containing interpretations of and commentaries on the Torah, or the first five books of the Bible. It includes many early Jewish traditions known from ancient texts.

Tvedtnes refers to Exodus 3:12, "When thou hast brought forth the people out of Egypt, ye shall serve God upon this mountain"; suggesting that the Lord wanted all Israel to meet Him on the mount. However he notes that only Moses, Aaron and his two eldest sons and seventy of the elders of Israel were allowed to ascend the mountain and enter into the presence of the Lord. He then explains why only these few were allowed to enter into God's presence.

> When God uttered the Ten Commandments, "…all the people saw the thunderings, and the lightnings, and the noise of the trumpet, and the mountain smoking: and when the people saw it, they removed, and stood afar off. And they said unto Moses, Speak thou with us, and we will hear: but let not God speak with us, lest we die" (Ex. 20:18-19).
>
> From this, it seems that the people were unwilling to communicate directly with God and wanted Moses to be their intermediary. By so doing, they rejected the responsibility of being a "kingdom of priests," rejecting the higher priesthood that holds the keys of communing directly with God (see DC 104:9a-10/107:18-20).

The Doctrine and Covenants gives us this insight:

> And this greater priesthood administereth the gospel and holdeth the key of the mysteries of the kingdom, even the key of the knowledge of God.
>
> Therefore, in the ordinances thereof the power of godliness is manifest; and without the ordinances thereof, and the authority of the priesthood, the power of godliness is not manifest unto men in the flesh; for without this, no man can see the face of God, even the Father, and live.
>
> Now, this Moses plainly taught to the children of Israel in the wilderness, and sought diligently to sanctify his people that they might behold the face of God (DC 83:3b-4a/84:19-23).

Author's comment: While we don't have an exact date, the Melchizedek priesthood was restored sometime between the 16th and the 28th of May in 1829. Joseph Smith and Oliver Cowdery were ordained under the hands of Peter, James and John. **With this priesthood restoration, God once again has bestowed upon mankind the opportunity to come into His presence.** This priesthood authority is not to be taken lightly as its purpose is to help prepare God's people to stand in His presence.

Tvedtnes says that some elements of this revelation (DC 83/84) is to be found in the Zohar:

Zohar Numbers 221a

> When Israel left Egypt, God desired to make them on earth like ministering angels above, and to build for them a holy house which was to be brought down from the heaven … and to plant Israel as a holy shoot after the pattern of the celestial prototype…
>
> But as they provoked God in the wilderness they died there and God brought their children into the land, and the house was built by human hands, and therefore it did not endure. …

> It is for this building that we are waiting, not a human structure which cannot endure. ... This work should have been completed when Israel first went forth from Egypt, but it has been deferred to the end of days in the last deliverance.[24]

Tvedtnes says Rabbinic tradition holds that all Israel heard the first two of the Ten Commandments directly from God but that Moses delivered the other eight. Likewise he says that this is reflected by the *Zohar*:

Zohar Numbers 261a-b

> For had not Israel drawn back and had they listened to the remaining words as to the first, the world would never have been laid waste subsequently and they would have endured for generations upon generations.[25]

Tvedtnes writes that Israel's disobedience at Mount Sinai can be compared to the fall of Adam and Eve. He says the observation makes sense when we consider that at the time of the fall, Adam and Eve were cast out of the garden, out of the presence of God. Likewise, at Sinai, the Israelites rejected the privilege of being in the presence of God.

It was only because of Israel's rejection of the higher law that God gave them the lesser law:

> For I spake not unto your fathers, nor commanded them in the day that I brought them out of the land of Egypt, concerning burnt offerings or sacrifices: but this thing commanded I them, saying, **Obey my voice, and I will be your God, and ye shall be my people:** and walk ye in all the ways that I have commanded you, that it may be well unto you. But they hearkened not, nor inclined their ear, but walked in the counsels and in the imagination of their evil heart, and went backward, and not forward (Jer. 7:22–24).

After the golden calf incident which caused Moses to destroy the first set of tablets, the Bible does record that Moses took steps to punish those responsible; he then returned to the mountaintop where he was instructed to prepare a second set of tablets. The KJV records this but the Inspired Version adds valuable information:

> And the Lord said unto Moses, Hew thee two other tables of stone, like unto the first, and I will write upon them also, the words of the law, according as they were written at the first on the tables which thou brakest; **but it shall not be according to the first, for I will take away the priesthood out of their midst;**
>
> **Therefore my holy order, and the ordinances thereof, shall not go before them; for my presence shall not go up in their midst, lest I destroy them.** But I will give unto them the law as at the first, but it shall be after the law of a carnal commandment; for I have sworn in my wrath, that they shall not enter into my presence, into my rest, in the days of their pilgrimage (Ex. 34:1–2 IV).

The Israelites, by refusing to commune directly with God, rejected the opportunity to receive the higher priesthood which meant that they would not be able to "endure His presence" (see DC 83:4b/84:24). The story of the second set of tablets is also found in Deuteronomy in the Inspired Version:

> At that time the Lord said unto me, Hew thee two other tables of stone like unto the first, and come up unto me upon the mount, and make thee an ark of wood. And I will write on the tables the words that were on the first tables, which thou breakest, **save the words of the everlasting covenant of the holy priesthood, and thou shalt put them in the ark** (Deut. 10:1-2 IV).

Tvedtnes then says:

> While New Testament writers taught that the law brought by Christ was higher than that taught by Moses, they did not suggest, as did Joseph Smith, that the higher law or covenant had already been offered to Israel but was removed when Moses destroyed the first set of tablets on which it was written.

The Zohar declares:

Zohar 114a

> Had not the tablets been broken, the world would not have suffered as it subsequently did, and the Israelites would have been in the likeness of the … angels above.[26]

The Zohar teaches that the law (Torah) will be made fully known only at the time of the Messiah.

Rabbi Simeon

(Zohar Genesis 117b-118a, Zohar Exodus 147a)

> … but when the days of the Messiah will be near at hand, even children will discover the secrets of wisdom.[27] "Blessed is this generation! There will be none other like unto it until King Messiah shall appear, when the Torah shall be restored to her ancient pride of place."[28]

Jesus – Sermon on the Mount

Jesus said in Matthew:

> "Think not that I am come to destroy the law, or the prophets: I am not come to destroy, but to fulfill" (Matt. 5:17).

He said it was important to keep the commandments found in the law but added:

> "…except your righteousness shall exceed the righteousness of the scribes and Pharisees, ye shall in no case enter into the kingdom of heaven" (Matt. 5:20).

He then went on to explain. Rather than simply prohibiting murder, he commanded his disciples to avoid anger. To avoid committing sexual sins, we should not have lustful thoughts. He said love is superior to revenge and honesty of speech is superior to swearing oaths.

Christ's message can be summed up by saying that in order to avoid sinful acts, we must begin by having pure thoughts. By emphasizing the internalization of God's commandments, Jesus was fulfilling the New Covenant prophecy in Jeremiah:

> But this shall be the covenant that I will make with the house of Israel; After those days, saith the Lord, I will put my law in their inward parts, and write it in their hearts; and will be their God, and they shall be my people (Jer. 31:33; also see Heb. 8:10-11).

Our motivation for obedience to the law of God should not be fear of punishment or hope of reward. Rather, we should be motivated by a love of God and our desire to do right (John 14:15; 1 John 5:2-3).

> "Blessed are they which do hunger and thirst after righteousness" (Matt. 5:6).

When we desire to do good as much as we desire to eat and drink and breathe, then and only then are we doing it for the right reason. Hence:

> "Not every one that saith unto me, Lord, Lord, shall enter into the kingdom of heaven....Lord, Lord, have we not prophesied in thy name? and in thy name have cast out devils? And in thy name done many wonderful works?" (Matt. 7:21-23).

The entire Sermon on the Mount can be summed up in Christ's commandment,

> "Be ye therefore perfect, even as your Father which is in heaven is perfect" (Matt. 5:48).

Author's comment: We can become perfect only through Christ and the Holy Spirit that He places in our hearts. That's what the New Covenant is all about - preparing us to dwell in the presence of God.

While all Christians believe that Christ brought a higher law, we also believe that this law had been known to earlier generations as well. Early Jewish and Christian texts that tell the same story were unavailable to Joseph Smith and have only come to our attention in later years.

Study Guide

1. For what reason did God give the lesser law instead of the originally intended higher law?

2. What is the ***Zohar*** and what does it tell us about God's original plan for Israel?

3. In what sense did Tvedtnes compare Israel's disobedience at Mount Sinai to the fall of Adam and Eve?

4. What is the significance of the restoration of the Melchizedek priesthood by Peter, James and John in 1829?

CHAPTER 4

The Two Roads

"I perceived that the right and left road will merge and the Jews and the Gentiles who are covenant people of the Lord will become one people." - Len Edwards

Like many who endeavor to write, I file away books and articles that I think might be of some future value. I realize fully the power of the Holy Spirit to recall to memory, at an appropriate time, that which should be written.

Early one morning as I was considering how to proceed and what should be written next, I first decided to insert a text into a draft of my initial chapter, "Making a New Covenant." Among the final words I added there was my belief that the Book of Mormon was not only "the keystone of our religion,"[29] as Joseph Smith contended; but that overall it was the "keystone in God's Plan of Salvation."

Then immediately thereafter, I turned my attention to that which should be written next. I began to shuffle through my files where a testimony written by Len Edwards of Lamoni, Iowa, stood out. I was drawn to its title – "The Book of Mormon is a Key in God's Plan of Salvation" which mirrored the words which I had just written. I felt the strong impress of the Spirit that I should include Len's testimony as I felt it no accident that I had just written those matching words. Len's testimony is appropriate to include because, in very simple and concise language, he gives a wonderful overview of the purpose of the Book of Mormon and how it fits into God's overall plan. It not only talks about how, as the scriptures prophesy, the sticks (books) of Judah (the Bible) and Joseph (the Book of Mormon) will one day be used as one in God's hands (see Ezek. 37:19), but it explains why these books needed to be separate in the first place. As stated in Len's testimony, the independent journeys of the Bible and Book of Mormon began as a road split in two, and will culminate when these two roads come together again.

Len's testimony is included with permission (with emphasis added).

The Book of Mormon is a Key In God's Plan of Salvation

By Len Edwards

Note: all Bible scripture references are from the Inspired Version (Joseph Smith Translation).

On the night of the 9th of March, 2000, I had read 2 Nephi 11:40-41/25:21-22 rather lightly.

> Wherefore, for this cause hath the Lord God promised unto me that these things which I write shall be kept and preserved and handed down unto my seed from generation to generation:
> That the promise may be fulfilled unto Joseph that his seed should never perish for as long as the earth shall stand.
> Wherefore, these things shall go from generation to generation as long as the earth shall stand:
> And they shall go according to the will and pleasure of God.

I marked the verses, then proceeded onward to Jacob 3:4-6/4:4-5.

> For this intent have we written these things:
> That they may know that we knew of Christ and we had a hope of His glory many hundred years before His coming,
> And not only we, ourselves, had a hope of His glory, but also all the holy prophets which were before us.
> Behold they believed in Christ and worshipped the father in His name,
> And also we worship the Father in His name,
> And for this intent we keep the law of Moses, it pointing our souls to Him;
> And for this cause it is sanctified unto us for righteousness,
> Even as it was accounted unto Abraham in the wilderness

> to be obedient unto the commands of God in offering up his son Isaac, which was a similitude of God and His Only Begotten Son.

It came to me that this was another reason for the plates to be preserved, in addition to the promise that Joseph's seed should never perish from the earth (Gen. 50:34). But I had always accepted that the records were kept as a second witness to the Christ and His eternal nature (Book of Mormon Title Page). Later I had learned that the book was to teach the covenant relationship with the Lord. But, I realized that I had never thought of the book as being a part of preserving the seed of Joseph. I returned to 2 Nephi 11:40/5:21.

A mental vision filled my mind as though it was a road.

As I read the passage again, I felt the Spirit of the Lord move within my soul and a mental vision of the Lord's incredible handiwork filled my mind as though it was a road. Abraham, Isaac, and Jacob had been promised that Abraham's seed would become a blessing to all mankind (Gen. 12:1-2; 28:13-14). Because they had remained faithful, God would not break His covenant promise with them (Alma 17:47-48/37:16-17). Joseph had been promised that his seed would never perish from the earth. He also had remained faithful and therefore God would not break His covenant promise. But, the Lord knew that Abraham's descendants in Israel would one day become so unrighteous that they would crucify Himself as the Son; Jesus who would be the Christ. So I perceived that the blessing of Joseph (Gen. 48:9-11, 13-27; 49:22-26) was according to God's carefully laid-out plan (1 Ne. 2:101/9:6).

I saw the plan as though it was a road that split into two when Lehi was commanded to go into the wilderness (1 Ne. 1:26, 29/2:2, 4). **Lehi and his family went onto the left road while the Jews proceeded on to the right. And I felt the words of the Lord say: "Though my covenant people have broken many covenants, I have never forgotten My covenant with Abraham, Isaac, Jacob and Joseph."** I watched as Lehi was commanded to send his sons back to Jerusalem to get the plates of brass (1 Ne. 1:60-62/3:2-4). I perceived that the plates were to begin the record of Lehi's descendants. They would be separated from the Jews in order to leave many of the Jewish traditions behind (2 Ne. 11:2-3/25:1-2; 3 Ne. 7:18/15:19). **This was to be done in order to prepare Abraham's descendants through Joseph's seed for the knowledge of the true nature of God and for the covenant relationship that would be rejected by the Hebrew followers of Moses** (Ex. 20:19).

I perceived that as the years and centuries past, Lehi's seed, the Nephites and Lamanites, moved within their agency and according to God's plan for Abraham's seed to become a blessing to all mankind (Gen. 12:2). **At God's command, all this was carefully and continually recorded upon plates of metal that would be preserved for a wise purpose** (1 Ne. 2:99/9:5; Enos 1:22-28/1:14-18; Omni 1:12/1:9).

Because Lehi's descendants did not teach their children the Jewish traditional concept of God as mysterious, distant and untouchable (Ex. 20:18-19), they knew him as tender (1 Ne. 1:23/20), personal (Jacob 2:49-50/3:1-2; 2 Ne. 11:95-96/26:23-24), willing to serve (Mosiah 8:26/14:11; 1 Ne. 6:38/21:8) and though mysterious (Jacob 3:10/4:8), eager to reveal Himself through the Son to those who are willing to embrace righteousness (Jacob 3:11/4:8). **I perceived that along the right road, because of their traditional perception and expectation of the prophesied Messiah, the Son was rejected and crucified by the Jews** (2 Ne. 11:21-22/25:12-13)**. But on the left, because they had not been taught the traditions of the Jews except as it pointed towards Christ** (Jacob 3:5-6/4:5), **He was welcomed and worshiped by the Nephites and Lamanites; Joseph's seed** (3 Ne. 5:11-17/11:9-17; 4 Ne. 1:3-4, 20/2-3, 17).

Then I perceived that once more, the Lamanites and Nephites became one people for a while, then fell away into iniquity and unbelief (4 Ne. 1:27, 53/24, 45). But the records of Lehi's seed continued (4 Ne. 1:56-59/47-49; Morm. 1:2-5; 2:25; 3:7-8/1:2-4; 4:23; 6:6) to be written upon plates of ore until the only remaining righteous descendant, Moroni, buried them under the earth (Morm. 4:1, 4, 17/8:1, 3-4, 13-14). I perceived that upon the left branch of the road, the records remain buried under the earth waiting for the appointed time in which they would be revealed according to God's plan (Morm. 4:19-21/8:15-17).

Upon the right branch, the apostles and the righteous believers in Christ wrote another record of Him. But, as the years passed, the believers in Christ formed denominations because of the contentions which were rooted in the ambitions of men and promoted by the adversary. They became abominations because they were built upon contentions and were used to glorify men in the name of God (2 Ne. 12:3-6, 13-16, 23-25/28:3-5, 11-14, 19-21; Acts 20:29-30; 2 Thess. 2:3; 2 Tim. 4:3-4).

I perceived that the Jews were considered by many within these churches to be rejected by the Lord since they had not recognized and had crucified His son (2 Ne. 12:44-52/29:2-5). But the Jews themselves, as though chained to their traditions, remained convinced that they were still the chosen people of God. They continue to await a Messiah that conformed to their traditions. Yet, **I perceived through the Spirit of the Lord, that they were not rejected, would be redeemed and the ancient covenant made with Abraham, Isaac, Jacob and Joseph would be fulfilled in accordance with the prophecies contained within the scriptures. I perceived that the Jews remained upon the carefully laid plan that appeared as a road to me.**

Under the influence of the Lord, the book that had been written by the Jews was brought to the land in which the Nephite plates were buried (1 Ne. 3:190-193/13:38-40). Then, at the appointed time, the plates were revealed to Joseph Smith, Jr., who, under the power and gift of the Lord, translated them into English (Morm. 4:17-21/8:13-17; 1 Ne. 3:250/14:26).

The Lord commanded Joseph Smith Jr. and his followers to take the translated record to the Indians; the remnants of Lehi's seed, whom the Lord called Lamanites (DC 18:3c; 27:3a/19:27; 28:8). They were to teach the Lamanites about the Christ and their ancient covenants with the Lord (DC 2:6a-e; 3:10c-13b/3:16-20; 10:46-51). The

Lamanites would then take the book of the Jews (the Bible) and the Book of Mormon and would perceive the true points of the fullness of the gospel (DC 3:15a-c/10:60-63). Assisted by the Gentiles, they would begin to establish a righteous people who would form a community called the New Jerusalem (3 Ne. 9:58; 10:1-3/20:22; 21:22-24). The children of Abraham would then be gathered to fulfill God's ancient covenant promise that they would be a blessing upon all mankind (3 Ne. 9:65, 67-68, 71/20:27, 29, 33). But Joseph Smith and his following came under the influence of unrighteous men to build up another church unto the Gentiles and so did not obey the Lord and came under condemnation which remains (DC 2:3b-c; 83:8a-c/3:5-7; 84:54-59).

I perceived that the right and left road will merge...

Then I perceived that the task would still be accomplished for the Lord will not break His covenant with those who remain faithful. The promise to Abraham will be fulfilled. The Book of Mormon will go to the Lamanites (2 Ne. 2:11-47/3:7-24) and one of them, named Joseph, whose father will be named Joseph, will perceive the true points of the fullness of the gospel (DC 3:15b/10:62). Then the Lamanites; the seed of Abraham, will, assisted by the Gentiles (3 Ne. 10:1-4/21:22-26), establish the New Jerusalem which will be a blessing upon all mankind. I perceived that the right and left road will merge and the Jews and the Gentiles who are covenant people of the Lord will become one people.

I was overcome with the plainness and simpleness of the perception that the Spirit of the Lord had laid before me. With amazement and joy, I heard myself saying over and over, "I can see! I can see! It's so plain!" Then I asked the Spirit of the Lord why the road had to split. Why could He not have led the Jews with a strong hand to believe in Jesus as the Christ and so have directly brought about the blessing promised to Abraham? Then I perceived that God must respect the agency He has given, even to the adversary. Therefore, His plan, while plain and simple, moves according to the agencies of all the creatures to which agency has been given.

The separation of Lehi and the creation and preservation of the records, the abridgment of which we know as the Book of Mormon, was according to the carefully laid plan of salvation which was laid before the foundation of the world. Adam's Redemption, Enoch's Zion, Noah's Ark and Abraham's Covenant have all been in accordance with this carefully laid plan made in accordance with the agencies of Adam, Enoch, Noah, Abraham and even the adversary. For the Lord must try his people, otherwise there is no agency.

The Book of Mormon must go to the Lamanites.

There are a few other things that I would like to share with you. I perceived that the Book of Mormon must go to the Lamanites. But, I knew that this was already happening through many avenues, yet I realize that the prophesied perception of the true points of the gospel had not come to pass. I was given to know that this work cannot be done except as the Spirit of the Lord directs, either through the covenant members of Christ's Church called specifically by Him for this work, or even through His Spirit alone. It is His Spirit that will determine the time, place and way. He also has led me to understand that though the Gentiles are to take the book to the Lamanites, it cannot be done with any shred of contention nor any pride associated with the perception of being from a superior culture nor imprinted with any desire for a name or denomination other than that of Jesus Christ. It must be done by a people who are full of humbleness, who recognize the Lord's hand in this work and are willing to teach only of Christ and His covenants, then are willing to assist, not lead, those they have taught, through their love for the Lord and all mankind. It is only in this way that Joseph, the son of Joseph will come forth.

[End Len Edward's testimony]

Comment

Len's testimony had been in my possession for several years. I had read it before several times and had been duly impressed. However, after much time had elapsed and I had studied more concerning God's covenants, I again read his experience as I considered it for inclusion in this book. It was only then that I realized how profound Len's experience was; that it contains many valuable insights to God's plan; insights that I might add are like the Book of Mormon itself; "plain and precious." Insights that caused Len to proclaim with amazement and joy, "I can see! I can see! It's so plain."

I felt it significant that we are told that Joseph's seed was separated from the Jews in order to leave many of the Jewish traditions behind. Lehi's descendants came to know that God was a personal, tender, loving God, as opposed to the Jewish traditional concept of God as being mysterious, distant and untouchable. Because they were taught the traditional concepts only as they pointed towards Christ; Christ was then "welcomed and worshiped by the Nephites and Lamanites" as he made his post-resurrection appearance among them.

One day soon their memories will be awakened.

We know that, as stated in the experience, that the Nephites and Lamanites fell into iniquity and unbelief. But, the truly important thing that God desired to happen took place, the record of the Book of Mormon was completed to come forth in the latter days to fulfill its God-given purpose. Even though the Lamanites became a "dark and loathsome" people, yet deeply ingrained in their DNA and their nature is the inclination to believe. They have a reverence for their traditions, for their ancestry, that will yet be awakened by their record, the Book of Mormon. One day soon their memories of the Christ that walked among them will be awakened, and as the Lord has said, "Before the great day of the Lord shall come, Jacob shall flourish in the wilderness; and the Lamanites shall blossom as the rose. Zion shall flourish upon the hills" (DC 49:5a-b/24-25). We read that: "**This was to be done in order to prepare Abraham's descendants through Joseph's seed for the knowledge of the true nature of God and for the covenant relationship that would be rejected by the Hebrew followers of Moses**" (Ex. 20:19).

Indeed, this book is about "the true nature of God" and the "covenant relationship" that God desires to have with His people. The covenant rejected by the Jews was the New Covenant, even "the very presence of God." Because of the Lamanite inclination in the past to believe, and because of the covenant that God has made with Joseph, this New Covenant will initially come to the Lamanites, and from there spread to the rest of the house of Israel and the house of Judah, fulfilling the covenant that God made with Abraham, that "...in thy seed shall all the families of the earth be blessed" (Gen. 28:14).

Through the Book of Mormon, which is in itself the New Covenant, God will move to fulfill all the covenants that He has made with the house of Israel. It is truly "the keystone of God's Plan of Salvation."

Study Guide

1. What promises did God make to Abraham and to Joseph?

2. In what way does God's plan, as seen by Len Edwards as splitting into two roads, serve to fulfill God's promises to Abraham and Joseph?

3. What reason was given as to why Jesus was welcomed by the Nephites and rejected by the Jews?

CHAPTER 5

The Song of Zacharias

> **There was in the days of Herod, the king of Judaea, a certain priest named Zacharias... and his wife was of the daughters of Aaron, and her name was Elisabeth.**
> **And they were both righteous before God, walking in all the commandments and ordinances of the Lord blameless.**
> **And they had no child, because that Elisabeth was barren, and they both were now well stricken in years** (Luke 1:5-7).

Little did Zacharias, a common village priest, dream that he would one day be at the center of an unfolding drama that would literally change the course of world history. He and his wife Elizabeth, also from a priestly family, were perhaps in their seventies or eighties. In order to fully appreciate the Song of Zacharias as given by Luke, we must look at the circumstances; not only for Zacharias and Elizabeth, but the circumstances that existed at that time in Israel.

Per William Barclay, there was as many as twenty thousand priests altogether; so, that meant that there was probably almost a thousand in Zacharias' section. A priest would serve at the temple twice each year, and only for a week each time. Within the sections all duties were allocated by lot. Every morning and evening sacrifice was made for the whole nation. Before the morning sacrifice and after the evening sacrifice, incense was burned on the altar of incense (see Ex. 30:1-10) so that, as it were, the sacrifices might go up to God wrapped in an envelope of sweet-smelling incense. This was one of the most solemn parts of the daily worship at the temple. It was quite possible that many a priest would never have the privilege of burning incense all his life; but if the lot did fall on any priest, that day was the greatest day in all his life, the day he longed for and dreamed of. On this day the lot fell on Zacharias and he would be thrilled to the core of his being.[30]

The Golden Altar of Incense sat in front of the curtain that separated the Holy Place from the Holy of Holies. The incense was a symbol of the prayers and intercession of the people going up to God as a sweet fragrance. While Zacharias was performing this sacred duty, the angel Gabriel appeared to announce that he and his wife Elizabeth would bear a son. This would truly be a miraculous event as the old couple were well beyond child-bearing years. According to the angel, their son was to be named John. He was to be the forerunner of the Messiah.

Zacharias was incredulous and asked for a sign saying "Whereby shall I know this? For I am an old man and my wife is stricken in years." The angel curiously answers him this way:

> I am Gabriel, that stand in the presence of God; and am sent to speak unto thee, and to shew thee these glad tidings (Luke 1:19).

I like how Stephen Davey frames Gabriel's response to Zacharias:

> There is a play on words in this verse that is lost to the English reader. Zacharias said, "I am an old man," and the angel said, "I am Gabriel."
>
> In other words, "You might be an old man, but I am Gabriel. Your wife might be advanced in years, but I stand in the presence of an eternal God."[31]

Gabriel then told Zacharias that for his unbelief, he would be struck dumb until these events came to pass. Perhaps Zacharias could be excused somewhat for his incredulity. This was certainly a dark time in the history of Israel. It had been over 400 years since the prophets had spoken; a time in history now known as "the four hundred years of silence."

Being well-versed in Old Testament theology, Zacharias was aware of the significance of what had just happened. This was to be the greatest moment in the history of Israel; indeed, in the history of mankind.

After the birth of baby John, on the eighth day they assembled in the Temple for the rite of circumcision. There, as Zacharias' tongue was loosed, and his pent-up emotions released; he began to praise

God. Luke 1:67-79 over the years has become known as "Benedictus" which is the Latin word for "blessed." It is Zacharias' song of praise to God.

This song of praise might appear on first glance to be an interruption of Luke's narrative but close examination reveals its great theological significance. Zacharias' praise serves to connect the Old and New Testaments pointing to the fulfillment of God's covenants made to the house of Israel.

As we look at Zacharias' praise to God, three verses stand out as covenantal verses. Verse 69 is an implicit reference to the Davidic covenant; while verse 73 refers to the covenant that God made with Abraham; and then finally verse 77 is a reference about the remission of sins, known as the New Covenant presented in Jeremiah 31.

For our purposes, we can then divide Zacharias' praise into those three parts. Part of it deals with the fulfillment of the Davidic Covenant, part deals with the fulfillment of the Abrahamic Covenant, and part deals with the fulfillment of the New Covenant.[32]

The Davidic Covenant

And hath raised up an horn of salvation for us in the house of his servant David (Luke 1:69).

Zacharias is very excited. He knows that the coming Messiah is the "horn of salvation"; "horn" meaning authority and power. He knew that the Messiah will come from the royal line of David, the great king who defined Israel at the height of its glory, and will restore David's kingdom. All Jews longed for and expected that restoration of his Kingdom when the Messiah would come.

In 2 Samuel 7, King David proposed to the prophet Nathan to build a house for the Lord. At first Nathan responds positively to David's suggestion, but that night Nathan received the word of the Lord declining David's offer. While David might have been disappointed initially that God did not allow him to build a house for Him; He instead gave David something quite wonderful, a living house that shall last forever.

> And when thy days be fulfilled, and thou shalt sleep with thy fathers, I will set up thy seed after thee, which shall proceed out of thy bowels, and I will establish his kingdom. He shall build an house for my name, and I will stablish the throne of his kingdom forever (2 Samuel 7:12-13).

God not only promises that David's son Solomon would build a house for the Lord, but also issues an irrevocable pledge to David that out of Solomon's lineage would come a greater Son who would have an eternal kingdom. This is the Davidic Covenant. There are over forty references in the Bible to 2 Samuel 7 and this eternal kingdom.[33] Prophets were excited about this coming kingdom.

> For unto us a child is born, unto us a son is given: and the government shall be upon his shoulder: and his name shall be called Wonderful, Counsellor, The mighty God, The everlasting Father, The Prince of Peace.
>
> Of the increase of his government and peace there shall be no end, upon the throne of David, and upon his kingdom, to order it, and to establish it with judgment and with justice from henceforth even for ever. The zeal of the Lord of hosts will perform this (Is. 9:6-7).
>
> And the Lord shall be king over all the earth: in that day shall there be one Lord, and his name one (Zech. 14:9).
>
> Behold, the days are coming, says the Lord, that I will raise unto David a righteous Branch and a King shall reign and prosper, and shall execute judgment and justice in the earth.... this is His name whereby He shall be called, THE LORD OUR RIGHTEOUSNESS (Jer. 23:5-6).

Jeremiah refers to the coming King as a righteous branch, not only because He himself is righteous, but because He makes His people righteous. This is a pointer to the New Covenant to be made with the house of Israel and the house of Judah.

Psalm 89 describes the nature of the Davidic Covenant, the promise of a King and a Kingdom, subduing the enemies of Israel and extending the reign of the Messiah forever and ever. The Messiah will be the Lord of all establishing a literal earthly kingdom. Justice, judgment, mercy and truth (v. 14) shall be the habitation of His throne.

The Abrahamic Covenant

The oath which he sware to our father Abraham... (Luke 1:73).

God's covenant with Abraham is irrevocable and eternal. It involves land, descendants and blessings to all nations of the earth. Of that covenant, John MacArthur has said, "It is the rock-bed foundation by which you can understand the whole of redemptive history...."[34]

> And I will make of thee a great nation, and I will bless thee, and make thy name great; and thou shalt be a blessing: And I will bless them that bless thee, and curse him that curseth thee: and in thee shall all families of the earth be blessed (Gen. 12:2-3).

This covenant was subsequently repeated to Abraham's son Isaac and to Isaac's son Jacob. Many theologians postulate that the Abrahamic Covenant was ultimately and completely fulfilled in the coming of Jesus and his death on the cross; which offered salvation to all who would believe. Others do stipulate however, that the covenant will not be completely fulfilled until Christ returns to bless and save His people Israel. It would then be through the nation of Israel that the blessings to all nations would be fulfilled.

As to when the Abrahamic Covenant will be fulfilled, the Book of Mormon supports the idea that the ultimate realization of Abraham's covenant is to come through the house of Israel.

> And behold ye are the children of the prophets; and ye are of the house of Israel; and ye are of the covenant which the Father made with your fathers, saying unto Abraham, And in thy seed, shall all the kindreds of the earth be blessed; The Father having raised me up unto you first, and sent me to bless you, in turning away every one of you from his iniquities; and this because ye are the children of the covenant.
> **And after that ye were blessed, then fulfilleth the Father the covenant which he made with Abraham**, saying, In thy seed shall all the kindreds of the earth be blessed...
> (3 Ne. 9:63-65/20:25-27).

The Abrahamic Covenant emphasizes mercy and blessing; while the Davidic Covenant concerns the Messianic reign and His sovereignty over the world.

Curses and Blessings – the Issue of Sin

And it shall come to pass, when all these things are come upon thee, the blessing and the curse, which I have set before thee, and thou shalt call them to mind among all the nations, whither the Lord thy God hath driven thee, And shalt return unto the Lord thy God, and shalt obey his voice according to all that I command thee this day, thou and thy children, with all thine heart, and with all thy soul (Deut. 30:1-2).

"Houston, we have a problem." These immortal words expressed by the Apollo 13 flight crew sum up the situation facing the Jews at the birth of Christ. The problem centered on the Law of Moses. By that law, the Jews were offered blessings if they obey; and curses if not. The purpose of the law was for it to come to an end in itself; to convict of sin; not to justify it. John MacArthur clarifies:

> You see, they didn't have any understanding about their true situation. They thought that because they were Jews and because the covenant of God to David and to Abraham was irrevocable, unalterable, the gifts and callings of God

> being without repentance and God being faithful – and they rehearsed that again and again and again that God is faithful to His promise and never breaks it – they assumed that therefore it was just a matter of the Messiah showing up and they would get it all... What they didn't know was they needed to be redeemed from sin.[35]

The problem is that no matter how hard the Jews tried, they both lacked understanding as to the purpose of the law, and their inherent inability to keep the law. It didn't really matter how great blessings God offered nor the severity of His threats. What would be needed then is another covenant that addressed both their need for forgiveness of sin, and to change their heart, their very nature, so that they could abide the Law of Love.

> One truth that the Bible makes abundantly clear, one truth the Bible makes unmistakably clear is that all men are sinners...and that their sin is not just a behavioral problem. It is not just an attitudinal problem. It is a deep-seated flaw in their nature. It's not a matter of just how they act, or how they speak. It's a matter of what they are.[36]

Deut. 30:1 quoted on the previous page gives a clue as to how the Jews would fare in keeping the law; as God says that they would eventually be scattered among all nations - scattered because of disobedience. However, verse 2 is again another pointer to a New Covenant that will allow Israel, His chosen people, to love God with all their heart and soul.

Zacharias knew what was going on. Before they could ever receive the promises of the Davidic and Abrahamic covenants, the issue of sin must be dealt with.

A New Covenant

And thou, child, shalt be called the prophet of the Highest: for thou shalt go before the face of the Lord to prepare his ways; To give knowledge of salvation unto his people by the remission of their sins... (Luke 1:76-77).

While the New Covenant is not explicitly mentioned in this passage from Luke, it is exactly what Zacharias and Luke are talking about. Again, this New Covenant is an everlasting covenant, irrevocable and eternal. We cannot do anything to earn it; it will be given according to the mercy of God.

As mentioned before, Zacharias was unbelievably excited because in his mind, he saw the fulfillment of all three of these covenants; Davidic, Abrahamic and the New Covenant. However, he had no way of knowing that the Jews would reject their Messiah, and thus they would need to wait until the latter days for covenant fulfillment.

With their rejection of Jesus as their Messiah, the New Covenant, the fullness of the gospel then transferred to the Gentiles. However, this would not be the last turning. Ultimately, last of all, the Jews will accept Jesus the Christ as their Messiah and thus receive all the covenantal blessings that will result in the kingdom of God on earth.

Zacharias then is referring to the last instance of the New Covenant, the covenant that God will make with the houses of Israel and Judah:

> But this shall be the covenant that I will make with the house of Israel; After those days, saith the Lord, I will put my law in their inward parts, and write it in their hearts; and will be their God, and they shall be my people.
> And they shall teach no more every man his neighbour, and every man his brother, saying, Know the Lord: for they shall all know me, from the least of them unto the greatest of them, saith the Lord: **for I will forgive their iniquity, and I will remember their sin no more** (Jer. 31:33-34).

We are told that with the Gentiles there will come a falling away (see 2 Thess. 2:1-3) and that eventually another instance of the New Covenant will be given to the Gentiles. And finally, the Book of Mormon says that the Gentiles will once again reject the fullness of the gospel; and then, for the last time, God will make a New Covenant with the house of Israel and the house of Judah.

Through Joseph Smith, Jr. we are told that this New Covenant is not new, but it is even that which has been from the beginning: "Behold, I say unto you, that all old covenants have I caused to be done away in this thing, and this is a new and everlasting covenant; **even that which was from the beginning**" (DC 20:1a/22:1). Zacharias is then prophesying of this last and final iteration (instance or occurrence) of the New Covenant to be made with the house of Israel and the house of Judah. This is when God's covenantal promises all come to fruition. God vows to be in their midst manifesting Himself in word and power such that He will remove their stumbling-blocks (sins).

> ...At that day when the Gentiles shall sin against my gospel...I will bring the fullness of my gospel from among them...And then will I remember my covenant which I have made unto my people, O house of Israel, and I will bring my gospel unto them... (3 Ne. 7:34-36/16:10-11).

To quote John MacArthur:

> The New Covenant has a unique application to the people of Israel. We are all New Covenant believers. Everybody who has ever believed has been saved by the terms of the New Covenant; that is by the sacrificial blood atonement of Jesus Christ on the cross. Everybody who has ever been saved through all of history has been saved by the death of Jesus Christ. **But the New Covenant as a special pledge to the people of Israel has not been fulfilled because Israel as a nation has not believed. But they will.**[37]

The Tender Mercy of God

Through the tender mercy of our God... To give light to them that sit in darkness and in the shadow of death, to guide our feet into the way of peace (Luke 1:78-79).

From just these few verses of praise in the Song of Zacharias, we have uncovered a profound insight into the fulfillment of God's covenants by a New Covenant yet to be made with the houses of Israel and Judah. We have discovered that the basis of fulfillment is the grace and tender mercy of God. We are of ourselves powerless to implement the necessary changes to our nature for us to be obedient to His commandments.

> For the mountains shall depart, and the hills be removed; but my kindness shall not depart from thee, neither shall the covenant of my peace be removed, saith the Lord that hath mercy on thee (Is. 54:10).
>
> I will greatly rejoice in the Lord, my soul shall be joyful in my God; for he hath clothed me with the garments of salvation, he hath covered me with the robe of righteousness… (Is. 61:10).
>
> And they shall call them, The holy people, The redeemed of the Lord: and thou shalt be called, Sought out, A city not forsaken (Is. 62:12).
>
> And the Redeemer shall come to Zion, and unto them that turn from transgression in Jacob, saith the Lord. As for me, this is my covenant with them, saith the Lord; My spirit that is upon thee, and my words which I have put in thy mouth, shall not depart out of thy mouth, nor out of the mouth of thy seed, nor out of the mouth of thy seed's seed, saith the Lord, from henceforth and for ever (Is. 59:20-21).

Study Guide

1. Zacharias was astonished at the angel message that he and Elizabeth would bear a son that would be the forerunner of the Messiah. He asked for a sign. What do you think of Gabriel's answer?

2. What are the three covenantal verses that stand out in Zacharias' song? Briefly mention the substance of each covenant.

PART II:

COVENANTS OF THE LORD

Covenants are the footsteps of God. They show us what He is doing and where He is going. Covenants reveal the plan of God and how He proposes to accomplish His purposes. Everything that God does is under Covenant and by the terms of the Covenant. This is a fundamental fact of life.

– Tom Nunn

CHAPTER 6

Covenants of the Lord

> As fine and as noble as people in the world may be now, unless they are harnessed to the covenants of God they are ineffective in face of the powers of destruction now prevailing. **For - mark it well - it is either the fulfillment of the covenants or it is the total destruction of the race. Take your choice**.[38]
>
> - Arthur Oakman[d]

It is somewhat ironic that the Book of Mormon, which our Lord has identified as embodying the New Covenant, unlike its scriptural counterparts in the Old and New Testaments and the Doctrine and Covenants, does not actually contain the words, "New Covenant." However, it is indeed woven into the fabric of its printed pages, but one must with spiritual discernment, look deeper into this mystery. It is a mystery for a reason; it is hidden for a reason.

For years I have read treatises on covenant by Ray Treat and others wherein I "obtained knowledge." Yet, I must confess that only during these past few months, the time in which I have been studying and praying about this New Covenant in preparation for writing this book, that only now a light has dawned and I have begun to say, "I can see! I can see!" Indeed the New Covenant can and should be taught; however full comprehension can only come through revelation.

As one spiritually discerns what the New Covenant is, all of scripture then begins to open unto them. Ray Treat (1934-2017), archaeologist and founder of Zarahemla Research Foundation, has said, "The covenant relationship is the most important subject in all scripture. Jesus Christ is the most important person but the covenant relationship is the most important subject." Referencing Hebrews 9:14-17, Treat says, "Christ came to die to make the

---

[d] Arthur Alma Oakman (1905-1975): British-born author and leader in RLDS Church. Served in Quorum of Twelve Apostles from 1938-1964.

covenant relationship available to anyone who would desire to believe, repent and come unto Him."[39]

It's difficult if not impossible for "casual believers" and new Christians to comprehend what the Lord has in mind for those who come unto Him without reservation. This revelation of the New Covenant comes only to those who hunger and thirst for righteousness; those who love the Lord with all their might, mind and strength. Really, it could not be any other way; otherwise, this understanding would only serve to condemn those who do not respond.

"Come unto Christ"

In 1993, Ray Treat wrote an article entitled, "The Hidden Principle: Come Unto Christ."[40] Like in the Book of Mormon, Treat does not specifically mention the "New Covenant"; however, in actuality, this is the subject of his article.

> "Come unto Christ" is an important phrase in the Book of Mormon. It is important because it occurs frequently, because Jesus emphasizes it and because it is so closely associated with the principles of the gospel such as repentance and baptism.
>
> To find out just how frequently it occurs we need to include all the variations on the phrase such as "come unto him," and "come unto me," referring to Jesus Christ. A preliminary search in the Book of Mormon reveals 43 references. In 17 of these references Jesus is speaking, or someone is quoting Jesus. In one case, Jesus is quoting the Father. Another important thing about these 43 references is that 26 of them are directly related to the covenant-making process that we see in the principles of the gospel and that the remainder are indirectly related.
>
> What does "come unto Christ" mean? After looking at the "come unto Christ"-type verses such as Omni 1:47/1:26, we learn that to "come unto Christ" means to **"offer your whole souls as an offering unto him**." This describes a covenant relationship. In other words, to "come unto Christ" means

> making a covenant with the Father through belief in and obedience to the words of Jesus Christ.

Interestingly, Treat makes the point that to repent and be baptized is not enough; that we cannot remove the covenant step which is equated to "becoming as a little child." Little children ask many questions, believe readily and are teachable.

> And again I say unto you, Ye must repent, and become as a little child, and be baptized in my name, or ye can in no wise receive these things.
> And again I say unto you, Ye must repent, and be baptized in my name, and become as a little child, or ye can in nowise inherit the kingdom of God (3 Ne. 5:39-40/11:37-38).

Treat points out that the order of "becoming as a little child" is reversed in the two verses above. The preferred sequence is: repent, become as a little child (covenant), and be baptized. The second sequence is for those who were baptized and did not understand the significance of making a covenant prior to baptism. Jesus is saying that rebaptism is not required; you can make your covenant with him now.

Finally, Treat asks the question, "If the covenant-making step is so important why have we not seen it in Hebrews 6:1-2, the famous reference to the six gospel principles?" He says that the answer is found in Nephi's vision:

> For behold, they have taken away from the gospel of the Lamb many parts which are plain and most precious; And also many covenants of the Lord have they taken away (1 Ne. 3:168-169/13:26).

Zion cannot and will not come without the New Covenant.

There appears to be a pattern here, as to those plain and precious parts taken from the New Testament; and, they all have to do with the New Covenant.

- Denying the power of God to make us perfect in Christ.
- Denying the existence of the higher priesthood (Melchizedek) which is essential to perfection; essential to coming in the presence of God.
- Taking away many covenants of the Lord.

Zion cannot come unless all the necessary pieces are in place. Zion cannot and will not come without the New Covenant (the covenant God will make with the houses of Israel and Judah, the Book of Mormon). Those plain and precious parts of the gospel which were removed are what Satan fears most.

> Behold, I have come unto the world to bring redemption unto the world, to save the world from sin: therefore whoso repenteth and cometh unto me as a little child, him will I receive; for of such is the kingdom of God (3 Ne. 4:51/9:21-22).
>
> Yea, come unto Christ, and be perfected in him, and deny yourselves of all ungodliness, and if ye shall deny yourselves of all ungodliness, and love God with all your might, mind and strength, then is his grace sufficient for you, that by his grace ye may be perfect in Christ; and if by the grace of God ye are perfect in Christ, ye can in no wise deny the power of God (Moro. 10:29/ 32).

As mentioned previously, the purpose of the New Covenant is to literally fulfill all previous covenants that God has made with the house of Israel. In the following chapters we will examine several selected covenants that are key to understanding the New Covenant purpose.

- The Everlasting Covenant
- The Abrahamic or Patriarchal Covenant
- The Horeb Covenant
- The Covenant to Restore Israel
- The Promised Land Covenant
- The New Jerusalem Covenant

- The Righteous Remnant Covenant

History and Destiny

In the words of Arthur Oakman:

> We must study history (DC 85:21/88:76-80), but along with our view of the panorama of history we must seek also the destiny which lies behind history. Perspective is everything. We must know something about the ends to which the forces of creation are allied. **We must know something of the covenants of the agreements made between God and man. These will give us insight into destiny. They will help us interpret the past and work in the present**. They will point toward the goals set in the course of time and devised in the mind of God.
>
> But when all this is said, the fact remains that man does not devise the covenants. Man neither conceives them nor does he stipulate any of the terms upon which they become operative. These covenants which still bear their potent testimony in history are fashioned in heaven. They grow out of the nature of God, and this fact guarantees their power and permanency. **For, mark it well, behind destiny dwells God.** Likewise, men who respond to divine persuasions and enter into covenant relations have power and immortality in the proportion that they abide in the covenants. Consolation and deep peace are afforded to those who go on their way in the strength of the Lord and the assurance that the "mountains shall depart, and the hills be removed; but My kindness shall not depart from thee, neither shall the covenant of my people be removed, saith the Lord that hath mercy on thee."[41]

Covenants are divine means to conserve and guarantee that man shall realize a glorious end.[42] - Arthur Oakman

Study Guide

1. Ray Treat mentions that the covenant relationship is the most important subject in all scripture. What reason then did he give as to why the covenant making step is omitted from the principles of the gospel (Heb. 6:1-2)?

2. In the words of Arthur Oakman, why is it important that we know the substance of the covenants between God and man?

CHAPTER 7

The Everlasting Covenant

(God's Plan of Salvation)

Creation and redemption were associate in the plan
devised by Me, hence came the need of pilgrimage for man.
And as creation on that clay My faultless "image" drew,
e'en so, redemption work shall bring My "likeness" into view.
(Inspired words given thru Joseph Luff, 1927)

G.N. Clark, in his inaugural lecture at Cambridge, said: "There is no secret and no plan in history to be discovered. I do not believe that any future consummation could make sense of all the irrationalities of preceding ages."[43]

Covenants are the footsteps of God.

Yes, it is true, when we look at the history of the world and the dysfunction that now exists, we can easily come to that same conclusion as Clark. However, when we look to the author and finisher of our faith, Clark's protestations notwithstanding, we will find that all things are fitting together quite nicely according to His word. Covenants are the footsteps of God. They show us what He is doing; where He has been and where He is going. Covenants reveal the plan of God and how He proposes to accomplish His purposes. Consider these words of R.C. Sproul:

> The Bible has much to say about God's activity "before" the world was made. The Bible speaks often of God's eternal counsel, of His Plan of Salvation and the like. It is a matter of theological urgency that Christians not think of God as a ruler who *ad libs* His dominion of the universe. God does not "make it up as He goes along." Nor must He be viewed as a bumbling administrator who is so inept in His planning that His blueprint for redemption must be endlessly subject to revision according to the actions of men. The God of Scripture has no "plan b" or "plan c." His "plan a" is from

> everlasting to everlasting. It is both perfect and unchangeable as it rests on God's eternal character, which is among other things, holy, omniscient, and immutable. God's eternal plan is not revised because of moral imperfections within it that must be purified. His plan was not corrected or amended because He gained new knowledge that He lacked at the beginning. God's plan never changes because He never changes and because perfection admits to no degrees and cannot be improved upon.[44]

We of the Restoration commonly associate "the everlasting covenant" to that covenant that God made with Enoch that only appears in the Inspired Version of the Bible.

> And this is ***mine everlasting covenant,*** that when thy posterity shall embrace the truth, and look upward, then shall Zion look downward, and all the heavens shall shake with gladness, and the earth shall tremble with joy;
> And the general assembly of the church of the firstborn shall come down out of heaven, and possess the earth, and shall have place until the end come. And this is ***mine everlasting covenant,*** which I made with thy father Enoch (Gen. 9:22-23 IV).

However, we should be aware that to someone not familiar with Restoration scripture, the term "everlasting covenant" (and sometimes known as the "eternal covenant," the "Covenant of Redemption" or the "Covenant of the Father and the Son") would be referring to a covenant made between the Father and the Son prior to creation. There are tantalizing hints in scripture of such a covenant, a covenant perhaps more explicitly made mention of, also in the Inspired Version.

> And he [Satan] came before me, saying, Behold I, send me, I will be thy Son, and I will redeem all mankind, that one soul shall not be lost, and surely I will do it; wherefore, give me thine honor.

> But behold, my beloved Son, which was my belove
> chosen from the beginning, said unto me; Father, thy v
> done, and the glory be thine for ever (Gen. 3:2-3 IV).

Christ, the Son of God, was the One chosen from the beginning, "the Lamb slain from the foundation of the world" (Rev. 13:8). The Apostle Paul puts it this way: "Who hath saved us… according to His own purpose and grace which was given us in Christ Jesus before the world began" (2 Tim. 1:9). And also, "Wherefore when he cometh into the world, he saith, sacrifice and offering thou wouldest not, but a body hast thou prepared me" (Heb. 10:5).

However, the clearest and best passages pointing towards this "Covenant of the Father and Son" are to be found in the Gospel of John. In the beginning, Jesus is declared to be the very word of God made flesh; the agent of creation (John 1:1-3). John subsequently records that Jesus would again and again say such things as "…I seek not mine own will, but the will of the Father which hath sent me" (John 5:30). "I speak to the world those things which I have heard of him" (John 8:26). "I must work the works of him that sent me" (John 9:4).

> Now is my soul troubled; and what shall I say? Father, save me from this hour: but for this cause came I unto this hour (John 12:27).

> Father, I will that they also, whom thou hast given me, be with me where I am; that they may behold my glory, which thou hast given me: for thou lovedst me before the foundation of the world (John 17:24).

The Book of Mormon is very explicit in naming numerous elements of *God's Plan of Salvation* extant from the very beginning, even from the foundation of the world:

The Way (1 Ne. 3:28/ 10:18)
Plan of Atonement (Mosiah 2:10-11/ 4:6-7)

Plan of Redemption (Mosiah 8:53/ 15:19; Alma 9:42-43/ 12:25; 9:49-50/ 12:30; 12:119/ 18:39; 13:45/ 22:13; 16:217/ 34:16; 19:81-117/ 42)
Plan of Happiness (Alma 19:81-117/ 42)
Plan of Mercy (Alma 19:81-117/ 42)
Priesthood (Alma 9:65-72/ 13:3-7)
Only Begotten Son, My well beloved, Jesus Christ, Only Begotten of the Father (Alma 9:68/ 13:5; Hel. 2:112/ 5:46-47; Ether 1:77/ 3:14; Alma 9:73/ 13:9; 3 Ne. 4:45/ 9:15)
Eternal purpose (Alma 19:108/ 42:26)
All things (3 Ne. 1:14/ 1:14)
Great things, Great and marvelous things (Ether 1:110-111/ 4:14-15)
Kingdom (Ether 1:116/ 4:19)
Little children alive in Christ (Moro. 8:13/ 8:12)
Adam and the plan of salvation (Alma 19:85-86/ 42:5)
Revelation from beginning of world until end thereof (2 Ne. 11:126/ 27:7)
Two stones which were fastened into the two rims of a bow (Mosiah 12:18-19/ 28:13-14)

Of note with the above list is the finite level of God's plan. The two stones mentioned in Mosiah, whose purpose was to translate ancient writings, point towards the Restoration Movement and the translation of the Book of Mormon and other ancient records yet to come forth. A revelation from the beginning of the world to the end thereof would certainly witness of God's plan. And then Jesus saying:

> Behold, I come unto my own, to fulfill all things which I have made known unto the children of men from the foundation of the world… (3 Ne. 1:14/ 1:14).

And then finally the words of Alma gives explicit reference to God's eternal plan:

> For behold, if Adam had put forth his hand immediately, and partook of the tree of life, he would have lived for ever,

> according to the word of God, having no space for repentance; Yea, and also the word of God would have been void, and the great plan of salvation would have been frustrated (Alma 19:85-86/ 42:5).

Per Tom Nunn, this "Covenant of the Father and the Son" made prior to creation is the foundational covenant that enables creation and the plan of redemption to take place."[45]

Also, we will find that there are other covenants that can rightly be referred to as "everlasting covenants," because they point to or reveal some aspect of this foundational everlasting covenant; or, perhaps because their realization is necessary to the fulfillment of the everlasting covenant. God's covenant with Enoch would be one of those covenants necessary to the fulfillment of this foundational covenant along with the New Covenant and several others.

The New Covenant: even that which was from the beginning.

Concerning the New Covenant, we will find it to be so connected with this foundational everlasting covenant such that they appear to be one and the same. In two places in the Doctrine and Covenants we are told this very thing; that the New Covenant is "even that which was from the beginning" (DC 20:1a/22:1; 49:2d/49:9).

Keeping in mind that since the Lord has labelled the Book of Mormon as the "New Covenant, even that which was from the beginning," this then gives us a sobering view of the vital importance of the Book of Mormon in God's plan; and why the Lord in Section 83/84 would say that the church is under condemnation because it has treated it lightly. When we reject or treat lightly the Book of Mormon, the fullness of the gospel, we in fact limit what God would do for us and in us, which is to create us in His own image.

As we offer quotations describing this foundational everlasting covenant, watch for points of intersection with what we know as the New Covenant; such as themes of redemptive love and mercy;

of spiritual maturation and perfection into the image of God wherein God would dwell with His children. **In short, the New Covenant allows God, in the person of His Son, to do for us what we cannot do for ourselves**. To begin, here is how Tom Nunn describes the New Covenant:

> Christ Jesus embodied and fulfilled within Himself all the covenants of God. He covenanted that he would, through his cross and resurrection and the outpouring of the Holy Spirit, so inhabit his people that he would thoroughly purge them of all sin, transgression and iniquity, and fulfill the covenants in them also. Through the ordinances of this covenant they are made to be the children of God. This is the everlasting covenant; it embodies all other covenants.[46]

From ***Present Truth Magazine*** we see these thoughts about the "everlasting covenant":

> Back of all the covenants and before all the covenants which God made with men stands a covenant which God made in the councils of eternity. He made this covenant with His eternal Son. From everlasting the Son of the eternal God, the second Person of the Godhead, was the Surety and Mediator of the everlasting covenant.
>
> This covenant with Jesus Christ is the foundation of all God's actions.
>
> Christ was appointed to the office of Redeemer from the foundation of the world (Rev. 13:8). The covenant of redemption was set up from eternity (Rom. 16:25). **In the councils of heaven the Father and the Son covenanted together that Christ should redeem the sinner by taking his place and fulfilling his obligations.** Redemptive love therefore preceded creative love. God's love carefully planned man's future and made provision for every emergency. The salvation of the human race has ever been the object of the councils of heaven. The covenant of redeeming mercy existed from all eternity. So, surely as there never was a time when God was not, so surely was

there never a moment when it was not the delight of the eternal mind to manifest His grace to humanity.

> **In God's eternal purpose He arranged that His fellowship with man would be based on a more enduring foundation than the stability of creature-righteousness... On the event of man's failure to render perfect righteousness in his relationship to God, Christ would stand Guarantor for man — that is to say, He would undertake to fulfill man's responsibilities in such a way that the perfect God-man relationship would endure for eternity.**[47]

R. C. Sproul further enlightens us:

> If we understand the fact that Jesus was sent and authorized by the Father, we understand something of what went on before God created the world, before God created Adam and Eve, before there was any kind of probation in the Garden of Eden. We talk in the first instance not about a covenant that God makes with us, but a covenant that was forged within the triune Godhead itself. In theological parlance, we call this the "covenant of redemption." It speaks to us about an agreement that has existed from all eternity among the persons of the Godhead with regard to God's Plan of Redemption."[48]

Here, we include excerpted thoughts from an article posted on the Wikibooks discussion website entitled, "The Everlasting Covenant":

> In all the covenants between God and man, God has taken the initiative and therefore has set the terms and conditions in which each will be fulfilled, and the promises or benefits in each specific covenant.
>
> The covenants which He has established with man are based solely on His unmerited favor and blessing which He has determined to bestow upon those who keep the terms of His covenants. The validity of every covenant God has made with man stands on the provision, the power and the resources of God, of which man is the beneficiary with nothing to contribute in return. Man is not an equal partner

with anything of substance to offer, other than his gratitude, devotion and service in return.

All of these covenants which God has made with man are based upon the initial and primary covenant which was made in heaven before the eternal purpose of God was actually set in motion in creation, and is called the Everlasting Covenant.

The whole plan of salvation and the intermediary covenants made with man in the process of the fulfilment of that initial Everlasting Covenant, are a means to that end. **The aim of the Everlasting Covenant is that the redeemed company of mature sons** [and daughters] **will reach a state of absolute perfection in order that we may live with a perfect and holy God for all of eternity to come.**

"He chose us in him before the foundation of the world, that we should be holy and without blame before Him in love having predestined us to adoption as sons by Y'shua the Messiah to Himself" (Ephesians 1:4-5). Although mankind had not entered into the reality of it, "the works were finished from the foundation of the world" (Heb. 4:3).[49]

It is awe-inspiring as we consider the implications of Hebrews 4:3 above wherein God's works were finished from the foundation of the world - and that God did rest the seventh day from all his works (Heb. 4:3-4). Concerning the everlasting covenant and God's completed plan of salvation that came forth from His word, we share these insightful and profound words from John Moody:

In the Holy Order we're dealing with something conceived by Infinite Intelligence, something of such breadth, depth and intricacy, whose elements are so interrelated, interconnected, and interdependent that it's difficult to define or sum it up in a few simple words.

Apostle Arthur Oakman had the awesome experience of being taken into the *Bosom of Eternity* where he saw the act of creation take place. As he heard the words *"Let there be light"* he witnessed something stream forth from the presence of God which was beyond the power of mortal language to adequately communicate. It encompassed all that we might call the Holy Order of God. Oakman was tempted to call it a living creature yet this was insufficient. It was spirit; it was the directed mind and will of God; it was the spiritual template; the primordial image; the archetype; the living pattern that would give rise to the universe, to our world with all its varied forms of life, and to mortal man.

It contained within it (like an acorn contains an oak tree) the everlasting covenant, the fullness of the gospel, the Church, priesthood, and all else necessary to raise mankind up from the dust to eternal life in celestial glory. And as this living creature/pattern/order proceeded forth from the presence of God it created all things spiritually before they were naturally upon the earth. It created time and the immensity of space; and in regards to this earth, it continues to roll on towards the climax of Zion, the Kingdom of God on earth - and ultimately the new heavens and earth *"like unto the old, save the old have passed away, and all things have become new"* (Ether 6:9/13:9-10).[50]

In this chapter so named "The Everlasting Covenant," we have spent our time thus far discussing aspects of that covenant prior to creation for three reasons. **One**, only in describing the New Covenant in its connection to the foundational "Covenant of the Father and Son," can we fully appreciate that which is shortly to come to pass (the New Covenant being made with the house of Israel and the house of Judah). **Two**, only in connection with this foundational covenant can we fully appreciate and value this precious treasure that God has placed in our hands, the Book of Mormon. And **three**, so that we might have a hope for the future, it's vitally important for us all to realize that yes, God does have a plan.

While it is important for us to consider, as we have, this foundational Covenant of the Father and the Son, it is also important for the world to know of the everlasting covenant that God made with Enoch (Gen. 9:22-23 IV); an account that only appears in the Inspired Version. John Moody tells us why it's important that all know of this covenant:

> It is small wonder that Satan wanted this great beacon of hope and promise taken from the Bible. It shows that *Zion* is possible for it has already been attained once in the days of Enoch; it shows that ultimately the wicked always destroy themselves; that in the latter days *Zion* and the power of holiness will be our *Ark* to save us from the great coming flood of destruction; and gives the tremendous promise that the faithful will dwell with Christ in peace for a thousand years.[51]

Enoch and the City of Zion

Now we'd like to turn our attention to the everlasting covenant that God made with Enoch. This covenant with Enoch is the earthly mirror-image of the heavenly everlasting covenant, a coming together of heaven and earth.

Sometime before the great flood where everyone perished except Noah and his family, a righteous man came along by the name of Enoch. Enoch walked and talked with God and built a holy city called Zion. So great was the language and the power of God that was with Enoch, that all nations stood in awe and fear of his city.

> And it came to pass, that Enoch talked with the Lord, and he said unto the Lord, Surely, Zion shall dwell in safety for ever. But the Lord said unto Enoch, Zion have I blessed, but the residue of the people have I cursed (Gen. 7:26 IV).
>
> And it came to pass, that Zion was not, for God received it up into his own bosom; and from thence went forth, the saying, **Zion is fled** (Gen. 7:78 IV).

However, God made an everlasting promise to Enoch that Zion would once again come upon the earth "...when thy posterity shall **embrace the truth and look upward**..." (Gen. 9:22 IV).

> And great tribulations shall be among the children of men, but my people will I preserve; and **righteousness** will I send down out of heaven; and **truth** will I send forth out of the earth, **to bear testimony of mine Only Begotten;** his resurrection from the dead; yea, and also the resurrection of all men. And righteousness and truth will I cause to sweep the earth as with a flood... (Gen. 7:69-70 IV).

The Book of Mormon, itself the new and everlasting covenant, is the truth sent forth out of the earth to bear testimony of the Son. In just under 800 pages, the Book of Mormon has almost 2000 references to our Lord. This averages almost three references per page using combinations of Christ, Redeemer, Son, Lord, Jesus, Lamb of God and Messiah. That the Book of Mormon witnesses of Christ is made clear in its pages:

> **... to the convincing of the Jew and Gentile that Jesus is the Christ, the Eternal God, manifesting himself unto all nations (Title Page).**

> **...that they may be persuaded that Jesus is the Christ, the Son of the Living God** (Morm. 2:41/5:14).

Because "his name" was known from the earliest periods in their sojourn from Jerusalem, the people of this land were "expecting him" and were receptive to his ministry after his resurrection. As a result Jesus was able to do many miracles among these people and a righteous society developed of which the Book of Mormon bears record.

The New and Everlasting Covenant

Per John Moody, "Although the Book of Mormon writers do not use the specific phrase 'Everlasting Covenant,' they placed the utmost importance on the covenants made with their ancestors:

> ***Which covenant the Lord made to our father Abraham, saying, In thy seed shall all the kindreds of the earth be blessed"*** (1 Ne. 4:29/15:18).

> ***And...this people will I establish in this land, unto the fulfilling of the covenant which I made with your father Jacob; and it shall be a new Jerusalem*** (3 Ne. 9:58/20:22).

"This is the Everlasting Covenant, which with all its subsidiary covenants, points toward the goal of Zion, the kingdom of God on earth. The Book of Mormon, as a repository of these covenants, can itself be called the Everlasting Covenant as we see in DC 83:8/84:57, ***'remember the new covenant, even the Book of Mormon.'*** The Everlasting Covenant made with Enoch notes the necessity for mankind to embrace the truth and keep all the commandments, i.e. *'the fullness of the gospel,'* as the Book of Mormon calls it. And in DC 66:1/2, we find this: *'...mine everlasting covenant, even the fullness of my gospel.'*"[52]

The Everlasting Covenant, the New Covenant, the fullness of the gospel and the Book of Mormon are all practically synonymous, and are part of the multi-faceted Holy Order that works towards the perfection of man in celestial glory.[53] When people totally embrace the truth in the Book of Mormon, then God's laws will be written in their hearts and minds resulting in Zion.

Postscript: Even That Which Was From the Beginning

Late in the process of writing this book, I received from a friend, Heather Fryer, a copy of two pages from Jonathan Cahn's book, ***The Book of Mysteries***. She sent these particular pages because she knew I was writing a book on the New Covenant. One page[54] offers us profound insights on the New Covenant, why it can be called new even though it has been "from the very beginning"; why it can be called new even though by now it is thousands of years old.

In one of his daily lessons, Cahn was asked by "the teacher" why the New Covenant is called the New Covenant. Cahn's reply was, "because it came after the old" [which makes perfect sense]. The teacher pointed out that the original Hebrew does not say "New Covenant," it says "brit haddashah." ***Haddashah*** **doesn't speak of**

a position in time, but a state of being. *Haddashah* means new and fresh. The teacher said that it could be translated as "the covenant of newness" or "the covenant of freshness." He said "the New Covenant is new not primarily because of when it came, but because of what it is. Its nature is to be new… to be fresh."

Cahn then said to the teacher, "So then the New Covenant is just as new now as it was when it first began thousands of years ago." The teacher concurred saying "No matter how long you've been in the New Covenant, it never grows old. It stays just as new as the day you first entered it."

Cahn then asked, "But, what if, for a believer, it's no longer something new?" The teacher replied:

> "If it's no longer new, then it's not the New Covenant. The only way to know the New Covenant is to know it newly, freshly, every day of your life. It must always be to you new. And if it is, then it will always renew your life, and you'll always walk in the newness of life, always young, always in the freshness of His presence. For the New Covenant is the covenant of newness…the always fresh covenant…the covenant of Haddashah."

The Everlasting Covenant involved two things – a program for the redemption of mankind and a kingdom for the redeemed. Christ was both Redeemer and King. – Verneil Simmons

Study Guide

1. Discuss and contrast the opposing viewpoints of G.N. Clark and R.C. Sproul as to whether or not history is proceeding according to plan.

2. Explain the purpose of the Everlasting Covenant and list other names by which it is known.

3. Tom Nunn states that this "covenant of the Father and Son" made prior to creation is the foundational covenant that enables creation and the plan of redemption to take place. The author says that this foundational covenant appears to be one and the same as the New Covenant. Discuss.

CHAPTER 8

The Patriarchal Covenants

(The Faith of Our Fathers)

Thus saith the Lord, Stand ye in the ways, and see, and ask for the old paths, where is the good way, and walk therein, and ye shall find rest for your souls (Jer. 6:16).

The Book of Mormon is the New Covenant, our inherited covenant promises that testify of Christ and his coming kingdom. The book's purpose is to encompass and fulfill all of the covenants that God has made with the house of Israel. It is then within its pages alone that loose ends are tied up, and that understanding and clarity come concerning the faith of our fathers.

It is significant that Joseph Smith received the Book of Mormon plates on September 22, 1827, coinciding with the Israelite Feast of Trumpets. This feast day was a time when Israel was to remember their covenant with God; and, in like manner, to ask God to remember His covenants with the ancient patriarchs, that He would regather His people.

Jewish scholars have said that the Feast of Trumpets signifies, 1) the beginning of Israel's final harvest, 2) the day God had set to remember His ancient promises to regather Israel, 3) **a time for new revelation that would lead to a New Covenant with Israel**, and 4) a time to prepare for the coming reign of the Messiah and the Millennium.[55] **Many Jewish scholars have taught that the final spiritual gathering of Israel would begin with the Feast of Trumpets.**[56]

These Jewish traditions concerning the Feast of Trumpets would be borne out by those things the angel Moroni told Joseph Smith on the night of his initial appearance, September 21, 1823 (the Day of Trumpets). That night, Moroni made four separate visits to Joseph, each time repeating the same verses of scripture that would begin Joseph's education for those things God was calling him to do.

Moroni taught Joseph that "the covenant which God made with ancient Israel was at hand to be fulfilled"; "that the preparatory work for the second coming of the Messiah was speedily to commence"; and "that the time was at hand for the gospel, in all its fullness to be preached in power, unto all the nations that a people might be prepared for the millennial reign."[57] How appropriate then, that the Book of Mormon plates would be delivered to young Joseph Smith early in the morning of September 22, 1827.

The Feast of Trumpets, with prayers pleading for God's remembrance of His still-exiled people, had begun at sundown the previous evening. The services continued that morning, with a worldwide sounding of the ram's horn. Unperceived by Judah, all that those horns represented was now to be fulfilled. On that very day, God remembered His people and set in motion His plan to regather them. On that day, God's final harvest began. On that day, new revelation was granted which would bring a return to renewed covenants. From that day onward, Israel would be called to repentance in preparation for Christ's return and reign. The Book of Mormon exists to serve these ends.[58]

On that first night of Moroni's appearance to Joseph (September 21, 1823), one of the verses that he would recite several times to Joseph was Malachi 4:6, which he would do with some variation from the King James Version:

> And he shall ***plant*** in the hearts of the children the promises made to the fathers, and the hearts of the children shall turn to their fathers. If it were not so, the whole earth would be utterly wasted at his coming[59] (as quoted by Moroni).

Here then is the authorized rendering of this verse from Malachi for purposes of comparison:

> And he shall turn the heart of the fathers to the children, and the heart of the children to their fathers, lest I come and smite the earth with a curse (KJV).

Moroni's adapted version specifically refers to the necessity to "plant" in the hearts of the children the covenants, or promises, that God made to our fathers. This is reflective of New Covenant language wherein God will ***write*** His laws into the hearts and minds of the children. Conversely, the KJV does not reference promises or covenants. The Hebrew word "shuwb" (Strong's 7725) has much more depth and breadth of meaning than conveyed by the English "shall turn." "Shuwb" also carries the meaning of "restore."

Unless this "planting" takes place, we have no future at all.

Finally, this very last verse in the Old Testament (Mal. 4:6) carries a warning that unless this planting of God's laws into our hearts and minds takes place, we have no future at all. Embracing the message of the Book of Mormon and the covenants of our fathers is no mere academic pursuit; it is literally the difference between life and death.

Before we begin our discussion of the covenant that God made with Abraham, it is useful to mention one additional point of information about trumpets. "Rosh Hashanah's trumpet blasts have been accepted by many Jews not just as a memorial of the ancient covenant revealed at Sinai, **but as a prelude to a new and future covenant to be revealed, one that would result in Israel's ultimate redemption**."[60]

The Book of Mormon, the book that came forth with trumpet blasts, is that "New Covenant" sent in answer to centuries of prayer to redeem His ancient covenant people.

Our Father Abraham

Look unto the rock from which ye are hewn... look unto Abraham your father" (Is 51:1-2).

Three of the world's major religions -- the monotheist traditions of Judaism, Christianity, and Islam -- were all born in the Middle East and are all inextricably linked to one another. New Testament Christianity was born from within the Jewish tradition, and Islam developed from both Christianity and Judaism.[61] Because Judaism, Christianity, and Islam all recognize Abraham as a great prophet and as an example of faith, they are called the Abrahamic religions. God's covenant with Abraham provides the central theme of the Old Testament, and is considered by many scholars as a pivot-point in redemptive history. The Apostle Paul is quite clear in Romans 4 (vv. 11-12, 16-17) that Abraham is the "spiritual father of all who believe," whether they be of the law (circumcision) or not.

After God destroyed the world in Noah's day, He put the next phase of His plan into action by selecting one man and thus one family through which He would be made known to the world. The Lord said to Abraham,

> Go from your country…and your father's household to the land that I will show you…and all the families on earth will be blessed through you (Gen. 12:1, 3 NIV).

Not much detail is known about the early life of Abram (Abraham). He was from Ur of the Chaldees in ancient Mesopotamia, the land between the Tigris and Euphrates rivers, which is in modern-day Iraq.[e] Legend has it that his father Terah was known as a maker of idols. Whether or not Abram was a believer in idols, we don't know; however, it would have been almost certain that Abram was a participant in the family business. What we know for sure is that in Joshua (24:2) it says that "they served other gods."

With his family background, he would have seemed an unlikely choice. Tom Nunn speculates as to why God would choose Abram:

> It is important to take particular notice of who God chose for His latest re-implementation of the Covenant. He did not choose those who might have been expected to have been chosen. Job is described as a perfect man. He might have been chosen, he was not. Melchizedek was a great high priest of God, so much so that his name is applied to the

---

[e] It should be noted here that many scholars now believe the Ur of Abraham to be located in northwest Syria or the area immediately across the border in southern Turkey, and not in southern Mesopotamia.

priesthood of the Holy One of God. But he was not found suitable to the purposes of God at this point either. The choice that God made is a surprising one. He chose idolaters (see Josh. 24:2-3).

Abram the Idolater: testament to God's grace.

The Lord had a reason for doing this. Had he chosen Job or Melchizedek or some other person of similar stature, then people could say, "Well, God could use them because of how good they were, but He couldn't use us because we don't measure up to such a stature." So, God picked two people who had no claim on God, who had nothing to recommend them, who were in no way a proper or logical choice. From this day on he could say, "Look what I did with Abraham and Sarah. They were nothing until I laid My hand on them. What I did with them I can do with anyone." In fact this is exactly what he said in the fifty-first chapter of Isaiah. He tells those who are searching for righteousness to look to Abraham and Sarah, a desert stone and a rock quarry, and see what the Lord did with them, if they wished to understand how the Lord wrought out His righteousness. This action of God was a testament to His work of grace. This is what John the Baptist was pointing out when he pointed to the Gentiles and said, "God is able of these stones to raise up children of Abraham." I know, it doesn't say that John pointed to Gentiles, but that is what he did.[62]

R.C. Sproul poses the question as to why God waited until Abraham was an old man and his wife was apparently barren before beginning to fulfill His covenant promise to make of Abraham a great nation.

The whole point of God's dealings with Abraham was to manifest clearly that the benefits of the covenant rest in the power and the grace of God alone. God was not saying, "Well, Abraham, if you really work at it, I'm going to help you become great, and I will be your cheerleader as you cooperate with the gifts that I give you so that you can become the head of a great nation." No, Abraham was

> incapable of receiving these covenant blessings apart from the supernatural intervention of God Himself…This is critical for us. Paul told us later that Abraham was not redeemed because of any of the works he performed in his lifetime. He was saved by faith, the same way any of us is saved.[63]

Abraham was a man of great faith who performed all that God called him to do; and thus, is an example to us. "Abraham believed God, and it was imputed unto him for righteousness: and he was called the Friend of God" (James 2:23). **We must share "the faith of Abraham" insomuch that he literally becomes our spiritual father. However Abraham was also a flawed human being, and as such, his story isn't really about the greatness of man, but the greatness and grace of God.**

Promised Blessings

Genesis 12:1, 3 records God's actual covenant with Abraham, "I will make of thee a great nation…and in thee shall all the families of the earth be blessed." This included the promise of land and the promise of descendants. Abram queried God as to how this was possible given that he and Sarai were beyond child-bearing years. The Lord replied, "…look now toward heaven, and tell the stars, if thou be able to number them: and God said unto him, 'So shall thy seed be'; and he believed in the Lord; and God counted it to him for righteousness" (Gen. 15:5-6). This promise was amplified in Genesis 17:6 where God promised that nations and kings would descend from the aged patriarch.

> And I will establish my covenant between me and thee and thy seed after thee in their generations for an ***everlasting covenant***, to be a God unto thee, and to thy seed after thee (Gen. 17:7).

Many if not most Christians have come to see the incarnation of Jesus Christ as representing the complete fulfillment of all God's promises to Abraham. Christ was indeed the ***Seed*** who blessed the whole earth, but this was not all that was to be involved in Abraham's seed blessing the earth. In Genesis 22:18 we are told that "*in thy seed* shall all the nations of the earth be blessed; because thou (Abram) hast obeyed my voice." Soon after his arrival in this land, Jesus made clear to the Nephites that God's covenant with Abraham had not yet been fulfilled, and that it would yet be fulfilled through ***his seed***:

> Behold, I do not destroy the prophets, For as many as have not been fulfilled in Me, verily I say unto you, shall all be fulfilled.... For behold, the covenant which I have made with my people, is not all fulfilled; but the law which was given unto Moses, hath an end in me (3 Ne. 7:7, 9/15:6, 8).
>
> And behold ye are the children of the prophets; and ye are of the house of Israel; and ye are of the covenant which the Father made with your fathers, saying unto Abraham, And ***in thy seed***, shall all the kindreds of the earth be blessed;
>
> **The Father having raised me up unto you first, and sent me to bless you, in turning away every one of you from his iniquities**; and this because ye are the children of the covenant.
>
> **And after that ye were blessed**, then fulfilleth the Father the covenant which he made with Abraham, saying, ***In thy seed*** shall all the kindreds of the earth be blessed... (3 Ne. 9:63-65/20:25-27).

To this we add the voices of Nephi, Mormon and Moroni:

> Wherefore, our father hath not spoken of our seed alone, but also of all the house of Israel, **pointing to the covenant which should be fulfilled in the latter days**;
>
> Which covenant the Lord made to our father Abraham, saying, In thy seed shall all the kindreds of the earth be blessed (1 Ne. 4:28-29/15:18).
>
> But behold, it shall come to pass that they [remnant of Lehi's seed] shall be driven and scattered by the Gentiles; and after they have been driven and scattered by the Gentiles, behold, ***then*** will the Lord remember the covenant which he made

> unto Abraham, and unto all the house of Israel (Morm. 2:49/5:20).
>
> And they are they who were scattered and gathered in from the four quarters of the earth, and from the north countries, and are partakers of the fulfilling of the covenant which God made with their father Abraham (Ether 6:12/13:11).

The Book of Mormon perspective on the Abrahamic covenant is both clear and unique. It plainly and repeatedly anticipates the fulfillment of the Abrahamic covenant ***in the last days***. But rather than constituting God's solution, traditional Christianity becomes a significant part of the problem precisely because it has lost many of the most "plain and precious parts" of Christ's gospel.[64]

As we continue our discussion, we shall find that Abraham's covenant is more than a covenant about land and descendants, it is an everlasting covenant, even that which was from the beginning. Our three books of scripture, the Book of Mormon, the Inspired Version of the Bible and the Doctrine and Covenants all provide additional details critical to our understanding, details not available in the Bible's Authorized Version (KJV).

Noel B. Reynolds, a professor at BYU[f], has written a paper entitled "Understanding the Abrahamic Covenant through the Book of Mormon," in which he identifies three distinct streams of covenant discourse throughout its pages. He says that all three streams are intimately connected with the Book of Mormon and its long-term mission. He says that all three are taught by multiple prophets and in the teachings of Jesus Christ himself to the Nephites. Reynolds says this about the three covenant streams:

> The ***first*** of these streams of covenant discourse is the Lord's promise to Lehi and his successors that, depending on their obedience, he will give them a chosen land of liberty in which they will be prospered as a people. The ***second*** is a version of the Abrahamic covenant—focused on Jacob's son Joseph as the ancestor of Lehi— which emphasizes (1) the

---

[f] Brigham Young University, Provo, Utah.

> promise to the house of Israel that they will ultimately be gathered home in peace and righteousness to their promised homeland and (2) the promise received originally by Abraham (and not much repeated in the Bible) that ***in his seed*** all the kindreds of the earth would be blessed. The ***third*** is the universal covenant the Father has offered to all his children as individuals, without respect to Abrahamic descent, that if they would accept his gospel and come unto him, they would receive eternal life.
>
> The Book of Mormon, to be produced by Lehi and his successors, was destined to become the primary means in the last days by which the gospel would come first to the Gentiles, and subsequently to the lost and scattered tribes of Israel, to gather them in—**becoming in that process a blessing to all nations**. That unifying vision of the three covenants was given to Lehi and Nephi, was re-articulated by Jesus himself in his visit to the Nephites, and provided the overarching structure for the final teachings and prophecies of Mormon and Moroni at the end of the record.[65]

Reynolds goes on to say that there are at least thirty-eight passages in the Book of Mormon where a prophet/writer restates, or alludes directly to the remnant prophecy as a way of invoking the perspective of the Abrahamic covenant for his readers.[66]

Jesus, in 3 Nephi (10:1-7/21:22-28) gives us a sequence; saying, that the New Jerusalem will be established by a small remnant of Jacob (Lehi's seed) and by repentant Gentiles; that the powers of heaven will be among them; next, that the word would spread to the remainder of that remnant of Jacob; and then to all the dispersed of "My people" (even the tribes that have been lost) and, finally, from there to all nations of the world. In that way shall "all the kindreds of the earth be blessed," thus fulfilling God's covenant with Abraham.

Of the Nephite prophets Reynolds says, **"Though they have failed to bring their own people to repentance, they are powerfully motivated by the knowledge that the abridgment of the Nephite**

record, that they have labored under seemingly impossible circumstances to compile, will in the last days prove to be the key instrument through which the Lord will restore the fullness of his gospel to the Gentiles and to all Israel, thereby fulfilling his ancient covenant with Abraham, that in his seed all the nations of the earth would be blessed."[67]

Abraham and the Everlasting Covenant

Towards the latter part of his paper, Reynolds makes this somewhat curious statement that deserves some comment:

> The Abrahamic covenant brings responsibilities for embracing and sharing the gospel of Jesus Christ. But it has no salvific force that can substitute for the gospel itself, which provides the only way "whereby man can be saved in the kingdom of God."[68]

The Abrahamic covenant pretends in no way to be a "substitute" for the gospel, it is in fact one and the same. We begin with Paul:

> What's more, the Scriptures looked forward to this time when God would declare the Gentiles to be righteous because of their faith. God proclaimed this good news to Abraham long ago when he said, "All nations will be blessed through you." So all who put their faith in Christ share the same blessing Abraham received because of his faith (Gal. 3:8-9 NLT).

And then we have this from the Book of Mormon:

> Behold, I say unto you, that none of the prophets have written, nor prophesied, save they have spoken concerning this Christ (Jacob 5:19/7:11).

In our beginning chapter, we made the statement that the New Covenant (and thus the everlasting covenant, even that which was from the beginning) has existed whenever and wherever an authorized high priesthood (that of Melchizedek) has existed since the fall of Adam. The Inspired Version and the Doctrine and Covenants give us insight into the priesthood of Abraham:

> Abraham was told "remember the covenant which I make with thee; for it shall be an everlasting covenant; and thou shalt remember the days of Enoch thy father" (Gen. 13:13 IV)..."And thou shalt observe to keep all my covenants wherein I covenanted with thy fathers" (Gen. 17:12 IV).

> [Melchizedek] "was ordained an high priest after the order of the covenant which God made with Enoch, It being after the order of the Son of God...Melchizedek was a priest of this order; therefore he obtained peace in Salem...And his people wrought righteousness, and obtained heaven, and sought for the city of Enoch..." (Gen. 14:27-28, 33-34 IV).

> ...Abraham received the priesthood from Melchizedek; who received it through the lineage of his fathers, even till Noah (DC 83:2e/84:14).

Reynolds points out, especially in his second day of ministry to the Nephites; that Jesus focused almost exclusively on the forgotten promise that in Abraham "all the kindreds of the earth would be blessed."

> He [Christ] proceeded on the second day to unfold a lengthy account of how he would fulfill the Father's covenant with Abraham in the last days....Jesus referred to "the Father" 38 times in making it clear that he was talking about "the covenant which the Father made with your fathers," "with your father Jacob," or "with Abraham."[69]

> He [Christ] cited the Abrahamic covenant explicitly twelve times! That includes one quotation from Isaiah that we should read as an allusion to the same covenant. Nowhere else in scripture do we have such an intensive and extensive treatment of the Abrahamic covenant.[70]

Christ points to the covenants of God, and the covenants of God point to Christ, and the Book of Mormon points to them both. The central role of the Book of Mormon is that the remnants of the house of Israel might know of the covenants of the Lord; and to the convincing of Jew and Gentile that Jesus is the Christ, the Eternal God. No other book so ably fulfills this dual role.

Isaac and Jacob

We will not go into great detail about the lives of Isaac and Jacob, but suffice it to say that God also confirmed and established the covenant with Isaac and Jacob because their father Abraham obeyed and followed God.

There came a famine in the land and Isaac was considering going down to Egypt. God spoke to Isaac and told him to remain in the Promised Land; and then he renewed the promise that He gave to Abraham:

> Sojourn in this land, and I will be with thee, and will bless thee; for unto thee, and unto thy seed, I will give all these countries, and I will perform the oath which I sware unto Abraham thy father; And I will make thy seed to multiply as the stars of heaven, and will give unto thy seed all these countries; ***and in thy seed shall all the nations of the earth be blessed;*** Because that Abraham obeyed my voice, and kept my charge, my commandments, my statutes, and my laws (Gen. 26:3-5).

We know the story of how Isaac's son Jacob, through stratagem, "bought" the birthright blessing from his older twin brother Esau with one hot meal (Gen. 27:36). When Isaac was blind and near death, and sought to give the blessing to Esau, his wife Rebekah conspired with her son Jacob, to receive the blessing. Perhaps appreciating Jacob's respect for the birthright blessing and Esau's apparent lack thereof, God would later appear to Jacob in vision confirming the original promise made to Abraham and renewed to Isaac:

> And thy seed shall be as the dust of the earth, and thou shalt spread abroad to the west, and to the east, and to the north, and to the south: ***and in thee and in thy seed shall all the families of the earth be blessed.*** And, behold, I am with thee, and will keep thee in all places whither thou goest, and will bring thee again into this land; for I will not leave thee, until I have done that which I have spoken to thee of (Gen. 28:14-15).

Study Guide

1. Discuss the Feast of Trumpets and the significance of Joseph Smith receiving the Book of Mormon plates on that day.

2. Discuss the implication of Moroni's different rendering of Malachi 4:6 in his appearances to Joseph Smith.

3. What do you think of Tom Nunn's assessment as to why God chose Abram?

4. What promises did God make to Abraham?

5. Discuss the different interpretations of "in thy seed shall the nations of the earth be blessed" and what part the Book of Mormon has to play.

CHAPTER 9

The Horeb Covenant

And Moses called all Israel, and said unto them, Hear, O Israel, the statutes and judgments which I speak in your ears this day, that ye may learn them, and keep, and do them. The Lord our God made a covenant with us in Horeb. The Lord made not this covenant with our fathers, but with us, even us, who are all of us here alive this day. The Lord talked with you face to face in the mount out of the midst of the fire (Deut. 5:1-4).

The Horeb covenant is perhaps the most important covenant that nobody has ever heard of. It's somewhat ironic that one of the most vivid word pictures painted in all of scripture, of what it means to have a personal relationship with God, is one that most people are not aware of. We need to review what happened at "the mountain of God," in the book of Exodus, because it has profound implications for our future relationship with God as He establishes a "new covenant with the house of Israel and the house of Judah" (Heb. 8:8).

Horeb: the most important covenant nobody has ever heard of.

Israel sojourned in Egypt for about 400 years. Eventually their numbers grew so large that the Egyptian rulers began to fear and persecute them. We will not attempt here to relate the entire story of Moses and the miraculous events that surrounded the deliverance of Israel from bondage. Suffice it to say that God raised up Moses for this very purpose.

When Egypt would not let the Israelites go, God, through Moses, visited them with plagues. Finally, they relented and agreed to let Israel go. After they left, Pharaoh changed his mind and pursued them. Then came the parting of the sea where the Israelites crossed on dry land; while the pursuing Egyptians were drowned as the parted waters collapsed upon them.

They travelled for several weeks until they came to the wilderness of Sinai. At that point, God made a covenant with the nation of Israel.

Most people are familiar with the Mosaic Covenant, the covenant that the Lord revealed to Moses with all its dietary laws and such; however, most don't realize that this is the second covenant God made with them at Sinai. This second covenant is also referred to as the Sinai Covenant.

This first covenant can be referred to as the Horeb covenant. Both Horeb and Sinai are used to refer to the "Mountain of God" where Moses ascended to meet with God. Most say Horeb and Sinai are the same mountain while others say they were different mountains or at least different peaks in the same range. One source says that Horeb is the name for the entire mountain range and that Sinai is one of the peaks in that range[71]. We just don't know for sure. However, "Horeb" and "Sinai" are useful terms used in distinguishing the two covenants God made with Israel on that mountain.

The prophet Malachi, in the last chapter of the last book of the Old Testament, is talking about the last days when he says:

> Remember ye the law of Moses my servant, which I commanded unto him in **Horeb** for all Israel, with the statutes and judgments (Mal. 4:4).

To be sure, Malachi is not referring to the second covenant, the Law of Moses with all its rules and regulations. Malachi, is saying that we should remember the first covenant made to the house of Israel at Horeb. Interestingly enough, Horeb can be seen as a synonym for Zion, for the Celestial Kingdom, while Sinai can be seen as referring to a lesser kingdom[g]:

---

[g] See the chapter "Living An Amazing Life" for further discussion of the three heavenly kingdoms (or glories) mentioned in 1 Cor. 15:40-42.

> Horeb is thought to mean glowing/heat, which seems to be a reference to the Sun…[72]

> … the general opinion of modern scholars is that the name "Sinai" is derived from the name of the Babylonian moon-god Sin.[73]

The Lord had taken the family of Abraham, Isaac and Jacob and cultivated them until they numbered in the hundreds of thousands[h]. Now He determined to set in motion the second stage of His great plan for Israel and the world. This people would now take its place among the nations of the world and would constitute the kingdom of God on earth. He would be their king, and they would be His people.

The New Covenant is not new.

After the resurrection of Jesus and before his ascension, you remember that his disciples asked him this question (Acts 1:6): "…Lord, wilt thou at this time restore again the kingdom to Israel?" Well, there at Mt. Horeb, God's intention was to do that very thing: to make a covenant with Israel and establish the kingdom of God on earth. This is what we are calling the New Covenant. The New Covenant is not new. It's the covenant that God wanted to make with Israel in the beginning.

If they agreed to this covenant they would become a special treasure to the Lord above all other people. This covenant with Israel was not to be because He loved them more than anybody else, but because He wanted a people to demonstrate to the world His power, His glory, His faithfulness, and His love. He wanted Israel to become a beacon of salvation for the world. He wanted Israel to become a witnessing nation, a nation of blessing. They were never to be an end in themselves; but a means to bring blessings "to all the nations of the earth."

---

[h] Ex. 12:37 says that there were six hundred thousand men on foot. Estimates of women, children and old men would then raise the total population upwards to over two million.

"Although the whole earth is mine, you will be for me a kingdom of priests and a holy nation" (Ex. 19:5-6 NIV).

Let's review now the sequence of events as God endeavored to make this first covenant with Israel, the covenant at Horeb:

Verses: Exodus 19

1-2 Israel arrived at Mountain of God and camped at the foot.

3 Moses as mediator went up the mountain.

4-6 The Lord made the offer of a covenant.

7 Moses conveyed God's offer to the people.

8 The people agreed to enter the Covenant and Moses reported that to the Lord.

9-13 The Lord said to prepare and in three days He would come in the cloud and speak to the people.

16-26 On the third day the cloud descended on the mountain and the Lord began to speak and Moses was called up.

Verses: Exodus 20

1-17 The Lord began speaking and delivered the Ten Commandments. **All the people heard Him speak. Each person was addressed individually**, so each person became personally a partner of and responsible for the Covenant.

18-19 The people stood far off. They were afraid and no longer wanted to hear the voice of the Lord. They appointed Moses to be their mediator and to hear the voice of the Lord.

Moses spoke to the people...

Moses would later remind the Israelites that no other people had ever had an experience like this.

33 Did *ever* people hear the voice of God speaking out of the midst of the fire, as thou hast heard, and live?

35 Unto thee it was shewed, that thou mightest know that the Lord he *is* God; *there is* none else beside him.

36 Out of heaven he made thee to hear his voice, that he might instruct thee: and upon earth he shewed thee his great fire; and thou heardest his words out of the midst of the fire (Deut. 4:33, 35-36).

Exodus 21-23

Moses went up the mountain to receive additional covenant instructions.

Verses: Exodus 24

3 Moses related all the words of the Lord to the people. They agree to comply with them.
4 Moses wrote the words in a book and built an altar.
5-6 Sacrifices were made and Moses took half the blood and poured it on the altar.
7-8 The Covenant book was read to the people and they agreed to it. Moses took the rest of the blood and sprinkled it on the people. This sealed the covenant.
8-11 The appointed party (Moses, Aaron, Nadab, Abihu and seventy of the elders of Israel), the representatives of Israel, went up the mountain, **saw the Lord in glory and did not die** (being in covenant) **and ate the covenant meal in His Presence**.
10 **And they saw the God of Israel**: and *there was* under his feet as it were a paved work of a sapphire stone…
11 **And upon the nobles of the children of Israel he laid not his hand: also they saw God, and did eat and drink** (Ex. 24:10-11).

This is the New Covenant. This is God's desire for us; that we might hear His voice and that He might dwell in our midst.

And I will dwell among the children of Israel, and will be their God.

> And they shall know that I am the Lord their God, that brought them forth out of the land of Egypt, that I may dwell among them: I am the Lord their God (Ex. 29:45-46).

Only Moses, Aaron, Nadab and Abihu and seventy of the elders of Israel were allowed to see God and eat the covenant meal in His presence. God's original plan was that the whole nation of Israel see Him and eat the covenant meal in His presence.

Sometime after that, Moses went up into the mountain again to receive additional instructions from the Lord concerning the Tabernacle and the garments of the priests. There the Lord wrote the Covenant Tables with His own finger. Moses remained there forty days and forty nights.

The Golden Calf

After that, everything changed. The Israelites, fearing that Moses would never return, persuaded Aaron to cast an idol that they could worship, a golden calf. Of course this displeased God and this first covenant then became null and void. Moses came down from the mountain and broke the tablets in the presence of the people. This was a legal act which pronounced the covenant null and void.

A death sentence was passed on Israel. Moses proceeded to persuade God not to carry out the penalty and to make another covenant with Israel.

It was only after Israel disobeyed that God imposed all those rules. God then made a covenant with Moses on behalf of the people – the Mosaic Covenant. Moses was faithful to God and he died a faithful person. Therefore, this covenant was structured so that Israel would never again have the death penalty pronounced on them. This covenant was made not with the people individually, but with Moses acting as a mediator on behalf of the nation of Israel. Later there would be other mediators such as Priests, Levites, judges, prophets and elders; but none would have the same status as Moses did and there would always be some distance between the Lord and His people.

However, God did not abandon the first covenant; instead, it became delayed until the latter days. It became obscured under the cover of the second one; however, it still existed in shadow form.

The purpose of all those rules God imposed on Israel was to constantly remind them of who they were and their calling. Those who seriously pursued the deeper meaning of the law would, by the influence of the Holy Spirit, begin to see the fuller revelation that was in it. In this way the time would come when they would be prepared to receive the Messiah and the kingdom of God.

One can wonder why God would try to restore the kingdom to Israel at that time when He no doubt knew it would fail. I think the reason was to leave us a record so that we could learn by their failure. So that we can know what is possible.

We know how Israel split up into two kingdoms, Israel and Judah, and how Israel was led away captive and scattered throughout the world and became the lost ten tribes. For the most part, the Jews rejected Jesus as their Messiah and were themselves banished from the land of Canaan and scattered throughout the world only to be reconstituted as a nation in 1948.

When Christ came, he came to restore the covenant made with Israel at Horeb. We do know that again things didn't work out the way the Lord desired because he was not accepted by the Jews. Instead the gospel went to the Gentiles.

By way of summary, I offer this comparison of the two covenants, Horeb and Sinai, as offered by Tom Nunn.

A Comparison of the Two Covenants

One is congregational in that it was made with each person directly. Moses was not initially a mediator of the covenant. He did not receive the covenant and then bring it to the people.

The first covenant [Horeb] was offered to and undertaken by the whole house of Israel. Moses brought the offer of the covenant to them and the whole congregation agreed to the proposal. On three separate occasions they expressed their willingness to enter into the covenant and observe its regulations. The last time was after the terms of the covenant had been recorded in their presence and read out to them. They were not blindly manipulated into something without being aware of what they were undertaking. When the Lord spoke to them from the mountain every member of the congregation heard the voice. This is the significance of the pronoun 'thou' in the commandments. The Lord was not simply addressing an aggregation of people, but was speaking to each individual person under the sound of His voice. He did not use the plural pronoun 'ye.' All of the people were involved in the sealing of the covenant and their lawful representatives participated in the covenantal meal. The covenant was congregational. It was made directly with the whole assembly and with each individual in the multitude who was of lawful age.

The second covenant not so. The people were not given an option; they did not participate in the sealing of the covenant and were not consulted. No representatives accompanied Moses up the mountain and no ceremony took place either before or after the event. In this instance Israel is little more than a none-to-innocent bystander. While the people see the smoke and hear the thunder only Moses is permitted to see the glory of God or hear His voice.

At the time of the making of the second covenant the people of Israel understand that they are under a sentence of death and their only hope is that the Lord will indeed deliver unto them a second covenant [i.e. a New Covenant]. This is why Paul can refer to it as a "ministration of death"; and a "ministration of condemnation" (2 Cor. 3:7, 9) as well as saying that the Law was "added because of transgressions" (Gal. 3:19). The purpose of the Sinai Covenant was to counter the violation of the Horeb Covenant.[74]

Study Guide

1. Were you previously aware that God had made two covenants with Israel in Sinai?

2. Why do you suppose God would offer the kingdom to Israel at Horeb when He obviously knew that effort would fail?

3. In what way does the first covenant at Horeb give us a preview of our future relationship with God?

4. Briefly discuss the differences between the two covenants made at Sinai.

CHAPTER 10

The Covenant to Restore Israel

For this intent have we written these things, that they may know that we knew of Christ, and we had a hope of his glory, many hundred years before his coming, and not only we, ourselves, had a hope of his glory, but also all the holy prophets which were before us. Behold, they believed in Christ, and worshiped the Father in his name; and also, we worship the Father in his name (Jacob 3:4-5/4:4-5).

The "Restoration of the House of Israel" speaks to the Work of the Father, or God's intent to fulfill the covenants He has made with the house of Israel, which ultimately includes a great gathering of His people to the promised lands of their inheritance, even a New Jerusalem. Central to the fulfillment of God's covenants is the awakening of a remnant of Lehi's seed to the knowledge had among their fathers; that "they believed in Christ, and worshipped the Father in His name." This knowledge shall come as the "record of their fathers" speaks to them out of the dust. At that day, the restoration of the house of Israel begins (see 1 Ne. 4:16-24/15:13-16).

God cannot deny the prayers of His righteous, as He has promised them that He will grant their wishes concerning the restoration of His people. The Lord had promised Joseph, the son of Jacob, that his seed would never be destroyed (2 Ne. 2:31/3:16). This was a physical as well as a spiritual promise. As Lehi blessed his young son Joseph, he passed along Joseph's blessing saying that likewise his seed should not be destroyed because "they shall hearken unto the words of the book" (2 Ne. 2:45/3:23).

A great blessing has been left upon this land and the remnant of Lehi's seed; that they will come to a knowledge of Christ their Lord and the fullness of the gospel. They will become a righteous remnant, a covenant people, a people of the book, and because of the prayers of their forefathers, the powers of heaven, even the presence of the Lord, will be in their midst. That through their blessing, they will become a blessing to all nations of the earth.

The restoration of the house of Israel is a phased process as the Book of Mormon first comes forth to the Gentiles. In the Doctrine and Covenants we find that the Gentiles are charged with a preparatory work; even "laying the foundation of a great work" (DC 64:6c/33); "laying the foundation, and of bearing record of the land upon which the Zion of God shall stand" (DC 58:3c/7). In a revelation given through Joseph Smith in June 1829, Oliver Cowdrey is told:

> Behold, I have manifested unto you, by my Spirit in many instances, that the things which you have written [i.e. the Book of Mormon as he served as a scribe for Joseph Smith] are true; wherefore you know that they are true;
> And, if you know that they are true, behold, I give unto you a commandment, that you rely upon the things which are written; for in them are all things written concerning the **foundation** of my church, my gospel, and my Rock;
> Wherefore, if you shall build up my church upon the **foundation of my gospel and my Rock**, the gates of hell shall not prevail against you (DC 16:1b-d/18:2-5).

The Book of Mormon then first becomes the pattern in laying the foundation of the Restored Church. Christ calls the Book of Mormon "the foundation of my gospel and my Rock"; against which, the gates of hell shall not prevail.

As one reads the Book of Mormon, it is clear that the process of the restoration of Israel cannot and does not begin in earnest until the chosen remnant of Lehi's seed first has the fullness of the gospel preached to them, and they are restored unto the knowledge of their fathers. The sequence of restoration is that it is to begin with a small remnant of Lehi's seed assisted by repentant Gentiles; which then spreads to all of Lehi's seed in this land; then to all the house of Israel, even the tribes that have been lost, and finally to all nations of the earth (see 2 Nephi 12:80-87/30:3-8; 3 Nephi 10:4-7/21:25-28).

It seems that it was clearly God's intention to accomplish the restoration of Israel early in the days of the Restoration. Beginning in the latter part of 1830, God commissioned a group to travel to the land of Missouri, the borders of the Lamanites, to take the Restored Gospel to the seed of Lehi (see DC 27, 29, 31/28, 30, 32). John Moody says this of their mission:

> When the first missionaries to the Lamanites started out on their assignment they thought nothing of taking time out to do intensive missionary work among the Gentiles, spending much more time at this than they did with the Indian tribes they met on their journey west.
>
> The lackadaisical response of so many of the Saints regarding their divine commission to the Lamanites, and to the work in general, would have great consequences.[75]

This failure was very substantial because, even though God continued to work with the church and there were indeed many spiritual high points to come, the fact remained that Zion could never be redeemed without the church being established among the Lamanites. Again, using the words of John Moody:

> You see it was originally Jews like the apostle Paul and others who brought the gospel to the Gentiles. Now Gentiles would be given the privilege of returning the favor by taking the gospel back to these American descendants of Israel. And furthermore, inasmuch as God has covenanted with Lehi that this Land of Promise is given to be the inheritance of his descendants "for ever" (2 Nephi 1:8/1:5), the Gentiles can have no permanent residence in America unless they perform this service of taking the Book of Mormon to the Indian people.[76]

In addition to this basic failure that would need to be rectified before the redemption of Zion could take place, there were other problems that would result in the expulsion of the saints from

Jackson County, Missouri, and their eventual scattering after the martyrdom of Joseph Smith, Jr. In June of 1834 we are told:

> "Therefore, in consequence of the transgression of my people, it is expedient in me that mine elders should wait for a little season for the redemption of Zion" (DC 102:3c/ 105:9).

Zion was put on hold for "a little season." Most probably those early saints thought this setback would only be for a short time. F. Henry Edwards said of this delay, "Subsequent experience and later revelation have shown that these years are just as few or as many as we make them[77]."

While God has given the Gentiles full opportunity to redeem Zion, the requirements have always been the same. We need to keep all of God's commandments - we need to be united and live according to the celestial law (DC 102:2b-c/105:3-5). God has said, "I will raise up unto myself a pure people" (DC 97:4d/ 100:16; Jacob 2:34/2:25). These requirements will be fulfilled as God makes "a New Covenant with the house of Israel and the house of Judah" (Heb. 8:8).[i]

"I Will Bring You Back..."

God made this promise to Jacob: "I am with you and will watch over you wherever you go, and I will bring you back to this land. I will not leave you until I have done what I have promised you" (Gen. 28:15 NIV).

The Exodus, God's deliverance of Israel from Egypt required many, many unforgettable miracles. Miracles so great that each year Israel observes an eight day festival called Passover, so that they will never forget. And yet, that will not compare to God's deliverance of the house of Israel in the last days.

---

[i] See 3 Nephi 7:34-36/16:10-11

> Therefore, behold, the days come, saith the Lord, that it shall no more be said, The Lord liveth, that brought up the children of Israel out of the land of Egypt;
> But, The Lord liveth, that brought up the children of Israel from the land of the north, and from all the lands whither he had driven them: and I will bring them again into their land that I gave unto their fathers (Jer. 16:14-15).

When Assyria captured the northern kingdom of Israel around 722 BC, they were carried away to the lands northward. This scripture from Amos clearly shows God's intention to restore all the tribes of Israel, not just Judah.

> ...I will sift the house of Israel among all nations, like as corn is sifted in a sieve, yet shall not the least grain fall upon the earth (Amos 9:9).

God's Plan of Salvation is an amazing one. As it says in Amos, over the course of millennia, God has been sifting the house of Israel among all nations. It is literally to be found in everyone, to a greater or lesser degree, with its DNA. What God will be searching out is for those who have a heart for Israel. He will be searching for those who will respond to His Spirit. If we respond, then we are chosen, we are of the house of Israel. As John Moody has said, "a person's spiritual/tribal inheritance is determined in heaven and not by DNA alone"[78].

> Behold, I will send for many fishers, saith the Lord, and they shall fish them; and after will I send for many hunters, and they shall hunt them from every mountain, and from every hill, and out of the holes of the rocks (Jer. 16:16).

More are the Children of the Desolate

> The children which thou shalt have, after thou hast lost the other, shall say again in thine ears, **The place is too strait for me; give place to me that I may dwell**. Then shalt thou say in thine heart, Who hath begotten me these, seeing I have lost my children, and am desolate, a captive, and removing to and fro? and who hath brought up these?

> Behold, I was left alone; these, where had they been? (Is. 49:20-21).
>
> Sing, O barren, thou *that* didst not bear; break forth into singing, and cry aloud, thou *that* didst not travail with child: for **more *are* the children of the desolate** than the children of the **married wife**, saith the Lord (Is. 54:1).

The Married Wife

Today, the Jews are the "married wife," the visible remnants of the house of Israel, the only ones we can positively identify. Over the centuries through war, persecution and assimilation, their population has been decimated. The number of Jews have made somewhat of a rebound from the holocaust of World War II. There are approximately fifteen millions Jews today.

It is estimated that 3 ½ million[j] came out of Egypt during the Exodus. During the time of Christ there were estimated to be about five million Jews. Shockingly, by around 1500 AD, the number had dropped to only about one million.

This seems to be saying that when the Lord restores all the house of Israel, that the married wife, Judah, will be literally amazed at all of her children. "More are the children of the desolate than the children of the married wife."

Who are the children of the desolate? These are the Gentiles. These are the lost tribes of Israel including the millions of Jews and their descendants over the centuries.

The Jews will be literally amazed by the gathering of the house of Israel. They will say, "Behold, I was left alone; these, where had they been?" They have suffered God's judgment and they have been persecuted all these centuries with Satan trying to destroy them so that God's Plan of Salvation would be thwarted. This will be a very emotional time for the Jews. They've seemingly suffered

---

[j] This estimate fluctuates wildly from a few thousand to a few million.

alone but suddenly, here are millions and millions of brothers and sisters of the house of Israel. They are no longer alone.[k]

We need to talk about Isaiah 41, verse 20, where it says "The place is too strait for me." From the Genesis description below, greater Israel would expand the present-day boundaries of Israel to the river of Egypt (the Wadi El-Arish), Iraq to the Euphrates, Jordan, most of Syria and approximately one-third of Saudi Arabia. Much of this land would be desert with limited areas suitable for cultivation. This is saying that even the historical, God-given boundaries of Israel will be much too small for all who want to gather to the Promised Land. This is where the land God gave to Joseph comes into play. We'll discuss this when we talk about the New Jerusalem covenant.

> ...the LORD made a covenant with Abram, saying, Unto thy seed have I given this land, from the river of Egypt unto the great river, the river Euphrates (Gen. 15:21 IV).

Israel Shall Live!

Ezekiel was shown an open valley littered with dry bones. The Lord told Ezekiel that these bones represent the WHOLE house of Israel. He then asked Ezekiel if these bones can live again. Ezekiel replied, "Only you know Lord." The Lord told him to prophesy over these bones. He began to prophesy and there came a shaking and a rattling as these bones began to come together. Then he saw flesh begin to cover the bones.[l]

But of yet, there was no breath in these bones. Ezekiel was told then to prophesy to the winds that they might come and breathe on these bones and bring them to life. The winds here represent the Holy

---

[k] John Moody remarks that the same could be said for Native Americans.

[l] Note: because this is a prophecy of our day and God says the WHOLE house of Israel, this is not just referring to historical Judaism and the lost ten tribes, but also to us of the Restoration, to latter-day Israel. While our situation may seem hopeless, God is saying, "Yes, these bones can live again!"

Spirit. As the winds came Ezekiel saw that these bones came to life and became an exceedingly great army.

Ezekiel 37:11-14

> Then he said unto me, Son of man, these bones are the whole house of Israel: behold, they say, Our bones are dried, and our hope is lost: we are cut off for our parts.
> Therefore prophesy and say unto them, **Thus saith the Lord God; Behold, O my people, I will open your graves, and cause you to come up out of your graves, and bring you into the land of Israel. And ye shall know that I *am* the Lord, when I have opened your graves, O my people, and brought you up out of your graves, And shall put my spirit in you, and ye shall live...** (Ezek. 37:11-14).

This is all described in Ezekiel 37, verses 1-15. Notice what Ezekiel talks about immediately thereafter: the stick of Ephraim, or, the stick of Joseph, which we proclaim to be the Book of Mormon; and, the stick of Judah, which is the Bible. This prophecy discusses a great change coming in the status of the Book of Mormon; and, that as a result of that union, a great change will come in the status of Israel. As the two sticks come together, then Israel is restored to the nation it was in the beginning. **The restoration of Israel is inseparably linked with the fate of the Book of Mormon, the New Covenant.**

Ezekiel 37:16-18

> **Moreover, thou son of man, take thee one stick, and write upon it, For Judah, and for the children of Israel his companions: then take another stick, and write upon it, For Joseph, the stick of Ephraim, and for all the house of Israel his companions: And join them one to another into one stick; and they shall become one in thine hand** (Ezek. 37:16-17).

Whose hands is the Lord talking about here? The Lord is talking to us – to all of us who use these two sticks as one. This is the situation we have today. We haven't yet had great success have we? Then, here's verse 18:

> **And when the children of thy people shall speak unto thee, saying, Wilt thou not shew us what thou meanest by these** (Ezek. 37:18)?

When Ezekiel refers to "the children of thy people," he is referring to the rebellious house of Israel (See Ezek. 12:9 and Ezek. 24:19). Verse 17 talks about the sticks of Ephraim and Judah being used as one in our hands. Verse 18 then is a transitional verse. Apparently some event will take place that brings the Book of Mormon to the children's attention - to the attention of the world. **Then**, they will ask; they will come to those of us who currently have stewardship over the Book of Mormon; and they will ask, "What's this all about?"

Ezekiel 37:19

> **Say unto them, Thus saith the Lord God; Behold, I will take the stick of Joseph, which is in the hand of Ephraim, and the tribes of Israel his fellows, and will put them with him, even with the stick of Judah, and make them one stick, and they shall be one in mine hand** (Ezek. 37:19).

This is when everything changes. **You see then that verse 18 is a transitional verse that stands between the two sticks as being used as one in our hands; and being used as one in God's Hands.**

Even in death, David Whitmer[m] continues to testify of the divinity of the Book of Mormon and of the time when the Book of Mormon and the Bible will be used as one in God's hands. On top of the tombstone we see a Bible with a Book of Mormon resting on top of it along with text saying:

THE RECORD OF THE
JEWS AND THE
RECORD OF THE
NEPHITES ARE ONE

TRUTH IS ETERNAL

---

[m] One of the three Book of Mormon witnesses.

The scriptures talk about this prophecy:

> The Lord hath **made** bare **his** holy arm in the eyes of all the nations; and all the ends of the earth shall see the salvation of our God (Is. 52:10).
>
> Wherefore, the Lord God will proceed to **make bare his arm** in the eyes of all the nations, in bringing about his covenants and his gospel, unto those who are of the house of Israel (1 Ne. 7:22/22:11).

This from 1 Nephi pulls several things together for us including the testimony of Tom Nyawere[n], Hebrews 8:8, Section 83/84 of the Doctrine and Covenants and Ezekiel 37. It specifically addresses what will happen in Ezekiel 37:18, our transitional verse.

What happens in Ezekiel 37:18, is that God will "bare His arm." Then in 37:19 God says "I will take the stick..." **God is intervening**

---

[n] See "Making a New Covenant" chapter.

in human history. Some unmistakable act of God has occurred that ties our two sticks together as one in God's Hands.

> And when that day shall come, it shall come to pass that kings shall shut their mouths; for that which had not been told them shall they see; and that which they had not heard shall they consider.
> For in that day, for my sake shall the Father work a work, which shall be a great and a marvelous work... (3 Ne. 9:94-95/21:8-9).

And, Nephi here says that the purpose of God "baring His arm" is to bring about His covenants and His gospel, to whom? To the house of Israel. That's the purpose of the New Covenant, which we now know is the Book of Mormon; to bring about the fulfillment of all the covenants that God has previously made with Israel.

An interesting aside here, is that traditionally, we Book of Mormon believers have all tried to "prove" the Book of Mormon by pointing to the Bible. **However, after God "bares His arm," as the Book of Mormon clearly says, it will be the other way around, the truth of the Bible will be verified by the Book of Mormon.**[o]

After the two sticks come together as one in God's Hands, then the gathering takes place. The two houses of Israel come together as one nation with one king. The kingdom comes on earth.

Ezekiel 37:21-22

> **And say unto them, Thus saith the Lord God; Behold, I will take the children of Israel from among the heathen** [i.e. the lost ten tribes – Gentiles], **whither they be gone, and will gather them on every side, and bring them into their own land:**
> **And I will make them one nation in the land upon the mountains of Israel; and one king shall be king to them all: and they shall be no more two nations,**

---

[o] See 1 Ne. 3:191/13:39; 2 Ne. 2:17-18/3:11

> **neither shall they be divided into two kingdoms any more at all** (Ezek. 37:21-22).

Here's the point being made in Ezekiel 37. **None of this happens without the Book of Mormon! According to God's plan, Israel does not come to life; Israel is not gathered and the kingdom does not come without the Book of Mormon.** The time is fast approaching when these two sticks will be joined together and be used as one in God's hands.

And, as you might expect, the Book of Mormon confirms the coming together of these two sticks, the Stick of Ephraim and Stick of Judah, to be used as one in God's Hands.

> And the words of the Lamb shall be made known in the records of thy seed, as well as in the records of the twelve apostles of the Lamb; **Wherefore, they both shall be established in one** (1 Ne. 3:195-196/13:41).

Ezekiel 37 Commentary

It should come as no surprise that non-Restoration sources would interpret the "sticks" in Ezekiel 37 differently from that of one representing the scriptural writings of the two houses. Various commentaries say such things of the sticks that they are "pieces of wood," "a prophetic sign," "a visual aid," "an emblem," "a writing tablet," "a symbol inscribed with tribal names," etc. A few commentaries merely say that the meaning is yet to be revealed; "events yet to come will further explain this prophecy." Most seem to agree that it is a prophecy of Israel and Judah coming together as one nation with Christ at the head. We know of course that sticks can refer to records or books. In ancient Israel records were written on tablets of wood or scrolls rolled upon sticks.[p]

One of Joseph Smith's early revelations makes the connection between the Book of Mormon and Ezekiel's "stick of Ephraim":

---

[p] See biblehub.com and studylight.org commentaries

> Behold, this is wisdom in me; wherefore marvel not, for the hour cometh that I will drink of the fruit of the vine with you on the earth, and with Moroni, whom I have sent unto you to reveal the Book of Mormon, containing the fullness of my everlasting gospel; to whom I have committed the keys of the record of the **stick of Ephraim** (DC 26:2a-b/27:5).

The Plates of Brass and the Stick of Joseph

> **And when the children of thy people shall speak unto thee, saying, Wilt thou not shew us what thou meanest by these? And the sticks whereon thou writest shall be in thine hand before their eyes** (Ezek. 37:18, 20).

Earlier, we identified Ezekiel 37:18 as a transitional verse wherein some event has miraculously occurred (God "baring His arm") that causes the children of Israel to ask a question almost certainly concerning the sticks of Joseph and Judah. Remember that their incredulous query in verse 18 comes between the two sticks being used as one in "thine hand" (verse 17) and one in "God's hand" (verse 19). Verse 20 then says those two sticks will be before their very eyes.

Events that follow the two sticks coming together include the restoration of the house of Israel to covenant status, the gathering, the second coming of Christ and the ushering in of the kingdom of God (see Ezek. 37:21-28).

I have no inside information as to what that precipitating event will be that brings the sticks together, however it is my belief that no other event could so ably serve that purpose than the discovery and coming forth of the Plates of Brass.

The Plates of Brass is a great treasure of inestimable worth. These records, being found not in Israel but in the Americas, could very well be the event wondered about in Ezekiel 37:18 that will cause the children of Israel to ask about the two sticks and thus cause them to be brought together. When these plates come forth, they will serve as a witness to the Bible, and will also testify to the truthfulness of the Book of Mormon; **it will testify to the Jews and all the house of Israel that Jesus is the Christ**. It does this by validating the testimony of the Book of Mormon that "none of the prophets have written nor prophesied, save they have spoken concerning this Christ" (Jacob 5:19/7:11).

Some have speculated that the Plates of Brass were in fact the "official scripture" of the Northern Kingdom of Israel that was used, as Len Edwards testified (see "The Two Roads" chapter), to begin the record of Lehi's descendants. These plates may have originated in the time of Joseph of Egypt and thus could be considered the original "Stick of Joseph." We know that Laban, the keeper of the plates, from whom Nephi and his brothers obtained the Brass Plates, was a descendant of Joseph (1 Ne. 1:168/5:16).

In an article entitled "The Plates of Brass," Robert Millett speculates that Laban may have been from the tribe of Ephraim (the birthright holder), while we know that Lehi's family was of Manasseh. In speculating how both parties ended up in Jerusalem (the Southern Kingdom), Millet surmises that Sidney B. Sperry is suggesting that "the prophets in both nations probably paid little attention to the political lines of division, **but it is improbable that all of them had their words recorded in the scriptures of both nations**...The Brass Plates may well have been the official scripture of the Ten Tribes."[79]
[80]

Millett goes on to quote Sperry: "The Northern Kingdom of Israel fell to the Assyrians when its capital of Samaria capitulated to Sargon II in 722 B.C. The forebears of Laban may have fled to Jerusalem to prevent the sacred records from falling into alien hands. Lehi's grandfather or great-grandfather may have left his northern home for Jerusalem in order to prevent his children from intermarrying and making religious compromises with foreigners brought into the land by Assyrians."[81]

Grant Hardy observes, "The plates of brass were the basic scriptures of the Nephite nation, and for centuries their prophets read them, quoted them in sermons, and excerpted material from them to enrich their own writings."[82] Much of the content of the Brass Plates has been incorporated into the Book of Mormon and has served to shape its people and history and thus has served to enrich all who read its message.

Lehi prophesied that "these Plates of Brass should go forth unto all nations, kindreds, tongues, and people who were of his seed. Wherefore, he said that these plates of brass should never perish; neither should they be dimmed any more by time" (1 Ne. 1:169-170/5:17-19).

The ancient Israelites' entire mode of existence was affected by their belief that throughout history they stood in a unique relationship with the Divine. The people of Israel believed that their response to the divine presence in history was central not only for themselves but for all humankind. The universal goal of the Jewish people has frequently expressed itself in messianism—the idea of a universal, political realm of justice and peace. In one form or another, messianism has permeated Jewish thinking and action throughout the ages. There is a general sense among Jews that they remain Jews not because of the force of anti-Semitism, but because of the attractiveness of their tradition and their common history and destiny.[83]

Indeed, it is their history that is the key to understanding Judaism. I can think of no other book that would present such a compelling witness to the Jews than that of the Plates of Brass. It may be Joseph's record, but it is THEIR HISTORY. It is "a record of the Jews from the beginning" to approximately 600 BC. It contains the first five books of Moses and an account of creation plus the prophecies of the holy prophets from the beginning. It contains many prophecies of Joseph of Egypt not in the Bible, and also writings of four prophets not found in the Bible; Zenos, Zenock, Neum, and Ezias (see 1 Ne. 1:159-163; 5:240-242; Hel. 3:54/5:11-13; 19:10; 8:19-20).

> And the Lord will set his hand again the second time to restore His people from their lost and fallen state. **Wherefore, he will proceed to do a marvelous work, and a wonder among the children of men. Wherefore, he shall bring forth HIS WORDS unto them**, which words shall judge them at the last day; **For they shall be given them for the purpose of convincing them of the true Messiah, who was rejected by them** (2 Ne. 11:28-31/25:17-18).

Other Books to Come Forth

> And it came to pass that I beheld the remnant of the seed of my brethren, and also the book of the Lamb of God, which had proceeded forth from the mouth of the Jew…And after it had come forth unto them, **I beheld OTHER BOOKS which came forth by the power of the Lamb**, from the Gentiles unto them, unto the convincing of the Gentiles, and the remnant of the seed of my brethren, and also the Jews, who were scattered upon all the face of the earth, that the records of the prophets and of the twelve apostles of the Lamb are true.
> And the angel spake unto me, saying, **These last records which thou hast seen among the Gentiles shall establish the truth of the first, which are of the twelve apostles of the Lamb** (1 Ne. 3:190-192/13:38-40).

> **And it shall come to pass that the Jews shall have the words of the Nephites, and the Nephites shall have the words of the Jews**…And it shall come to pass that my people which are of the house of Israel, shall be gathered home unto the lands of their possessions; and **MY WORD** also shall be gathered in one (2 Ne. 12:71, 73/29:13-14).

Per Keith Meservy, "Not only did Ezekiel [representing Judah] know that each of these tribes would keep records, but Joseph of old also knew that he and Judah would be keepers of special records. The Lord had told him that '...**the fruit of thy loins shall write; and the fruit of the loins of Judah shall write; and that which shall be written...shall grow together'** (2 Ne. 2:19-20/ 3:12). Lehi reported this to his children, so the Nephites knew that they would keep records which would be joined with Judah's records. Similarly, Ezekiel taught the Jews that God would join those records together to carry out His work. Thus, the Lord clearly told the two tribes the fate and importance of the records they were keeping."[84]

And then shall the Jews look upon me and say, What are these wounds in thy hands, and in thy feet? Then shall they know that I am the Lord; for I will say unto them, These wounds are the wounds with which I was wounded in the house of my friends. I am he who was lifted up. I am Jesus that was crucified. I am the Son of God. And then shall they weep because of their iniquities; then shall they lament because they persecuted their King (DC 45:9a-d/51-53).

Study Guide

1. Discuss the implications of the Lord calling the Book of Mormon "the foundation of my gospel and my Rock" (see DC 16: 1b-d/18:2-5).

2. What are the New Covenant implications of DC 64:6c/33 wherein the Gentiles are charged with "laying the foundation of a great work"?

3. In light of Ezekiel 37, discuss the implications of the "two sticks" finally being used as one in God's Hands.

4. Nephi spoke of "other books" coming forth that would convince us that the Bible, the records of the prophets and of the twelve apostles of the Lamb are true (see 1 Ne. 3:190-192/13:38-40). What do you think of the author's speculation that one of those books could be the Plates of Brass?

CHAPTER 11

Other Covenants of the Lord

Every covenant of God leads to JESUS CHRIST, THE KING OF ISRAEL, and every covenant of God goes back to the Everlasting Covenant of the Beginning.[85] – Tom Nunn

---

"THE FOUNDING OF A SOCIETY"[86]

Henry Drummond, a 19th century Scottish evangelist, says that the danger we Christians face is that we take out of context the work of Christ. That we often take out of the larger structure "a stone" [a single text of scripture] and insist that it represents Christ's whole purpose. He implores us to not allow any isolated text to keep us from trying to understand Christ's program as a whole.

Drummond reveals that it is a startling thought to consider that "Christ probably did not save many people while he was here." While he was able to minister to individuals, this was not the whole aim he had in view. "His immediate work was to enlist men in his enterprise, to rally them into a great company, or society for the carrying out of his plans. The name by which this society was known was, ***The Kingdom of God***." Christ's great cause was the kingdom of God.

CHRIST'S GREAT CAUSE

WAS THE KINGDOM OF GOD

"One hundred times it occurs in the Gospels. When He preached He had almost always this for a text. His sermons were explanations of the aims of His Society, of the different things it was like, of whom its membership consisted, what they were to do or to be, or not do or not be. And even when He does not actually use the word, it is easy to see that all He said and did had reference to this....Though one time He said He came to save the lost, or at another time to give men life, or to do His Father's will, these were all included among the objects of His Society.

The sense of belonging to such a Society transforms life.

"Tens of thousands of persons who are familiar with religious truths have not noticed yet that Christ ever founded a Society at all. The reason is partly that people have read texts instead of reading their Bible, partly that they have studied Theology instead of studying Christianity, and partly because of the noiselessness and invisibility of the Kingdom of God itself. Nothing truer was ever said of this Kingdom than that "It cometh without observation." Its first discovery, therefore, comes to the Christian with all the force of a revelation. The sense of belonging to such a Society transforms life. It is the difference between being a solitary knight tilting single-handed, and often defeated, at whatever enemy one chances to meet on one's little acre of life, and the *feel* of belonging to a mighty army marching throughout all time to a certain victory. This note of universality given to even the humblest work we do, this sense of comradeship, this link with history, this thought of a definite campaign, this promise of success, is the possession of every obscurest unit in the Kingdom of God."[87]

The Promised Land Covenant

By faith Abraham, when he was called to go out into a place which he should after receive for an inheritance, obeyed; and he went out, not knowing whither he went. By faith he sojourned in the land of promise, as in a strange country, dwelling in tabernacles with Isaac and Jacob, the heirs with him of the same promise: **For he looked for a city which hath foundations, whose builder and maker is God** (Heb. 11:8-10).

Abraham fully understood the grand scope and purpose of the promises God made to him; but also he realized that, in the flesh, he would not live to see their fulfillment; yet, "he looked for a city which hath foundations, whose builder and maker is God." Fundamental to God's ultimate purpose was the covenant of land and descendants; and ultimately a "city of God" in which all nations of the earth would be blessed.

God made a covenant with Enoch, that when his posterity shall embrace the truth and look upward, then shall Zion, the heretofore earthly city of Enoch whom God caught up into the heavens, shall once again look downward, and with the general assembly of the church of the firstborn, come down out of heaven and possess the earth (Gen. 9:22-23 IV).

> And the Lord said unto Enoch, Then shalt thou and all thy city meet them there; and **we will receive them into our bosom; and they shall see us, and we will fall upon their necks, and they shall fall upon our necks, and we will kiss each other;** And there shall be mine abode, and it shall be Zion (Gen. 7:71-72 IV/Moses 7:63-64).

Before Enoch's city can come again and possess the earth, its earthly counterpart must come into being; this city Abraham was searching for; a city whose builder and maker is God. Without a Promised Land and a city where the saints of God can gather, Zion cannot be, neither can God's covenant with Enoch be fulfilled; nor God's covenant with Abraham that in his seed should all nations of the earth be blessed. Since Israel's very beginning, Zion, the coming together of heaven and earth, has been God's goal. Jesus taught us to pray, "Thy Kingdom come, thy will be done on earth, as it is in heaven."

We have made several mentions about how God, in His infinite wisdom, has separated the pathways of Israel and Judah. While the world sees the house of Israel only through the trials and travails of the Jews, God has been quietly laying the foundation for a great and marvelous work that will astound; that will take the world completely by surprise. This is when "kings shall shut their mouths, for that which had not been told them, shall they see…" (3 Ne. 9:93/ 21:7).

In the chapter, "The Covenant to Restore Israel," we alluded to the fact that even with the original, expanded boundaries of Israel (see Gen. 15:18), well beyond that of the present-day boundaries; that even that land would still be much too small for all who would gather in the last days. Quoting Isaiah, "The place is too strait for me; give place to me that I may dwell" (Is. 49:20).

God's provision for the limited area of land in Palestine is a promised land bequeathed to Joseph, wherein the tribes of the northern kingdom, the lost ten tribes, can safely dwell.

> Moreover I will appoint a place for My people Israel, and will plant them, that they may dwell in a place of their own, and move no more; neither shall the children of wickedness afflict them anymore, as before time (2 Sam. 7:10; 1 Chron. 17:9).

The mystery of this prophecy is that at the time, Israel was already secure in its own land and Israel as a whole was prospering under the reigns of David and Solomon. So, on the surface this would seem to make no sense. However, the time would come when Assyria would invade and disperse the northern kingdom of Israel and they would no longer have a land of their own; at least, until that time when God would gather them again to Joseph's land.

Jacob (Israel) adopted the sons of Joseph, Ephraim and Manasseh (see Gen. 48:13-16), gave them his name Israel, and blessed them. As Jacob blessed Joseph's sons he prophesied that Ephraim and Manasseh would receive the birthright blessings of Gen. 35:11; that Manasseh would become a "great nation" and that Ephraim would become a "company of nations":

> Manasseh's descendants will also become a great people. But his younger brother will be greater than he, and his descendants will become great nations (Gen. 48:19).

> And God said unto him, I *am* God Almighty: be fruitful and multiply; a nation and a company of nations shall be of thee, and kings shall come out of thy loins (Gen. 35:11).

Jacob, in blessing Joseph, said:

> Joseph is a fruitful bough, even a fruitful bough by a well; whose branches run over the wall [over the sea]... The blessings of thy father have prevailed above the blessings of my progenitors unto the utmost bound of the everlasting hills: they shall be on the head of Joseph, and on the crown of the head of him that was separate from his brethren (Gen. 49:22, 26).

Lehi, the offspring of Manasseh, was the one separated from his brethren; "But behold I [Lehi] have obtained a land of promise, in the which things I do rejoice" (1 Ne. 1:150/5:5).

The New Jerusalem Covenant

We believe in the literal gathering of Israel and in the restoration of the Ten Tribes**, that Zion will be built upon this continent**, that Christ will reign personally upon the earth, and that the earth will be renewed and receive its paradisiac glory[88] – Joseph Smith Jr.

"Early on, Stalin built a village in Poland called Nowa Huta, or 'New Town,' to demonstrate the promise of communism. He could not change the entire country at once, he said, but he could construct one new town with a shiny steel factory, spacious apartments, plentiful parks, and broad streets as a token of what would follow. Later, Nowa Huta became one of the hotbeds of Solidarity[q], demonstrating instead the failure of communism to make just one town work.

"What if Christians used that same approach in secular society and succeeded? 'In the world the Christians are a colony of the true home,' said Bonhoeffer. Perhaps Christians should work harder toward establishing colonies of the kingdom that point to our true home. All too often the church holds up a mirror reflecting back the society around it, rather than a window revealing a different way."[89]

Many visionaries have come to recognize the need for Zion, a city that indeed would give us a foretaste of our future home, and that would hasten the redemption of the world. The good news is that this "kingdom colony" has been a part of God's plan from the very beginning.

Chronologically speaking, the first indication that Zion would be built on this continent comes near the end of recorded Jaredite history (c. 600 – c. 120 BC).

> … this land, it became a choice land above all other lands, a chosen land of the Lord. Wherefore the Lord would have that all men should serve him, who dwell upon the face thereof; and that **it was the place of the New Jerusalem, which should come down out of heaven, and the holy sanctuary of the Lord** (Ether 6:2-3/13:2-3).

The Book of Mormon contains over seventy references to the Americas using terms such as "promised land," "choice land" and "New Jerusalem." Besides the record of the Jaredites, Nephi received a testimony from the Lord that God would lead them to a "land of promise; yea, even a land which I have prepared for you; yea, a land which is choice above all other lands" (1 Ne. 1:54/2:20).

---

[q] A Polish trade union founded in 1980 that contributed greatly to the fall of communism – Wikipedia.

Later, but still before their sea voyage to the Promised Land, Nephi has a vision as an angel of the Lord appears to him and prophesies of things to come. Nephi is shown that the Gentiles also will be led to the Promised Land "which is choice above all other lands" (1 Ne. 3:176/13:30). Finally, in a post-resurrection appearance to the Nephites, Christ affirms the location of the New Jerusalem:

> And behold, this people will I establish in this land, unto the fulfilling of the covenant which I made with your father Jacob; and it shall be **a New Jerusalem**.
> And the powers of heaven shall be in the midst of this people; yea, even I will be in the midst of you (3 Ne. 9:58-59/20:22).

After the church was restored and the Book of Mormon was published, undoubtedly members had read and understood that the New Jerusalem would be located in America although the exact location was not known.

> And now, behold, I say unto thee, that it is not revealed, and no man knoweth where the city shall be built, but it shall be given hereafter. Behold, I say unto thee that it shall be on the borders by the Lamanites (DC 27:3c-d/28:9).

Through a revelation given February 9, 1831, they were told, "Thou shalt ask, and it shall be revealed unto thee in mine own due time, where the New Jerusalem shall be built" (DC 42:17b/62). After the June 1831 conference of the church at Kirtland, Ohio, a revelation (DC 52) was received through Joseph Smith Jr. that directed several elders to go to the land of Missouri where the Lord would reveal the Center Place of Zion. The missionaries were directed to go two by two taking different routes and leaving at different times. Shortly after their arrival, the following was received:

> Behold, the place which is now called Independence, is the Center Place, and the spot for the temple is lying westward upon a lot which is not far from the courthouse (DC 57:1d/3).

DC 57 directs that Sidney Rigdon consecrate and dedicate the spot of the temple unto the Lord. The saints were directed to gather money to purchase not only the site of the temple but the whole region of country as soon as time and money would permit - this for the gathering of the saints (DC 58).

An Ensign on the Mountains

All ye inhabitants of the world, and dwellers on the earth, see ye, when he lifteth up an ***ensign*** on the mountains; and when he bloweth a trumpet, hear ye (Is. 18:3).

I say unto you that Zion shall flourish, and the glory of the Lord shall be upon her, and she shall be an ***ensign*** unto the people, and there shall come unto her out of every nation under heaven (DC 64:8a/41-42).

And it shall come to pass that I will establish my people, O house of Israel. And behold, this people will I establish in this land, unto the fulfilling of the covenant which I made with your father Jacob; and it shall be a New Jerusalem (3 Nephi 9:57-58/20:21-22).

To make cities - that is what we are here for. To make good cities - that is for the present hour the main work of Christianity. For the city is strategic. One Christian city, one city in any part of the earth whose citizens, from the greatest to the humblest, live in the spirit of Christ, where religion has overflowed the churches and passed into the streets, inundating every house and workshop, and permeating the whole social and commercial life - one such Christian city would seal the redemption of the world[90] - Henry Drummond.

The Righteous Remnant Covenant

Wherefore, thus saith the Lord, I have led this people forth out of the land of Jerusalem, by the power of mine arm, that I might raise up unto me a righteous branch from the fruit of the loins of Joseph (Jacob 2:34/25).

In four appearances to Joseph Smith, three on the evening of September 21, 1823 and one the next day, the angel Moroni cited the same scriptures to Joseph, including this scripture which he said was about to be fulfilled:

> And I will shew wonders in the heavens and in the earth, blood, and fire, and pillars of smoke. The sun shall be turned into darkness, and the moon into blood, before the great and the terrible day of the Lord come.
> And it shall come to pass, *that* whosoever shall call on the name of the Lord shall be delivered: for in mount Zion and in Jerusalem shall be deliverance, as the Lord hath said, and in the **remnant** whom the Lord shall call (Joel 2:30-32).

Today, we are recipients and beneficiaries of the Book of Mormon, the resultant Restoration Movement and the fullness of the gospel, all because God purposed to raise up a righteous remnant of the seed of Joseph. God had in mind all along that this righteous remnant would embrace the truth of the Book of Mormon and thus would be the catalyst to gather the entire house of Israel home to their promised lands so that the Everlasting Covenant might be fulfilled:

> And this is mine everlasting covenant, that ***when thy posterity shall embrace the truth,*** and look upward, then shall Zion look downward, and all the heavens shall shake with gladness, and the earth shall tremble with joy;
> And the general assembly of the church of the firstborn shall come down out of heaven, and possess the earth, and shall have place until the end come. And this is mine everlasting

> covenant, which I made with thy father Enoch (Gen. 9:22-23 IV).

The Everlasting Covenant that God made with Enoch centers around his posterity "embracing the truth." In another place we are told what that truth is, even the truth "sent forth out of the earth" (Gen. 7:69 IV/Moses 7:62). Furthermore, we know that this truth from the earth, the Book of Mormon, is explicit from its title page through its very last chapter where Moroni begins by saying, "And I write unto my brethren the Lamanites…" (Moroni 10). It clearly says that the restoration of the house of Israel is to begin with the seed of Lehi, the remnant of Joseph:

> Yea, let us remember the words of Jacob, before his death; for behold he saw that a part of the remnant of the coat of Joseph was preserved, and had not decayed.
> And he said, Even as this remnant of garment of my son hath been preserved, <u>so shall a remnant of the seed of my son be preserved by the hand of God</u>… (Alma 21:56-57/46:24).

Currently, there are only two identifiable remnants of the house of Israel, one visible and one not; the Jews being visible while the Native American remnant of Joseph's seed is not yet discernible to the world. The word "preserved" God used in connection with this remnant of Manasseh is not to be taken lightly. Because this remnant is at the heart of God's plan to restore Israel, He did not allow Lehi's seed to be completely destroyed. When in Egypt, Jacob blessed Joseph by saying:

> Therefore, O my son, he hath blessed me in raising thee up to be a servant unto me, **in saving my house from death**… For thou shalt be a light unto my people, to deliver them in the days of their captivity, from bondage; and to bring salvation unto them, when they are altogether bowed down under sin (Gen. 48:8, 11 IV).

In the words of Jacob, he acknowledges the providence of God in raising up his son Joseph to save "my house" from famine and death. Then, Jacob prophesied as to how this literal salvation of Israel would be a "type" for Israel's salvation in the latter days. That when Israel would be bowed down under sin; that a remnant of Joseph's descendants (of Ephraim and Manasseh), would be a light to his people and deliver them from sin. Likewise, Moroni had reference to this prophecy, this "type" of salvation that would occur in the latter days:

> And that a New Jerusalem should be built up upon this land, unto the remnant of the seed of Joseph, for which things there has been a **type**... Wherefore the Lord brought a remnant of the seed of Joseph out of the land of Jerusalem, that he might be merciful unto the seed of Joseph, that they should perish not, **even as he was merciful unto the father of Joseph, that he should perish not** (Ether 6:6-7/13:6-7).

Just as God, through the providential act of Joseph's brothers selling him into slavery, **sent him ahead to Egypt** to prepare for the eventual salvation of the house of Israel; God, even so, has provided for His people Israel in these last days by **sending ahead a remnant of Joseph to this land**; that a New Jerusalem might be established that would once again provide salvation to Israel.

> And the love of men shall wax cold, and iniquity shall abound; and when the time of the Gentiles is come in, **a light shall break forth** among them that sit in darkness, and it shall be the fullness of my gospel (DC 45:4b/27-28).

> ...and the whole world lieth in sin, and **groaneth under the darkness and under the bondage of sin** (DC 83:7f/84:49).

> ...and ye must needs be led out of bondage by power, and with a stretched out arm; and as your fathers were led at the first, even so shall the redemption of Zion be (DC 100:3e/103:17-18).

As we read above, Lehi, a descendant of Manasseh, was the one prophesied to become a great nation, that would be "separated from his brethren" (Gen. 49:22, 26) and thus inherit a land of promise (1 Nephi 1:150/5:5). While Ephraim's descendants would become a multitude of nations, in time, many of their number chosen by God, would be led to and be united with Manasseh's remnants in the Promised Land of America; thus reconstituting the house of Joseph to fulfill its God-given role of redeeming the house of Israel when "they are altogether bowed down under sin."

A Covenant with Joseph

While the specific covenant is not recorded in the Book of Mormon, at some point God made a covenant with Joseph that out of the fruit of his loins He "would raise up a **righteous branch <u>unto the house of Israel"</u>**; a branch "to be broken off nevertheless to be remembered in the covenants of the Lord"; a branch wherein the Messiah, in the last days, would be manifest in the spirit of power which would bring them out of darkness into the light (2 Nephi 2:7-9/3:5).

A record would be kept by this branch of Joseph that, in the last days, will be instrumental not only in restoring the covenant to Joseph's descendants, but in uniting this record with that of the Bible in order to bring blessings to all nations. From their number will come a great leader who will be an instrument in God's hands to work mighty miracles and to help restore of the house of Israel.

> Wherefore, because of this covenant thou art blessed: for thy seed shall not be destroyed, for they shall hearken unto the words of the book.
> And there shall raise up one mighty among them, who shall do much good, both in word and in deed, being an instrument in the hands of God, with exceeding faith,
> To work mighty wonders, and do that thing which is great in the sight of God, unto the bringing to pass much restoration unto the house of Israel, and unto the seed of thy

brethren (2 Nephi 2:45-47/3:23-24).

These resultant mighty wonders and restoration of Israel come about because this remnant shall "hearken unto the words of the book." They will embrace the Book of Mormon which is the New Covenant, the fullness of the gospel.

> And I will shew unto thee, O house of Israel, that the Gentiles shall not have power over you, but I will remember my covenant unto you, O house of Israel, and ye shall come unto the knowledge of the fullness of my gospel (3 Nephi 7:37/16:12).

The day Christ "remembers" his covenant with the remnant of Lehi, is the day when he makes a new covenant with the house of Israel (Hebrews 8:8); and, on that same day, the stick of Joseph and the stick of Judah will become one in God's hands (Ezek. 37:19). Afterwards, the nations of Judah and Israel will become one nation with Christ at their helm, and he will be their prince forever.

> Moreover I will make a covenant of peace with them; it shall be an everlasting covenant with them: and I will place them, and multiply them, and will set my sanctuary in the midst of them for evermore. My tabernacle also shall be with them: yea, I will be their God, and they shall be my people (Ezek. 37:26-27).

The Book of Mormon along with its intended "righteous remnant" is perhaps the pivotal work in all of history. - Tom Nunn

Study Guide

1. What do you think of Henry Drummond's assessment as to the methodology of Christ employed in his earthly ministry?

2. Discuss the implications of God promising Israel a land of their own at a time when they were already secure in their own borders (see 2 Sam. 7:10; 1 Chron. 17:9).

3. Henry Drummond said that a city where its citizens, from the greatest to the humblest, live in the spirit of Christ – "one such city would seal the redemption of the world." Discuss the necessity of such a city that would be "an ensign on the mountain."

4. Discuss the Righteous Remnant covenant from the aspect of it being "a type" of salvation like wherein the house of Israel was saved in the days of Joseph of Egypt.

PART III:

THE NEW COVENANT LIFE

Thus far we have discussed the broad scope of God's Plan of Salvation, primarily looking at God's covenants on a collective basis, those covenants made with the house of Israel that will ultimately be fulfilled by a New Covenant that God will soon be making with the house of Israel and the house of Judah.

However, these far-ranging, magnificent covenants can only be fulfilled as the New Covenant promise is placed in the heart of each individual that has made the effort to learn what the New Covenant life is, and has come to desire this life for themselves. Zion will come one heart at a time.

We live in the climax-time of history and therefore have a unique opportunity not only for a fulfilling life, but for being an eternal benefit to all of God's creation.

The chapters in this next section are of prime importance and lie at the heart of the purpose of this book. I believe that the material in these few chapters, prayerfully read, can be life-changing. These chapters offer invitation, instruction and inspiration. Hopefully, you, the reader, might come to desire to avail yourselves of the riches of God's abundant grace; and that He might fulfill His New Covenant promise in you, as He "writes His laws in the tables of your heart."

THE TIME IS NOW!

CHAPTER 12

Invitation to an Amazing Life

Firstly, the rich and the learned, the wise and the noble; and after that cometh the day of my power; then shall the poor, the lame, and the blind, and the deaf, come in unto the marriage of the Lamb, and partake of the supper of the Lord, prepared for the great day to come. Behold, I, the Lord, have spoken it (DC 58:3e-f/ 10-12).

Israel's stunning victory in the 1967 Arab-Israeli war was certainly against all odds. For so many, the Six-Day war ultimately came down to the battle for Jerusalem. It is the most sacred place in Jewish history. The fight for its control was desperate and difficult.

Once the war began to turn in favor of the Israelis there was enormous international pressure not to attempt a capture of the old city of Jerusalem for fear of Muslim world-wide retaliation; but Israel's history with this city could not go unheeded. There was more passion toward this conquest than any other battle in the war.

One of those called on to liberate Jerusalem became one of the war's greatest heroes. Yoram Zamosh was a young paratrooper assigned to the capture of the Temple Mount. He was asked about how he felt when he learned he was about to fight for the liberation of the city. This is his recollection:

> Maybe, more than others, I had a sense of longing for this city – to think we were about finally to fight in Jerusalem, to liberate it. Remembering our parents, our grandparents back in Auchwicz, this was the climax of their wishes. When we spoke among ourselves we felt we were touching history, and even making history.
>
> The Jordanians were waiting for us. We killed eighty during that first battle the night before we ourselves arrived inside the old city. It was a very difficult battle. We lost a third of

our unit. There were more than eighty-six casualties while hundreds were wounded.

As our group of Israeli soldiers approached, the old city seemed deserted but there was a danger of snipers everywhere. The way to the Wailing Wall was through a green door which we found locked. An old Arab man stepped forward and, speaking in Hebrew, greeted us. He said he wanted peace in the old city, and he unlocked the door for us.

Twenty centuries of prayers had finally been answered.

For several minutes we were at the wall's courtyard, just a handful of us soldiers. Those first minutes were so quiet, no gunshots. We all prayed, even those of us who weren't great believers, we all wanted to be part of the Jewish people at that point.

We were the messengers of the entire Jewish people throughout all generations. We haven't arrived at this point by accident.

It was June 7, 1967, news of the liberation spread like wildfire throughout the country. Tank commanders stopped to pray. Soldiers on the frontlines cheered, the nation celebrated. Around the world faithful Jews and Christians alike wept for joy at the news twenty centuries of prayer had finally been answered.[91]

The Greatest Generation

"The Greatest Generation" is a term popularized by journalist Tom Brokaw with the publication of his book by the same name in 1998. Brokaw profiles that generation born from around 1901 to 1924 who grew up enduring the deprivation of the Great Depression of the late 1920s and early 1930s; and then went on to fight in World War II, as well as those on the home front, who through sacrificial effort, made a decisive material contribution to the war.

Clint Pumphrey, in his review of ***The Greatest Generation*** summarizes Brokaw's assertions about this generation.

> Tom Brokaw argues that the World War II generation's perseverance through difficult times is a testament to their extraordinary character. Their remarkable actions, during times of war and peace, ultimately made the United States a better place in which to live. Born and raised in a tumultuous era marked by war and economic depression, Brokaw asserts, these men and women developed values of "personal responsibility, duty, honor and faith." These characteristics helped them to defeat Hitler, build the American economy, make advances in science and implement visionary programs like Medicare. According to Brokaw, "at every stage of their lives they were part of historic challenges and achievements of a magnitude the world had never before witnessed."
>
> Brokaw credits ***The Greatest Generation*** with much of the freedom and affluence that Americans enjoy today. "They have given the succeeding generations the opportunity to accumulate great economic wealth, political muscle, and the freedom from foreign oppression to make whatever choices they like," he writes. Despite these achievements, however, Brokaw believes that ***The Greatest Generation*** remains remarkably humble about what they've done. He concludes, "It is a generation that, by and large, made no demands of homage from those who followed and prospered economically, politically, and culturally because of its sacrifices."[92]

Perhaps some would take issue with Brokaw's lofty assessment of this generation. Nonetheless, this generation met very difficult challenges at a pivotal point in human history, where the distinction between good and evil was made starkly clear.

There have been many generations, individuals, empires and events that have played critical roles in world history. Trying to list and rank the greatest would be futile. All have played crucial roles in getting us to where we are today.

Without a doubt the most meaningful and impactful event in human history is the incarnation of our Lord. This is true regardless of one's religious views. Christ has impacted all our lives individually and collectively. He has influenced how we govern and how we treat each other.

It is interesting to note that the purpose of our dating system (B.C. – 'Before Christ' and A.D. – 'in the year of our Lord') is to make the birth of Jesus Christ the dividing point of world history. Throughout eternity, Christ's sacrifice on the cross for us will remain the focal point of God's love and redemption. It is said of him that, in heaven, he will be the only one disfigured.

Our Generation

Certainly those believers who encountered Christ during his earthly ministry were blessed to be able to see and hear those things which the prophets of old so much desired. Jesus said this to his disciples:

> For verily I say unto you, That many prophets and righteous men have desired to see those things which ye see, and have not seen them; and to hear those things which ye hear, and have not heard them (Matt. 13:17).

These words of Jesus can be projected from his first advent to his next advent. Certainly those who loved the Lord and foresaw his latter day coming would have longed to be part of it. Hebrews 11 is the great chapter on faith in the Bible. It mentions those of faith who didn't live to see the promises fulfilled nevertheless looked forward to them with a longing that exceeded their desires for the things of the present world.

> For he [Abraham] looked for a city which hath foundations, whose builder and maker is God....These all died in faith, not having received the promises, but having seen them afar off, and were persuaded of them, and embraced them, and confessed that they were strangers and pilgrims on the earth... For they that say such things declare plainly that they seek a country....a better country, that is, an heavenly: wherefore God is not ashamed to be called their God: for he hath prepared for them a city (Heb. 11:10,13,14,16).

"...for he hath prepared for them a city (v. 16)." This would seem to indicate that these ancients were longing for the Zion of the last days.

> And these all, having obtained a good report through faith, received not the promise:
> God having provided some better thing for us, that they without us should not be made perfect (Heb. 11:39-40).

These saw Christ from afar off in types and shadows. Most were under the old covenant but God has provided something better for us; that being the New Covenant in Christ. In their day none of these had fulfilled to them the manifestation of the Messiah in the flesh. They hoped for a city whose builder and maker is God.

All of which serves to bring us to this day, our day, the last days; perhaps the very time these men and women of faith would have desired to see and be a part of. No matter how important and pivotal those past generations, individuals, ideas, inventions, and events might have been, like a funnel, they have all been distilled to a point in time, our day – the time of the restitution of all things. Peter said of our Lord:

> Whom the heaven must receive until the times of restitution of all things, which God hath spoken by the mouth of all his holy prophets since the world began (Acts 3:21).

We are of the generation that has the privilege of living in this the climactic time of history. There has not been, nor will there be, any more important generation in history than our own. This generation, because of the imminent fulfillment of God's covenant with Israel, unquestionably **WILL** be remembered as a great generation, one that responded to God's Spirit and became new creatures in Christ. God **WILL** make a new covenant with the house of Israel that, as a stone cut out of the mountain without hands, **WILL** roll forth and fill the whole earth as Daniel saw in vision (Dan. 2:31-45).

Both ancient and modern prophecy point to this time with the declaration, "Lift up your heads and rejoice, for...your redemption draweth nigh." It can be said, then, with conviction that we live in the most fascinating generation of history.[93] – Arthur Oakman

The Zohar is a mystical book, or set of books, composed in Spain in the 13th century containing interpretations of and commentaries on the Torah, or the first five books of the Bible. It includes many early Jewish traditions from ancient texts. Concerning this last generation, our generation, the Zohar says this:

Rabbi Simeon
(Zohar Genesis 117b-118a, Zohar Exodus 147a)

> ...but when the days of the Messiah will be near at hand, even children will discover the secrets of wisdom. "**Blessed is this generation! There will be none other like unto it until King Messiah shall appear**, when the Torah shall be restored to her ancient pride of place."

Prophetically speaking of this closing generation, we quote from a revelation received by Joseph Luff, June 12, 1923:

> **Blessed in that hour** shall he be who hath made the word of the Lord his study and in that hath found contentment, for his face shall shine with the glory of its fulfillment, and his feet shall be beautiful in the light of its vindication.
>
> His lips and his tongue shall minister as in the stead of his Master and in these shall the heavens have delight. Their words shall mean accomplishment, for upon them shall the heavens wait and their eloquence shall be as the noise of the Holy Ghost.
>
> They shall not be known by the name given them of their fathers, but as the messengers of God, for in them shall He be discerned...[94]

The only question for you then is whether or not you will choose to be a part of this great generation. God calls you to greatness and glory. He calls you by name. He calls you to "Have done with lesser things. To give heart and soul and mind and strength, To serve the King of Kings."[95] He offers you a personal invitation to the marriage supper of the Lamb, He requests a reply; you must give an answer. What will it be?

Precious blessings I have given,
richer far await my grace.
For ye now behold my presence,
With the veil before thy face;
But the time is shortly coming,
when this veil shall be removed,
Nothing then shall separate me
From the ones whom I have loved.

Answer this, my invitation,
To be present where I am,
Ye are all again invited,
To the marriage of the Lamb;
Then put on the white apparel,
Robe of righteousness all wear,
Children, are you making ready,
Will you all be present there?

(Song given by Spirit through
Russell Archibald, June 23, 1912)

Study Guide

1. Do you agree with the statement of Arthur Oakman that "we live in the most fascinating generation of history"? If not, what other generation would you have desired to be a part of?

2. What did Rabbi Simeon say about the generation when the days of the Messiah will be at hand?

CHAPTER 13

Living an Amazing Life

> **Zion cannot be built up unless it is by the principles of the law of the celestial kingdom, otherwise I cannot receive her unto myself ...** (DC 102:2c/105:5).

In Jesus' earthly ministry he made many "radical" statements challenging to saints and sinners alike. Calls to leave their homes, abandon their jobs, risk their lives and even give up their families for him. Perhaps the most controversial statement of all is: ***"I am the way and the truth and the life. No one comes to the Father except through me."*** This is a challengingly exclusive statement that doesn't leave room for equivocation – you either believe or you don't. How one answers this question lies at the heart of what it means to be a Christian.

"Be ye therefore perfect..."

For believers however, there's another statement of Jesus that is perhaps even more controversial. In his ***Sermon on the Mount,*** Jesus gives many beautiful, comforting beatitudes such as blessed are they that mourn, blessed are the meek, blessed are the merciful, blessed are the pure in heart and blessed are those who hunger and thirst after righteousness. However, in the verses that follow, we come to some sayings that are not quite as comforting as they appear to challenge our very nature. Besides reciting the command to not kill, we are told that we are in danger of judgment if we are even angry with our brother. We are told not to commit adultery, but also not even to have lustful thoughts. We are to love our enemies, bless those who curse us, and do good to those who hate us. And then for the *coup de gras,* Jesus concludes this series of sayings with this:

> ***Be ye therefore perfect,*** even as your Father which is in heaven is perfect (Matt. 5:48).

To say the least, this injunction of Jesus is very controversial; a true mystery of the gospel that is oftentimes misunderstood, explained away, or just plain ignored. Even for those who advocate for a literal interpretation, who say that it means what it says, oftentimes there appears to be a denial that this state of perfection can be achieved in our mortal lives but would wait until after the resurrection.

Alan Medinger[96] makes the point that Jesus' call for us to be perfect is the only standard he could possibly set for us, and yet at the same time, Medinger says, <u>it is an impossible standard to meet</u>. "Could he have said, 'Be, therefore, 75% unselfish, 90% chaste, 98% honest…'? Or, how about, 'Be loving and charitable to the extent that it feels right to you'? No, a righteous and loving God can neither accept sin, nor can He allow us - given our sinfulness - to set our own standards."

Medinger then postulates that "<u>perfection is truly an impossible standard</u>, one that none of us will achieve in this life. Our sin nature, our tendency to act selfishly, runs too deep."

He then states that there is only one possible answer as to how this seemingly unbridgeable gap between God and man can be bridged - grace. "Between what we are and what we are called to be spans the glorious arch of God's grace. It is both a covering over us, and a bridge to the Father - His priceless, yet freely offered gift."

Yes, the answer is Grace. However, many seem to think that when the word is used in the scriptures, it means a "give away" program from the Lord; that we can sin and that the Lord will automatically forgive us because we are "saved by grace."

C.S. Lewis is one that seemingly advocates for a literal interpretation but even he allows that perfection is a process that will not be completed in this lifetime. Lewis says that God intends to get us as far as possible along perfection's path before death.

> That is why He [Jesus] warned people to "count the cost" before becoming Christians. "Make no mistake," He says, "if you let me, I will make you perfect. The moment you put

> yourself in My hands, that is what you are in for. Nothing less, or other, than that. You have free will, and if you choose, you can push Me away. But if you do not push Me away, understand that I am going to see this job through. Whatever suffering it may cost you in your earthly life, whatever inconceivable purification it may cost you after death, whatever it costs Me, I will never rest, nor let you rest, until you are literally perfect— until my Father can say without reservation that He is well pleased with you, as He said He was well pleased with me. This I can do and will do. But I will not do anything less."[97]

Even a Restoration leader writing an article entitled, "Be Ye Perfect - Eventually," likewise suggests our "potential" to achieve perfection with God in eternity. He suggests that the command to be perfect, in part at least, is to be a tribute to Who and what God is and what we can achieve with Him in eternity. He suggests we ought to strive for "steady improvement" without obsessing over "toxic perfectionism."[98]

Historical Perspective

Former Community of Christ apostle, Andrew Bolton, examines for us the attitudes towards the Sermon on the Mount in Christian history:

> It is clear that the Sermon on the Mount was very important for early Christians. How, though, did they interpret it? Origen[r], for example, saw the sermon quite straightforwardly as something to be obeyed. Jesus, argued Origen, "conveys no other meaning than this, that it is in our power to observe what is commanded. And there we are rightly rendered liable to condemnation if we transgress those commandments which we are able to keep." Thus the early church saw the Sermon on the Mount as the literal commandments of Jesus to be obeyed. How did later Christians understand the Sermon on the Mount?

---

[r] Origen (184-253 AD) – "the most important theologian and biblical scholar of the early Greek church." – Encyclopedia Britannica

> Constantine, the first Christian Roman Emperor, came to power in 312 C.E. Before this time Christians were a minority. To be a Christian was a voluntary decision that could mean risking persecution. After Constantine, Christians became the majority and non-Christians were persecuted. But once people had little or no choice but to be a Christian, how did this new situation affect how they now understood the Sermon on the Mount?
>
> For the first time questions were raised as to how practical an ethic the Sermon on the Mount was. Could it still be kept by all Christians, many of whom were not particularly committed? From this time onward there developed a "double standard" interpretation.
>
> **Two Callings**
>
> One way of dealing with the Sermon on the Mount was to say there are two callings. One was the calling of clergy, monks, and nuns who would keep the sermon fully. The calling of the majority of "lay" Christians did not require the Sermon on the Mount to be kept fully.
>
> Reinhold Niebuhr, an important American theologian in the first half of the twentieth century, argued that the Sermon on the Mount was an impossible possibility. Some Christians already had argued that its purpose was to set up an impossible standard that we could never achieve. This would then make us throw ourselves on the grace of God and accept personal salvation through faith alone. The Sermon on the Mount has done its job when we realize we are sinners and have been brought to our knees and God's grace.[99]

Concerning the New Covenant and the possibility of living a life of obedience, Andrew Murray says this:

> It is just because this, the essential part of the New Covenant, so exceeds and confounds all human thoughts of what a covenant means; that Christians, from the Galatians downwards, have not been able to see and believe what the New Covenant really brings. They have thought that

> human unfaithfulness was a factor permanently to be reckoned with as something utterly unconquerable and incurable, and that the possibility of a life of obedience, with the witness from within of a good conscience, and from above of God's pleasure, was not to be expected. They have therefore sought to stir the mind to its utmost by arguments and motives, and never realized how the Holy Spirit is to be the unceasing, universal, all-sufficient worker of everything that has to be wrought by the Christian.[100]
>
> And, if we ask for the cause of the unbelief, that prevents the fulfillment of the promise, we shall find that it is not far to seek. It is, in most cases, the lack of desire for the promised blessing. Where the law (the old) has done its full work, where the actual desire to be freed from every sin is strong, and masters the heart, the promise of the New Covenant, when once really understood, comes like bread to a famishing man. **The subtle unbelief, that thinks it impossible to be kept from sinning, cuts away the power of accepting God's provision of a New Covenant.**[101]
>
> **The New Covenant is meant to meet the need for a power of not sinning, which the Old could not give**. Come with that need; it will prepare and open the heart for all the everlasting [New] Covenant secures you. It will bring you to that humble and entire dependence upon God in His Omnipotence and His Faithfulness, in which He can and will work all He has promised.[102]
>
> Let us beseech God earnestly that He would reveal to us by the Holy Spirit the things that He hath prepared for them that love Him; things that have not entered into the heart of man; the wonderful life of the New Covenant.[103]

Tom Nunn, in his book, ***Covenants of the Lord,*** offers some additional historical insights:

> It has been the business of Christianity for centuries to soften His words and back away from His stand, to make faith and loyalty as easy as possible, to cater to every whim and desire and to reduce the demands of Jesus to virtually

nothing. There is no vigor to most of Christianity today and this is the source of the impotence.[104]

> **"There is no vigor to most of Christianity today…" – Tom Nunn**

Israel is that People who are engaged in a struggle with God to learn His will, to discover their strength, to find the real meaning of history and life, to know the truth of any matter and of life, to expose our weaknesses and deal with them, to come to a solid and sound resolution of any decision while there is yet time. Israel is both a people and it is those individuals who are becoming that people. If and when we avoid this struggle and begin to look for the easy way, then we are among those of whom Paul said, "They are not all Israel who are of Israel."[105]

Whereas the proscriptions of the Sermon on the Mount were initially rigorously enforced, in time they began to lose their authority in the lives of the average Christian, so that through various interpretations they were set off as being statements for those who aspired to a special holiness, or as being descriptions of what things would be like in the kingdom of God to come, but were not intended for the present day, or with other such disclaimers.[106]

Admittedly I have not done exhaustive search concerning various opinions today about Jesus' admonition to be perfect; however, in the searching I have done, I have not found many opinions that this state of perfection can be achieved in our mortal lifetime.

As we shall see, there is a sense in which this is true, that we cannot receive a fullness of glory in this lifetime, but more importantly for Zion's sake, this perfection in the flesh, this adherence to the Celestial Law <u>must take place</u> for its redemption (see DC 102:2c/105:5). This perfection lies at the heart of the New Covenant that God will make with the house of Israel and the house of Judah.

The Secret Revealed

Tom Nunn assesses for us the secret of a true covenant relationship with God:

> Jesus, the man of the covenant, was constantly going off to pray, to spend time with God, to seek for and draw upon the solace, the joy, the counsel, the power of that companionship. He loved His father and He knew the strength of the joy of His presence.
>
> This is the secret of the true people of the covenant: to continually and diligently seek Him. This is not to try to learn things about Him. It is to pursue knowing Him, to become interested in the things which interest Him, taking them into ourselves and making them our interests. It is to be fascinated with Him and with His ways. It is to rejoice in His Presence and in His friendship. It is to want to know what it is that pleases Him and to attempt doing it. It is to really know that He is interested in us and that He is seeking to care for us according to all His ability. It is to lay aside those things which, however desirable they might be to us, are offensive to Him. This is pursuing the Lord, the lover of our souls, and this is how we may come to a knowledge of the secrets of the covenant. This is what worked for Jesus of Nazareth and it is what will work for us.[107]

WHEN OUR DEEPEST DESIRE IS NOT THE THINGS OF GOD, OR A FAVOR FROM GOD, BUT GOD HIMSELF, WE CROSS A THRESHOLD.[108]

The Celestial Life

We, of the Restoration, are most fortunate to have other scriptures that offer us great insight into what the celestial life is and what it entails. We are especially blessed to have Section 76 of our Doctrine and Covenants, which is a record of a vision revealed to Joseph Smith and Sidney Rigdon concerning the eternal glories and how man is to be judged.

For those not familiar with Restoration scripture, Joseph and Sidney were given a glimpse of the three glories as described in 1 Corinthians:

> There are also celestial bodies, and bodies terrestrial: but the glory of the celestial is one, and the glory of the terrestrial is another. There is one glory of the sun, and another glory of the moon, and another glory of the stars: for one star differeth from another star in glory. So also is the resurrection of the dead (1 Cor. 15:40-42).

In short, **Celestial Glory** (the glory of the sun) is the Church of the Firstborn; those who will dwell in the very presence of God and His Christ forever and ever (see DC 76:5b-r/51-62). **Terrestrial Glory** (the glory of the moon) are those who receive of the presence of the Son but not the fullness of the Father. These are the honorable men of the earth; those who were not valiant in their testimony of Jesus. Also, these are ones who "died without law"; who did not receive of the testimony of Jesus in the flesh but afterwards received it (see DC 76:6a-h/71-80). Of **Telestial Glory** (glory of the stars), these are the ones who received not the gospel of Jesus Christ in their lifetime. They are thrust down to hell, not having denied the Holy Spirit. They shall receive of the Holy Spirit through the ministrations of ones from the Terrestrial kingdom. The glory of this kingdom varies as do the stars in the heavens (DC 76:7a-g/81-90).

Of immediate concern, is the description we receive of the celestial life, the type of life God desires that we live and the requisite life necessary for the redemption of Zion. Here we will cite background information on the reception of Section 76 and then offer a brief description of celestial life that Joseph and Sidney were commanded to write. The following are Joseph Smith's words cited in the LDS preface to Section 76:

> "Upon my return from Amherst conference, I resumed the translation of the Scriptures. From sundry revelations

> which had been received, it was apparent that many important points touching the salvation of man had been taken from the Bible, or lost before it was compiled. It appeared self-evident from what truths were left, that if God rewarded every one according to the deeds done in the body the term 'Heaven,' as intended for the Saints' eternal home, must include more kingdoms than one. Accordingly ...while translating St. John's Gospel, myself and Elder Rigdon saw the following vision."

From this preface Joseph tells us that many important points concerning salvation have been taken from the Bible or lost before it was compiled. No wonder then the confusion concerning salvation. In Section 76 Joseph states:

> "For while we were doing the work of translation, which the Lord had appointed unto us, we came to the twenty-ninth verse of the fifth chapter of John, which was given unto us as follows: 'Speaking of the resurrection of the dead, concerning those who shall hear the voice of the Son of man, and shall come forth; they who have done good in the resurrection of the just, and they who have done evil in the resurrection of the unjust'" (DC 76:3c-d/15-17).

After reading the above from John, this caused them to marvel and the Lord touched their eyes of understanding and the vision opened. They beheld the glory of the Son, on the right hand of the Father, and saw the holy angels; and they who worship God and the Lamb forever and ever. The following is a brief summation of the celestial life that ensued (with RLDS and LDS verse references):

These are they who...(DC 76)

- **Received the testimony of Jesus...**(5b/51)
- **Received the Holy Spirit...**(5c/52)
- **Overcome by faith, and are sealed by the Holy Spirit of promise, which the Father sheds forth upon all those who are just and true...**(5d/53)
- **Are the Church of the Firstborn...**(5e/54)

- **Into whose hands the Father has given all things...**(5f/55)
- **Are priests and kings, who have received of his fullness ...**(5g/56)
- **Overcome all things...**(5h/60)
- **Shall dwell in the presence of God and his Christ forever and ever...**(5j/62)
- **Come unto Mount Zion, and unto the city of the living God, the heavenly place, the holiest of all...**(5n/66)
- **Are they whose bodies are celestial, whose glory is that of the sun, even the glory of God the highest of all...**(5r/70)
- **Are JUST MEN MADE PERFECT THROUGH JESUS THE MEDIATOR OF THE NEW COVENANT...**(5q/69).

That Dimmest Star

Verily I say unto you, among them that are born of women there hath not risen a greater than John the Baptist: notwithstanding he that is least in the kingdom of heaven is greater than he (Matt. 11:11).

In our attempt to describe the unsurpassed glory of the celestial life that God calls us to, we find that we are totally incapable of going beyond what Section 76 is telling us. However, by way of contrast, if we examine what God has in mind for the least person in the kingdom of heaven, we will be even more amazed.

In Matthew 11:11, we read above that the least person in heaven will be greater than John the Baptist, the greatest of all having been born of women. This is how Section 76 describes the three glories:

- Telestial – (the glory of the stars) **its glory surpasses all understanding...**(7g/89)
- Terrestrial – (the glory of the moon) excels in all things the glory of the telestial, even in glory, and in power, and in might, and in dominion (7h/91)
- Celestial – (the glory of the sun) excels in all things; where God, even the Father, reigns upon his throne for ever and ever (7i/92)

The glories of these three kingdoms are such Joseph testified that "man is [not] capable to make them known" (8b/116). Even the glory of the telestial "surpasses all understanding" (7g/89). The Apostle Paul concurs as he relates the experience of visiting the third heaven (see 2 Cor. 12:2) (or paradise as he subsequently called it). Paul said that he heard unspeakable words (see 2 Cor. 12:4) which were not lawful to utter; words not in our vocabulary or capable to be understood with our earthly understanding.

The glories of the telestial kingdom vary according to the brightness of the stars in heaven, from the very brightest to the dimmest of stars. Section 76 describes telestial glory this way:

- These are they who received not the gospel of Christ, neither the testimony of Jesus…(7b/82)
- They deny not the Holy Spirit…(7c/83)
- These are they who are thrust down to hell…(7d/84)
- These are they who are liars, and sorcerers, and adulterers, and whoremongers, and whosoever loves and makes a lie…(7o/103)
- These are they who suffer the wrath of God on the earth…(7p/104)
- These all shall bow the knee, and every tongue shall confess to him who sits upon the throne for ever and ever (7u/110)
- In the mansions which are prepared [for them], they shall be servants of the Most High, but where God and Christ dwell they cannot come…(7v/111-112)

Of telestial glory we are told that its numbers are as numerous as the stars in heaven, or as the sand on the seashore (7t/109). Of all the billions and billions of people who have ever lived, try to imagine the least person of all, the dimmest of stars in heaven. Now, compare that dimmest of stars to the brightness of the sun at noonday. Amazing!

Now here's the really marvelous thing about the grace, mercy and love of God: the glory of that dimmest star surpasses our human language to describe. Every inhabitant of telestial glory will spend countless ages singing of God's amazing love. Following is a testimony shared by Jim Hobbs concerning that dimmest of stars:

> In 1986 I took a period of 40 days to go to the mountains of west Texas and seek some answers from the Lord. During the third week at night there was a full moon and I was able to walk around the campground without any light. The next morning the Lord woke me up early in the morning before daylight and told me to "get up and go outside and look at the sky." So I got up and got dressed and went outside and squatted down behind a wall to get out of the wind. I looked up into the sky and there was hardly any space that you could stick a pen without hitting a star. There was all sizes and brightness of stars. Then as the sun began to come up the stars began to fade away. There was probably only two or three stars left just before the sun broke over the horizon. After the sun came up you could see no stars at all. After about thirty minutes I got up and went back to my camper. I spent the day praying, studying and hiking. At the end of the day I retired for the night. Again about five AM the Lord woke me up and told me to "go outside and look at the sky." I told the Lord it was cold outside and I knew what I would see. I then asked Him what it was He was trying to show me or to get me to understand. He said, "You remember the tiniest star you saw in the sky." I said yes. He said, "I died on the cross for the person who would receive me with that smallest amount of light."[109]

Study Guide

1. First, discuss the historical perspectives provided by Andrew Bolton concerning Christ's Sermon on the Mount.

2. Next, from a practical, day-to-day point of view, express your feelings about the practicality of living Christ's Sermon on the Mount.

3. Examine the various viewpoints expressed concerning this statement of Christ: "Be ye therefore perfect, even as your Father which is in heaven is perfect" (Matt. 5:48). What viewpoint most reflects your feelings about this commandment?

4. What is Tom Nunn's reason for stating "There is no vigor to most of Christianity today."

5. Discuss Tom's statement "revealing the secret" of a true covenant relationship with God.

6. Lastly, discuss what Section 76 reveals about the celestial life – the life necessary for the redemption of Zion.

CHAPTER 14

Having a Form of Godliness

This know also, that in the last days perilous times shall come. For men shall be lovers of their own selves, covetous, boasters, proud, blasphemers, disobedient to parents, unthankful, unholy, Without natural affection, trucebreakers, false accusers, incontinent, fierce, despisers of those that are good, Traitors, heady, high minded, lovers of pleasures more than lovers of God; Having a form of godliness, but denying the power thereof: from such turn away (2 Tim. 3:1-5).

For forty years the New Testament Church was predominantly Jewish so they had an understanding of the history of Israel and of the covenants. However, in the second generation, the Jewish War with the Romans (70 AD) disrupted the affairs of the church and gradually a shift in leadership took place, from Jewish to Gentile. Unfortunately these Gentile leaders did not have the background for a complete understanding of the Israelite heritage of the church, the gospel, or of the scriptures, and this became increasingly so with each new generation. **This shift away from the Jewish roots of the church is one of the reasons for the proliferation of heresies that pummeled the church in the second century of its existence.** Although the church put up a valiant defense against these intrusions, it was not equipped to adequately deal with them and gradually outside elements crept in.[110]

The Emperor Constantine became the sole ruler of the Roman Empire in 324 AD. In 313 AD his Edict of Milan legally ended the pagan persecution of Christians. Because Constantine favored Christianity it gradually became the dominant religion in the empire. With this seeming triumph however, the fate of an already wounded church was sealed as Constantine began to blend paganism with Christianity.[111]

Apostasy gradually spread, teachings were corrupted and the authentic priesthood of God was taken from the earth. The ancient prophet Amos had foretold such a time of apostasy and spiritual darkness.

> **"Behold, the days come, saith the Lord God, that I will send a famine in the land, not a famine of bread, nor a thirst for water, but of hearing the words of the Lord: and they shall wander from sea to sea, and from the north even to the east, they shall run to and fro to seek the word of the Lord, and shall not find it"** (Amos 8:11–12).

In 1820, one of those seeking the word of the Lord that had been lost was fourteen year old Joseph Smith, Jr. The Smith family lived in the rural community of Palmyra, New York, which was experiencing a great religious revival, where the established religions of the day were actively seeking converts. Several of Joseph's family united with the Presbyterians. While he became somewhat partial to the Methodists, his confusion was very great, such that he ultimately despaired as to his ability to come to a conclusion as to who was right and who was wrong.

One day he read from James 1:5, ***"If any of you lack wisdom, let him ask of God, that giveth to all men liberally, and upbraideth not; and it shall be given him."*** He subsequently determined that his only recourse was to do as James directed; to ask of God.

Joseph retired to the woods and began to offer up his desires to God, when he was seized by a power that seemed to doom him to destruction. Joseph exerted all of his strength to call upon God for deliverance. Suddenly there appeared over his head a pillar of light brighter than the sun that gradually descended upon him.

He saw two personages, whose brightness and glory defy all description… One of them called him by name, pointing to the other saying; "This is my Beloved Son. Hear Him." After composing himself, Joseph asked the two personages which of all the sects was right (for at that time it had never occurred to him that they were all wrong) – and which he should join.

> "I was answered that I must join none of them, for they were all wrong; and the Personage who addressed me said that all their creeds were an abomination in His sight; that those professors were all corrupt, 'they draw near to Me with their lips, but their hearts are far from Me, they teach for doctrines the commandments of men, ***having a form of godliness, but they deny the power thereof.***'"[112]

The Apostle Paul (see 2 Tim. 3:1-5 in opening scripture) echoed these words about the apostasy that would occur in the last days where there would be a form of godliness that denies the power of God. This, of course was the reason Joseph was told to join none of them; so that the church through him could be restored along with all the attendant spiritual gifts and power of God.

Continuing to Deny the Power of God?

The restoration of the church indeed saw the return of spiritual gifts not seen perhaps since the days of Pentecost and the beginnings of the New Testament church. Although the level of spiritual gifts have lessened considerably over the years, no doubt the universal opinion of all connected with any faction of the Restored Church would be that, "we do not deny the power of God."

Our protestations notwithstanding; in spite of clear teachings in all three of our books, I am convinced that in one crucial area, we of the Restoration join with our Christian brothers and sisters in continuing to deny the power of God. We continue to explain away and deny the power of God to make us perfect – IN THIS LIFE. In short, we deny the possibility of living a Celestial Life, a New Covenant life, the life necessary for the redemption of Zion. **It is one thing to admit that of ourselves we cannot be perfect as our Lord commands; but, it is entirely another thing to say that God cannot make us perfect. Is this not denying the power of God?**

Jesus answered and said unto him, If a man love me, he will keep my words: and my Father will love him, and we will come unto him, and make our abode with him (John 14:23).

If ye keep my commandments, ye shall abide in my love; even as I have kept my Father's commandments, and abide in his love (John 15:10).

..and Zion cannot be built up unless it is by the principles of the law of the celestial kingdom, otherwise I cannot receive her unto myself (DC 102:2c/105:5).

If thou lovest me, thou shalt serve me and keep ***all*** my commandments (DC 42:8a/29).

And the bow shall be in the cloud; and I will look upon it, that I may remember the everlasting covenant, which I made unto thy father Enoch; that, when men should keep ***all*** my commandments, Zion should again come on the earth, the city of Enoch which I have caught up unto myself (Gen. 9:21 IV).

Faith (or Grace) vs. Works

God "will repay each person according to what they have done" (Rom. 2:6).

While searching various websites on the subject of faith and works, I offer these excerpts from an article written by Steven Cole entitled "Judged by Your Deeds (Rom. 2:6-11)."

During my college years, several of my friends and I knew an attractive coed who was Roman Catholic. She called us her "minister friends," because we were always talking to her about the gospel. After hours of spiritual conversations, I persuaded her to read the Gospel of John. I told her that as she read, she should ask God to show her how she could have eternal life.

> Shortly after that she came up to me beaming and said, "I did as you said. I asked God to show me how to have eternal life, and He did!" I thought, "Yes! She came to John 3:16 and discovered that those who believe in Jesus have eternal life!" But instead, she took me to John 5:28-29, where Jesus says, "…for an hour is coming, in which all who are in the tombs will hear His voice, and will come forth; those who did the good deeds to a resurrection of life, those who committed the evil deeds to a resurrection of judgment." She said, "I will get eternal life if I do good deeds!"
>
> How would you have answered her? That sounds like what Jesus is teaching there. And, it seems to be what Paul is teaching in our text (Rom. 2:6-11). He says that those who persevere in doing good receive eternal life. Those who do evil will incur God's wrath. Is salvation by grace through faith *alone,* as the Reformers insisted? Or is it by grace through faith *plus* works, as the Roman Catholic Church has taught?
>
> Here is where we [must] come to grips with the question: "Is Paul contradicting himself?" Is he saying here that we're saved by works? But later, he clearly says that we're saved by faith (Rom. 3:20-28; 4:4-5; Gal. 3:11; Eph. 2:8-9; Phil. 3:9; etc.). Which is it?
>
> **"Is Paul contradicting himself?"**
>
> Good works do not earn salvation, but they are the essential evidence that a person is on the path to glory, honor, and immortality. We have to lean on God's grace not only for salvation, but also for perseverance in good works. So we will be judged by our works, which reveal whether our faith in Christ is genuine or mere empty profession. Paul and James say the same thing: your faith is demonstrated by your works.[113]

What do you think of Steven Cole's answer that we are judged by our works because they reveal whether our faith in Christ is genuine or not? How would you have answered her? The topic of faith and works, because of apparent scriptural contradictions (i.e. John 3:16 vs. John 5:28-29), is especially difficult to understand even for those of us who have studied the scriptures all our lives. It is a difficult topic even for those of us who are blessed to have Section 76 in the Doctrine and Covenants. It is a difficult topic for Christians because over the millennia our Bible has been corrupted. As previously stated in "Living an Amazing Life," the vision that Joseph Smith and Sidney Rigdon received, which resulted in Section 76, was engendered because they had been reading scriptures that said if God rewarded everyone according to the deeds done in the body, that the term "heaven" should encompass more kingdoms than one. To them, it became apparent that many important points touching the salvation of man had been taken from the Bible, or lost before it was compiled; a point confirmed in the Book of Mormon:

> Wherefore, thou seest that after the book hath gone forth through the hands of the great and abominable church that there are many plain and precious things taken away from the book, which is the book of the Lamb of God… Because of these things which are taken away out of the gospel of the Lamb, an exceeding great many do stumble, yea, insomuch that Satan hath great power over them (1 Ne. 3:171,175/13:28-29).

I want to reiterate here my concurrence with Joseph, Sidney and Nephi. **I now believe that this doctrinal point of denying God's power to make us perfect, happens to be towards the top of the list when it comes to the "plain and precious things taken away" that causes God's people to stumble and fall.**

Personal Reflections

As a young man I remember a time at my place of employment, when I had a conversation with a young Southern Baptist lady concerning our topic of faith and works. She said that she believed that "we are saved by grace, but rewarded for our works." At the time, that seemed to me to be an entirely reasonable answer. So, over the years, that has come to epitomize my personal belief (a belief that I now believe to be somewhat lacking). Sometime afterwards I came across this same teaching by well-known Southern Baptist minister Charles Stanley. Here I quote myself from a subsequent sermon:

> In his book, *Eternal Security,* Stanley writes of an experience of preaching a sermon in which he said that while we are saved by grace, we are rewarded for our works. He said that everyone does not receive the same reward in heaven. There was a particular young man in his congregation that this hit like a ton of bricks. This young man indeed thought that because he had accepted Jesus that this was all he needed to do. He thought that because he had accepted Jesus he could then do anything he liked because after all, we are saved by grace and grace alone. Because of this sermon he realized that it does make a difference how we live our lives. He said that he stopped drinking and partying and began to witness and invite his friends to church.

The bottom line is that our beliefs matter. They have a direct bearing on how we live our lives. The above by Charles Stanley illustrate the importance of coming to an understanding of this vital topic.

My experience in writing two previous books is to always look closely at any articles or books I encounter along the way. I have found that many, many times God has in one way or another directed to me material He wished to call to my attention. In preparing to write this book, the pattern has continued. In early 2017, I received an article written by Daniel Muhlenkamp entitled, "THE OTHER COMFORTER... AND PERFECTION." I read this with interest at the time and filed it away in my memory banks. Sure enough as ideas for this book developed, I had decided to write about how amazing the New Covenant life would be (i.e. "Living an Amazing Life"). I had determined that to live such a life where one is personally taught by God (Heb. 8:10-11) would indeed call for living a Celestial Life, as I knew that no unclean thing can come into God's presence. This then led to an examination of Christ's Sermon on the Mount which led to Christ's statement: "Be ye therefore perfect, even as your Father which is in heaven is perfect" (Matt. 5:48).

One of the primary functions of the Holy Spirit is to call to our mind those things we need in the time that we need it. The Holy Spirit then "reminded" me of Daniel's article which is germane to the topic at hand. Daniel and his mentor, Robert Johnson, have written extensively about the topic of "The Other Comforter and Perfection." I have found in Daniel's writings material I believe helps explain one of the great "mysteries" of the gospel, which is Christ's admonition to "be perfect." As I mentioned above, because of this material which is discussed in the following chapter, I have had to alter or qualify the mantra I've used for years which is, "we are saved by grace but rewarded for our works." Our examination of Daniel's article (plus inclusion of other material that we've shared) I believe can be life-changing and vital knowledge necessary for the redemption of Zion. I invite your prayerful consideration.

Study Guide

1. The Apostle Paul said that in the last days there will be "a form of godliness, but denying the power thereof." The author states that there is one specific way in which we continue to deny the power of God. Do you agree?

2. Discuss Steven Cole's story of how he and his minister friends interacted with a young college coed concerning how she could have eternal life. In what way was the coed's answer surprising?

3. Discuss this statement: "We are saved by grace but rewarded for our works."

CHAPTER 15

The Other Comforter and Perfection Part I

Master, which is the great commandment in the law? Jesus said unto him, Thou shalt love the Lord thy God with all thy heart, and with all thy soul, and with all thy mind. This is the first and great commandment. And the second is like unto it, Thou shalt love thy neighbour as thyself. On these two commandments hang all the law and the prophets (Matt. 22:36-40).

As mentioned in the closing words of the previous chapter, this topic of "The Other Comforter and Perfection" stems primarily from an article entitled the same written by Daniel Muhlenkamp. Also included is material from subsequent communications with Daniel along with material written by his mentor, Robert Johnson. On a limited basis, I will also include my own thoughts and commentary. Of necessity, the material has been rearranged and summarized. Daniel has graciously given me permission to write and use what I wish without attribution. To some extent, I will avail myself of his generous offer as it will lessen the time required to write this material.

P R E F A C E

Personally, I must say that this material has been a "revelation" to me. Like Daniel when he first came to know these concepts, I was and am familiar with most all of the individual scriptures, but putting it all together to understand the overall concept, to understand this mystery of the gospel proves to be somewhat challenging. Daniel testifies that, despite being in a class with Robert Johnson, his mentor, for a period of six months, he still was not understanding what it was that he was teaching. When he confided his confusion to him, he just told him to "stay with it," to fast and pray. Johnson told him that it had taken him about forty years to understand it himself; that he had even asked an apostle once for the interpretation of Ephesians 2:8-9 (a scripture that is at the very core of the controversy about faith, works and perfection) that says:

> **"For by grace ye are saved, through faith; and that not of yourselves; but it is the gift of God; Not of works, lest any man should boast."**

Johnson said that the apostle told him, "To tell you the truth, I'm not exactly sure myself, but if you find out what it means before I do, will you let me know?"

I haven't heard whether Johnson ever got back to the apostle or not with the answer, but this writing attempts to answer that question along with many more related questions. Daniel says that he subsequently had a spiritual experience where the Lord revealed to him the "code" as it were of such things as Grace, Justification, Election, The Royal Law, the Other Comforter, Perfection, and the Perfect Law of Liberty. In short, the mystery of the two great commandments taught by our Lord (see Matt. 22:36-40 above); the mystery of such passages as:

> But if ye be **led of the Spirit**, ye are not under the law (Gal. 5:18).
>
> If therefore **perfection** were by the Levitical priesthood (for under it the people received the law), what further need was there that another priest should rise after the order of Melchisedec, and not be called after the order of Aaron? (Heb. 7:11).

Daniel testifies that one day he came home after church and was reading some scriptures from class, when all of a sudden in an instant, all of the perplexities of understanding he had before literally vanished; the Lord opened "that thing" up to his understanding. The veil of darkness he had felt before was removed. It was like an atom bomb went off! He cried out loud, "OH - MY - GOD!" In the same breath he said, also out loud [without even thinking that he should say it out loud, it just came out of his mouth], "THIS THING IS EVERYTHING!"

Daniel cautions that there is and will be a certain amount of resistance to these teachings, even among the saints. He says that there is a certain aversion to the idea that something they have scarcely heard of before in their entire life in this church might be the very core of the doctrine of the kingdom to which they aspire; the idea being, "Then why haven't we heard about this before?"

Daniel says that while these things can and should be taught, that each person, with no exception, must come to a spiritual understanding on his or her own; these concepts, in the end, must be taught by the Spirit. The reader then is invited to prayerfully consider what is taught here.

Personally, I believe and accept these concepts because they are scriptural. They tie together seemingly diverse scriptures and make an understandable whole.

Faith (or Grace) vs. Works (continued)

In the previous chapter, we began our discussion of faith and works and the seemingly contradictory scriptures we encounter.

> For by ***grace*** are ye saved through faith; and that not of yourselves: it is the gift of God: Not of works, lest any man should boast (Eph. 2:8-9).
>
> For the Son of Man is going to come in the glory of His Father with His angels, and then he shall reward every man according to his ***works*** (Matt. 16:27).

The scriptures are replete with such examples, such seeming contradictions. **Daniel's writing points us to the true definition of grace, a definition which in itself completely changes how one looks at the topic of faith and works.**

Strong's #5485: charis (pronounced khar'-ece) from 5463; graciousness (as gratifying), of manner or act (abstract or concrete; literal, figurative or spiritual; **especially the divine influence upon the heart, and its reflection in the life; including gratitude**):--acceptable, benefit, favour, gift, grace(- ious), joy, liberality, pleasure, thank(-s, -worthy).

It is of interest to note here that most secular dictionary sources primarily define grace as "gracefulness" or "unmerited favor" while ascribing a secondary meaning of "divine influence upon the heart and its reflection in the life." However, the Merriam-Webster online dictionary offers this as their primary definition of grace: "**unmerited divine assistance given to humans for their regeneration or sanctification.**"[114] In twenty first century language this means "God touches your heart and changes you. When that change is reflected in your life: That's Grace!!"[115]

> "Grace is not simply leniency when we have sinned. **Grace is the enabling gift of God not to sin. Grace is power, not just pardon**."[116] – John Piper

> "Grace isn't just what Jesus did for us on the cross. **Grace is God giving to us the Holy Spirit, Who enables us and gives us the POWER TO OVERCOME sin**."[117] – Jeff Fenske

With this new concept of grace as our guide, we can now discern the true meaning of the Ephesian scripture above. **This "divine influence upon the heart" can have no other meaning than the Spirit of God, or the "Holy Spirit."** Nothing else explains the nature of grace because there is no other way mentioned in the scriptures in which His "divine influence" can come "upon the heart," and its "reflection in the life, including gratitude," except by His Spirit. This includes the various "gifts of the Spirit," and is the reason they are so-named.

> "But the ***manifestation of the Spirit*** is given to every man ***to profit withal...*** But all these [GIFTS] worketh that one and the selfsame ***Spirit,*** dividing to every man severally as he will" (1 Cor. 12: 7, 11).

In the book of Mosiah, a prophet by the name of Abinadi had come to the Land of Nephi prophesying the destruction of King Noah and his people unless they repented. Abinadi was to be put to death because of his testimony but Alma, a priest, believed Abinadi and pleaded with the king to spare Abinadi's life. This made the king very angry and he sought to take Alma's life also. He and other believers found a hiding place in the land of Mormon near a fountain of pure water. In Mosiah 9 is recorded Alma's baptismal charge to those willing to make a covenant with the Lord in the Waters of Mormon.

> If this be the desire of your hearts, what have you against being baptized in the name of the Lord, as a witness before him that ye have entered into a covenant with him that ye will serve him and keep his commandments; **that he may pour out his Spirit more abundantly upon you?** (Mosiah 9:41/18:10).

A few verses later, the following was written where, instead of saying that they were filled with the Holy Spirit after baptism, they were filled with the grace of God:

> Yea, and they were baptized in the waters of Mormon, and were **filled with the grace of God** (Mosiah 9:48/18:16).

For by the Holy Spirit ye are saved through faith.

Returning to our Ephesians 2:8-9 scripture, we can then substitute "Holy Spirit" for "grace" to more accurately discern its true intent: "...for by the ***Holy Spirit*** ye are saved through faith; and that not of yourselves: it is the gift of God; Not of works, lest any man should boast." I was literally amazed as to how this simple substitution clarifies and changes our view of salvation.

In the previous chapter I mentioned my inherited Southern Baptist mantra of "we are saved by grace and rewarded for our works." After discovering this new definition of grace I realized that this belief is entirely wrong, not only in my understanding of grace but as we shall see below, I had an incorrect understanding of works. I would now say something like:

> **We are saved by the Holy Spirit and rewarded by the Holy Spirit** (in other words, our salvation is entirely a work of God, a work of the Holy Spirit, the flesh accomplishes nothing).

Here I want to emphasize an important point concerning grace. All creation operates under the umbrella of God's grace; hence "for by grace ye are saved" is not incorrect. As the scriptures say, "God makes the sun to rise on the evil and on the good, and sendeth rain on the just and on the unjust" (Matt. 5:45). This grace of God is unmerited as there is nothing we can ever do to repay God for our existence; we are the workmanship of His Hands. By emphasizing this new understanding of God's grace as being synonymous with the Holy Spirit, we do not mean to imply that we should disregard the conventional understanding and definition of grace that it is the "unmerited favor" of God. Even with our substitution of Holy Spirit for grace above we still read in our Ephesians scripture that ultimately salvation is a gift of God (albeit a gift that requires a response on our part). However, when it comes to our salvation, we will shortly discover that without our new understanding of grace we cannot resolve our question as to whether we are saved by grace or our works or a combination thereof. We will now see that without this new understanding of grace that the concept of "continuing in grace" (Acts 13:43) or "receiving grace for grace" (see below) would make little sense.

"Grace is God giving us the Holy Spirit which is the power to overcome sin."[118] – Jeff Fenske

Receiving Grace for Grace

So, using grace and the Holy Spirit interchangeably we can rightly say that, "the closer one is to God then the greater amount of grace they receive." In the statement above I also substituted the Holy Spirit for works because the works we are rewarded for, the works of which God approves, are really Holy Spirit inspired works, works that we do while obeying His commands. You remember that Jesus "only did those works and said those words commanded of him by the Father" (see John 5:19; 12:49-50). Therefore, speaking of righteous works, "our works" are accomplished through the Holy Spirit and through our faith and obedience. So, Eph. 2:9 is literally correct: "Not of works, lest any man should boast."

> And he who obeyeth the truth, ***the works which he doeth they are of God*** (John 3:22 IV).

This "revelation" was amazing to me because it tied seemingly incompatible scriptures together to make a coherent whole. **Works and grace are therefore not contradictory. The works we are judged by are not our works, but the works of the Spirit.** It is all about God's Grace; "not of works lest any man should boast." I emailed Daniel my observation about receiving grace upon grace and got this response:

The process is known as "receiving grace for grace."

> What you say in your email, "the closer one is to God the greater amount of grace we receive" is right. **The sense of it is that the more we yield to His will for us, or to His Spirit, then the more of that Spirit we will receive,** and this process continues as we are able to receive more "until the perfect day." The process is known as "receiving grace for grace" which is another way of saying that we "put on the Lord Jesus Christ," or, we are replacing our carnal mind, or spirit, with the mind or Spirit

of God and of Christ. The Lord teaches this idea in several places in the scriptures, such as in the Doctrine and Covenants Section 90/93, where John testifies that Jesus himself grew from grace to grace—that is, he didn't receive of the fullness of the Spirit of his Father at the first, but grew from grace to grace until he received of the fullness—then in the same section, the Lord testifies that we are here to do the very same thing:

> I give unto you these sayings that you may understand and know how to worship, and know what you worship, that you may come unto the Father in my name, and in due time receive of his fullness, for if you keep my commandments you shall receive of his fullness and be glorified in me as I am in the Father: therefore, I say unto you, You shall receive ***grace for grace*** (DC 90:3b-c/93:19-20).

The idea is that when we keep His commandments we get "credit[s]" for keeping them, and the Lord is then justified in giving us more of his Spirit which always brings some kind of "revelation" of His will for us, or of some additional understanding of some aspect of the gospel (line upon line). As we come to recognize His Spirit which is synonymous with "His voice," and as we seek to follow it, to implement it into our lives, we get more "credit" as it were, and we receive more of His grace or a greater degree of His Spirit, until we come to receive of a fullness and become "one with Him," or "born again." **This is the end result and is synonymous with becoming "sealed" by the Holy Spirit of Promise** (re: DC 76:5d/53).

[s] "Credit" is not being used here to imply that the process described is transactional in nature. We don't "receive" just because we "do." This is a spiritual, growth-oriented process, wherein we receive "grace for grace."

The term "grace" then is synonymous with the "Spirit of God," which is "revelation." Paul, in giving an account of how he received the gospel, uses these terms interchangeably.

> ***But by the grace of God I am what I am***: and his ***grace*** which was bestowed upon me was not in vain; but I laboured more abundantly than they all: ***yet not I, but the grace of God which was with me*** (1 Cor. 15:10).

> But I certify you, brethren, that the gospel which was preached of me is not after man. For I neither received it of man, neither was I taught it, but by the ***revelation*** of Jesus Christ (Gal. 1:11-12).

King Benjamin, in his farewell address to his people, sums up our eternal indebtedness to God:

> ***I say, if ye should serve him with all your whole soul, yet ye would be unprofitable servants....*** And now, in the first place, he hath created you, and granted unto you your lives, for which ye are indebted unto him. And secondly: he doth require that ye should do as he hath commanded you, for which if ye do, he doth immediately bless you; and therefore, he hath paid you. And ye are still indebted unto him; and are, and will be, for ever and ever; therefore, of what have ye to boast? ***And now I ask, Can ye say aught of yourselves? I answer you, Nay*** (Mosiah 1:54, 57-60/2:21, 23-25).

In his own way, King Benjamin is saying that we receive "grace for grace." We receive grace initially from God and then each time we respond to God's grace, He immediately gives us more so that we are always in His debt.

Shortly before his martyrdom by Emperor Nero around 68 AD, the Apostle Peter was compelled to write a second letter to the churches in Asia Minor who had been the recipients of his first letter. It appears that Peter had received reports of false teachers who were trying to deceive the saints. Peter knew that his death was imminent (2 Pet. 1:14) and that God's people were facing many dangers. He wanted them to have his written record that they might always have "these things in remembrance" (see 2 Pet. 1:15). After his initial salutation in verse one, Peter begins his letter with this:

> **Grace and peace be multiplied unto you** through the knowledge of God, and of Jesus our Lord, **According as His divine power hath given unto us all things that pertain unto life and godliness**, through the knowledge of him that hath called us to glory and virtue: Whereby are given unto us exceeding great and precious promises: **that by these ye might be partakers of the divine nature**, having escaped the corruption that is in the world through lust (2 Pet. 1:2-4).

"Grace and peace be multiplied unto you..." God rewards us with His Grace, not on a one to one basis, but with multiples of grace. We receive God's grace on an exponential basis, a crescendo that keeps building until that perfect day. As Peter says, we have received these great and precious promises that we "might be partakers of the divine nature."

Peter warns us that we in the last days face similar dangers of false teachers; that we should always keep in mind the words spoken of by the holy prophets and the apostles of the Lord (see 2 Pet. 3). Peter is telling us in his letter that we should pursue spiritual maturity through the Word of God as a remedy for false teaching.

John Ortberg, in his audio disk *FLOW*[119], gives us this understanding of grace:

- Grace is experienced first as mercy and forgiveness. Then, as we become a Christian, we experience grace as POWER.

- It is an illusion that saints do not need much grace because they do not sin much. In reality, it's the other way around!
- **SAINTS BURN MORE GRACE THAN ANYBODY ELSE <u>because</u> that's what they're living on!**

It is God's grace, this infused Spirit of God that we receive in this life that will have the power to raise us in the resurrection to come. If we have a celestial spirit, we shall be raised a celestial body, even a fullness thereof.

> ...for that same spirit which doth possess your bodies at the time that ye go out of this life, that same spirit will have power to possess your body in that eternal world (Alma 16:232/34:34).

More on Grace

The true meaning of grace is revealed in the scriptures, but again, the disciple of Christ must continually keep in mind the fact that the gospel is hidden purposely by the Lord.

> And he said unto them, Unto you it is given to know the mystery of the kingdom of God: but unto them that are without, all these things are done in parables: That seeing they may see, and not perceive; and hearing they may hear, and not understand; lest at any time they should be converted, and their sins should be forgiven them (Mark 4:11-12).

The problem is that many "believers" want to be saved, but on their own terms. They want to hang on to their enjoyable life and their incorrect understanding of the gospel that allows them to feel secure in the state of their imperfection, while still "owning Jesus" at the same time. So, to them, he doesn't reveal himself, but lets them believe a lie. To some, this may seem cruel, but in their heart of hearts they have no desire to be saved – and Jesus honors that desire, he honors their exercise of agency.

> And for this cause God shall send them strong delusion, that they should believe a lie:
> That they all might be damned who believed not the truth, but had pleasure in unrighteousness (2 Thess. 2:11-12).

The Book of Mormon records that many "plain and precious" things were taken away from our New Testament (see 1 Ne. 3:171,175/13:28-29), things which cause the Gentiles to stumble. **The meaning of grace, which is at the heart of the gospel of Jesus Christ, has been changed to falsely represent a non-existent "give-away" program; where salvation comes at no cost; where salvation is devalued and thought to be of little worth.** To change this meaning of "grace" is to undermine the gospel of Jesus Christ as presented by all the holy prophets and apostles from the very beginning. Yet, a false rendition of "grace" is what many Christians have come to believe. The Bible warns of this very situation:

> Beloved, when I gave all diligence to write unto you of the common salvation, it was needful for me to write unto you, and exhort you that ye should earnestly contend for the faith which was once delivered unto the saints.
> For there are certain men crept in unawares, who were before of old ordained to this condemnation, ungodly men, turning the grace of our God into lasciviousness, and denying the only Lord God, and our Lord Jesus Christ (Jude 1:3-4).

They deny the power of God, that is available through His Grace, to make them perfect, or one with Him, or pure "even as He is pure" (see 1 John 3:1-3). The understanding many Christians have of grace is that we can never be perfect and will therefore always be sinners, and thus it is only through His grace that we are saved. As such, they deny the power of God because they are taught by false teachers who do not believe the plan of salvation as contained in the scriptures. ***The truth is that we are sinners to the extent that we have not yet "put on the Lord Jesus Christ."*** ***Grace is the power, from God, to become perfect***.

We are told however, that in the last days, a time when the love of men shall wax cold and iniquity shall abound, when the time of the Gentiles is come in..."a light shall break forth among them that sit in darkness, and it shall be the fullness of my gospel" (DC 45:4b/28). Jeremiah says of the last days, in the day of affliction:

> ...the Gentiles shall come unto thee from the ends of the earth, and shall say, Surely our fathers have inherited lies, vanity, and things wherein there is no profit" (Jer. 16:19).

[TO BE CONTINUED IN PART II]

Study Guide

1. This chapter addressed the seeming contradictory scriptural statements concerning salvation: whether we are saved by grace or works. After reading this chapter, did your viewpoint change at all? Are we saved by grace, works, or some combination thereof?

2. Discuss the definitions of grace that are given. Are they surprising to you? Does this change your concept of salvation?

3. Was your concept of works changed at all? (See John 3:22 IV) What motivates our good works: the Holy Spirit or reward?

4. Would you now concur with the following statement? "We are saved by the Holy Spirit and rewarded by the Holy Spirit."

5. Explain and discuss the concept of "receiving grace for grace."

6. Do you agree with John Ortberg's statement that "saints burn more grace than anybody else"?

7. Discuss how grace has been changed to falsely represent a non-existent "give-away" program.

CHAPTER 16

The Other Comforter and Perfection Part II

Now what is this other Comforter? It is no more nor less that the Lord Jesus Christ Himself; and this is the sum and substance of the whole matter.[120] – Joseph Smith, Jr.

Another Comforter – The Holy Spirit of Promise

Previously we have discussed the confusion, or the mystery surrounding the seemingly contradictory scriptural statements concerning grace and works. As we address this next topic of "Another Comforter" or "The Holy Spirit of Promise," I must freely admit that this concept has always been a source of confusion for me. As we quote the following words of Joseph Smith, Jr., we will see that apparently this is a topic that few have understood:

> The other Comforter spoken of is a subject of great interest, and perhaps understood by few of this generation. After a person has faith in Christ, repents of his sins, and is baptized for the remission of his sins and receives the Holy Ghost (by the laying on of hands), **which is the first Comforter**, then let him continue to humble himself before God, hungering and thirsting after righteousness, and living by every word of God, and the Lord will soon say unto him, Son, thou shalt be exalted. When the Lord has thoroughly proved him, and finds that the man is determined to serve Him at all hazards, then the man will find his calling and his election made sure, **then it will be his privilege to receive the other Comforter,** which the Lord hath promised the Saints, as is recorded in the testimony of St. John, in the 14th chapter, from the 12th to the 27th verses. Note verses 16, 17, 18, 21, and 23:

> "16. And I will pray the Father, and He shall give you another Comforter, that he may abide with you forever;
> "17. Even the Spirit of Truth; whom the world cannot receive, because it seeth him not, neither knoweth him; but ye know him; for he dwelleth with you, and shall be in you.
> "18. I will not leave you comfortless: I will come to you. ***
> "21. He that hath my commandments, and keepeth them, he it is that loveth me: and he that loveth me should be loved of my Father, and I will love him, and will manifest myself to him.
> "23. If a man love me, he will keep my words: and my Father will love him, and we will come unto him, and make our abode with him."
>
> **Now what is this other Comforter? It is no more nor less that the Lord Jesus Christ Himself; and this is the sum and substance of the whole matter;** that when any man obtains this last Comforter, he will have the personage of Jesus Christ to attend him, or appear unto him from time to time, and even He will manifest the Father unto him, and they will take up their abode with him, and the visions of the heavens will be opened unto him, **and the Lord will teach him face to face**, and he may have a perfect knowledge of the mysteries of the Kingdom of God; and this is the state and place the ancient Saints arrived at when they had such glorious visions—Isaiah, Ezekiel, John upon the Isle of Patmos, St. Paul in the three heavens, and all the Saints who held communion with the general assembly and Church of the First Born.[121]

There is much to digest in these words of Joseph Smith which explains the conditions for receiving this Other Comforter. **The astounding revelation is that this Comforter is nothing less than the Lord Jesus Christ himself who will make his abode with us; who will teach us face-to-face. This is the crux of the New Covenant that God will make with the house of Israel and the house of Judah; that He will teach us face-to-face.** Perhaps this is the meaning of Jesus' statement concerning the gathering to Zion; that "I also will be in the midst" (3 Ne. 10:4/ 21:25).

Joseph stated above that we are sealed with this Other Comforter after we are baptized for the remission of sins and receive that first Comforter, the Holy Ghost, by the laying on of hands.

Thereafter, we must continue to hunger and thirst after righteousness and live by every word of God. This concurs with these words of Nephi:

> For the gate by which ye should enter is repentance and baptism by water: and then cometh a remission of your sins by fire, and by the Holy Ghost…And now, my beloved brethren, after ye have gotten into this strait and narrow path, I would ask, if all is done? Behold, I say unto you, Nay; for ye have not come thus far, save it were by the word of Christ…Wherefore, if ye shall press forward, feasting upon the word of Christ and endure to the end, behold, thus saith the Father: "Ye shall have eternal life" (2 Ne. 13:24, 27-28, 30/31:17-20).

As Daniel Muhlenkamp comments, **"This 'Other Comforter' then, is the 'secret weapon' or medium the Lord uses to 'seal us His.' The means by which He bridges the great gulf that separates us from Him and makes us immune from the deception and power of Satan."** Section 85/88 expresses it as the promise we receive from God of eternal life, even celestial glory:

> Wherefore I now send upon you another Comforter, even upon you, my friends, that it may abide in your hearts, even the Holy Spirit of promise, which other Comforter is the same that I promised unto my disciples, as is recorded in the testimony of John.
> This Comforter is the promise which I give unto you of eternal life, even the glory of the celestial kingdom; which glory is that of the church of the Firstborn, even of God, the holiest of all, through Jesus Christ, his Son (DC 85:1c-2a/88:3-5).

ADMONITION: Christ in Us

In 2008, the then pastor of the Waldo Congregation in Independence, Missouri, Jim Hobbs, received what he calls "ADMONITION OF THE LORD: Counsel to the Children of the Lord." In that inspired counsel, a few things are mentioned that are of particular interest to the subject-matter of this book. Here and in a couple of places to follow I will quote applicable excerpts. So that the reader may understand quoted excerpts in context, I have reproduced the entire document as Appendix A. The following excerpt concerns the Other Comforter, Christ in us.

> *I would bless you beyond measure if you would allow My Spirit to live in you. That is, My Father and I will come and live in you, that which My Apostle Paul calls a mystery, Christ in you (Col. 1:27). I want to perform My Works, My Strange Acts through you. For that to happen My Spirit must live in you. You must accept My Love and My Grace for yourselves that My Love may radiate through you to others.*
>
> *I poured out My Heart in prayer for My Disciples because they perceived not the great work I had for them. And I promised them another comforter to help them accomplish My Work. You too perceive not the great work I have for you to do. And now I offer to you the same comforter I gave to My Disciples if you will gather together as one, as My disciples did in the upper room. They were of one heart and mind in desiring My Comforter. So you must come together in prayer and supplication as one, with one purpose, that is to receive My Spirit.* (emphasis added)

The Other Comforter – One or Two?

In the interest of full disclosure, it must be said there is no clear consensus as to whether or not there is one or two comforters. That being the case, the principle remains the same. Many who recognize only one comforter would agree that Other Comforter

Jesus promised his disciples (John 14:12-27) represents a much greater degree of the Holy Spirit than they previously experienced. This greater reception of the Holy Spirit would then be referred to as being sealed by the Holy Spirit of Promise. The *Encyclopedia of Mormonism* identifies the Holy Spirit of Promise "with a separate function of the Holy Ghost."[122]

Both Joseph Smith and Jim Hobbs in his experience make direct and indirect reference to the greater power of the Holy Spirit being the presence of Christ living within us; that which Paul refers to as a mystery:

> Whereof I am made a minister, according to the dispensation of God which is given to me for you, to fulfil the word of God;
> Even the mystery which hath been hid from ages and from generations, but now is made manifest to his saints:
> **To whom God would make known what is the riches of the glory of this mystery among the Gentiles; <u>which is Christ in you</u>, the hope of glory:**
> Whom we preach, warning every man, and teaching every man in all wisdom; **<u>that we may present every man perfect in Christ Jesus</u>**:
> Whereunto I also labour, striving according to his working, which worketh in me mightily (Col. 1:25-29).

Section 76 appears to separate the initial reception of the Holy Spirit by the laying on of hands from the act of being sealed by the Holy Spirit of Promise "**which the Father sheds forth upon all those who are just and true**" (DC 76:5c-d/52-53). "This Comforter [or Holy Spirit of Promise] is the promise of eternal life, **<u>even the glory of the celestial kingdom"</u>** (DC 85:2a/88:4). Alma, the high priest of the Church of Christ received this promise of the Lord: "Thou art my servant: and I covenant with thee, that thou shalt have eternal life" (Mosiah 11:127/26:20).

God only knows the heart so it would be in His infinite wisdom as to if or when this promise is given to a particular individual. In the wisdom of God it is certainly possible for this promise of celestial glory to be given at the time of confirmation, but it seems highly unlikely that this would be the normal circumstance. If one examines Section 76 and ascertains the relatively few numbers of those who would receive celestial glory in relation to the lower glories, then again, it would seem highly unlikely that this promise would be concurrent with confirmation in normal circumstances.

In 1990, by action of the RLDS world conference, Section 107 of the Doctrine and Covenants was removed from the main body and relegated to the Appendix for historical value only. The primary reason being the ordinance concerning baptism for the dead. Of interest here is a verse concerning the Holy Spirit of Promise which would seem to indicate as stated above that it is not necessarily conferred at the same time as the laying on of hands received at the time of baptism.

> First, I give unto you Hyrum Smith to be a patriarch unto you, to hold the sealing blessings of my church, even the Holy Spirit of promise, **whereby ye are sealed up unto the day of redemption,** that ye may not fall, notwithstanding the hour of temptation that may come upon you (DC 107:38/124:124).

Receiving the Holy Spirit of Promise would appear to be synonymous with being born of God wherein, through the grace of God we have overcome, we have become his sons and daughters with no more desire to sin:

> And now, because of the covenant which ye have made, ye shall be called the children of Christ, his sons, and his daughters: For behold, this day he hath spiritually begotten you; for ye say that your hearts are changed through faith

> on his name; therefore, ye are born of him, and have become his sons and his daughters (Mosiah 3:8-9/5:7).

> And now behold, I ask of you, my brethren of the church, Have ye spiritually been born of God? Have ye received his image in your countenances? Have ye experienced this mighty change in your hearts? (Alma 3:27-29/5:14).

> And they did all declare unto the people the self-same thing; that their hearts had been changed; that they had no more desire to do evil (Alma 12:176/19:33).

> I have written unto you, fathers, because ye have known him that is from the beginning. I have written unto you, young men, because ye are strong, and the word of God abideth in you, and ye have overcome the wicked one (1 John 2:14).

> Whosoever is born of God doth not commit sin; for his seed remaineth in him: and he cannot sin, because he is born of God (1 John 3:9).

> Ye are of God, little children, and have overcome them: because greater is he that is in you, than he that is in the world (1 John 4:4).

> Beloved, let us love one another: for love is of God; and every one that loveth is born of God, and knoweth God (1 John 4:7).

Resurrection and Without Sin Perfection

The scriptures teach that God desires to be in the presence of His people and indeed gives several examples where this has happened. We also know that no unclean thing can come into the presence of God. The scriptures also teach that it is impossible for the "natural man" to come into God's presence lest he wither and die. We see that in the case of Moses who came into God's presence upon an exceedingly high mountain. The glory of God was upon Moses who was transfigured so that he could endure God's presence. Moses desired to know about the heavens and the earth, all of God's works. He was told that no man can behold all of God's works and yet remain in the flesh upon the earth. Nevertheless God condescended to show Moses about this earth. As with the eye of God, he beheld all the earth, every last particle. He beheld all the children of men who were and are created of which he greatly marveled and wondered (see DC 22/ Moses 1). After God's glory withdrew from Moses, he fell to the ground and it was several hours before he regained his natural strength.

What the above discourse tells us is that there is a difference between the "completeness" we will receive with our perfect, resurrected body, and the mortal body we presently have which will one day wither and die. It tells us that in this life, while under certain conditions, we can come into God's presence, but we cannot behold all of God's glory while in the flesh.

Again, keeping in mind that no unclean thing can come into God's presence, Daniel, in his article, differentiates between "Resurrection Perfection" and "Without Sin Perfection." The idea of Resurrection Perfection is found in the words of our Lord:

> And he said unto them, Go ye and tell that fox [Herod], Behold, I cast out devils, and do cures today and tomorrow, and the third day I shall be perfected (Luke 13:32).

Again, quoting from Daniel: **"'Without Sin' perfection is attainable in this life and is in fact the function and purpose of the gospel concerning us in our present mortal state."**

The Two Commandments

To further our discussion of perfection ("Without Sin"), we will now turn back to where we began this chapter (Part I), by quoting the words of Jesus from Matt. 22:36-40, where he answers the query of a lawyer concerning, "Which is the great commandment in the law?" Jesus answered that the first and great commandment is, "Thou shalt love the Lord thy God with all thy heart, and with all thy soul, and with all thy mind... And the second is like unto it, Thou shalt love thy neighbor as thyself. On these two commandments hang all the law and the prophets."

In agreement with the words of Jesus, all of the laws that were ever written, and all prophesies ever given are based on these two commandments. These two commandments are taught and their respective ordinances performed by the two orders of priesthood, the Melchizedek or Holy Priesthood, and the Aaronic (Levitical) Priesthood.

The Aaronic Priesthood is to teach the Royal Law which is the Ten Commandments, or the civil law of a nation. It is called the "Royal Law" because it is the law that is governed by the king and has to do with our relations with each other - this is the commandment from the Lord to "love thy neighbor." We are not saved by this law; but we must keep it in order to be saved. It is also called the "The Law of Sin and Death." It is called thus because under Moses, the penalty for violating this law was death by stoning.

> If ye fulfil the royal law according to the scripture, Thou shalt love thy neighbour as thyself, ye do well: But if ye have respect to persons, ye commit sin, and are convinced of the law as transgressors. For whosoever shall keep the whole law, and yet offend in one point, he is guilty of all. For he that said, Do not commit adultery, said also, Do not kill. Now if thou commit no adultery, yet if thou kill, thou art become a transgressor of the law. So speak ye, and so do, as they that shall be judged by the law of liberty (James 2:8-12).

James equates the Royal Law with the law to "love thy neighbor as thyself" spoken of by Jesus in Matt. 22:39. The Ten Commandments are synonymous with the Royal Law. He says that if you keep the Royal Law or the Ten Commandments, which is to "love thy neighbor as thyself," ye do well. He says that we need to keep all the law, that if we fall short even one iota, then we are equally guilty as if we are guilty of the whole law. The reason for this is that if we break one of the Ten Commandments, or the law to "love thy neighbor as thyself," it means we have not "put on Christ," but still have the lust of the "natural man" within us.

Rich Young Ruler

> And, behold, one came and said unto him, Good Master, what good thing shall I do, that I may have eternal life? And he said unto him, Why callest thou me good? There is none good but one, that is, God: but if thou wilt enter into life, keep the commandments. He saith unto him, Which? Jesus said, Thou shalt do no murder, Thou shalt not commit adultery, Thou shalt not steal, Thou shalt not bear false witness, Honour thy father and thy mother: and, Thou shalt love thy neighbour as thyself. The young man saith unto him, All these things have I kept from my youth up: what lack I yet? Jesus said unto him, If thou wilt be perfect, go and sell that thou hast, and give to the poor, and thou shalt have treasure in heaven: and come and follow me. But when the young man heard that saying, he went away sorrowful: for he had great possessions (Matt. 19:16-22).

This is a real live example of how keeping the Ten Commandments alone cannot save us. He wasn't willing to hear and obey the voice of the Lord. His heart was set upon his earthly possessions, or the things of this world, more than it was on the Lord. As we learned in the James 2 scripture above, we do well if we obey the whole law (the Royal Law or the Ten Commandments), yet we will still be judged by the Law of Liberty which is, "Thou shalt love the Lord thy God with all thy heart, and with all thy soul, and with all thy mind."

Perfect Law of Liberty

The Perfect Law of Liberty mentioned in the scriptures is the essential link in this process of becoming perfect, without which perfection would not be possible. Its name says it all. Since sin is bondage, this law, administered through the Holy Priesthood, frees us from this bondage of sin. That is, obedience to this law brings liberty which in turn brings perfection, which is why it is also called "perfect." It involves replacing our sinful spirit or will with the Spirit of God and of Christ, and with their will for us; which is why it is also called the Law of the Spirit. This process is described throughout the scriptures as "putting on Christ." It is to be taught by the Holy (Melchizedek) Priesthood:

> And this greater priesthood administereth the gospel and holdeth the key of the mysteries of the kingdom, even the key of the knowledge of God. Therefore, in the ordinances thereof the power of godliness is manifest; and without the ordinances thereof, and the authority of the priesthood, the power of godliness is not manifest unto men in the flesh; for without this, no man can see the face of God, even the Father, and live (DC 83:3b,c/84:19-22).

> The power and authority of the higher, or Melchizedek, priesthood, is to hold the keys of all the spiritual blessings of the church; to have the privilege of receiving the mysteries of the kingdom of heaven; to have the heavens opened unto them; to commune with the general assembly and church of the Firstborn; and to enjoy the communion and presence of God the Father, and Jesus the Mediator of the new covenant (DC 104:9a-b/107:18-19).

> And he gave some, apostles; and some, prophets; and some, evangelists; and some, pastors and teachers; For the ***perfecting of the saints***, for the work of the ministry, for the edifying of the body of Christ: Till we all come in the unity of the faith, and of the knowledge of the Son of God, unto a ***perfect*** man, unto the measure of the stature of the fulness of Christ (Eph. 4:11-13).

> If therefore ***perfection*** were by the Levitical priesthood (for under it the people received the law), what further need was there that another priest should rise after the order of Melchizedek, and not be called after the order of

> Aaron? For the priesthood being changed, there is made of necessity a change also of the law (Heb. 7:11-12).

According to this scripture from Hebrews, along with this "change in priesthood" comes a "change also of the law." The proper name of this other law, the law described by Jesus in Matthew 22:36-37 as the law to "love the Lord thy God with all thy heart, and with all thy soul, and with all thy mind," is revealed here in James:

> Wherefore lay apart all filthiness and superfluity of naughtiness, and receive with meekness **the engrafted word, which is able to save your souls**.
> But be ye doers of the word, and not hearers only, deceiving your own selves. For if any be a hearer of the word, and not a doer, he is like unto a man beholding his natural face in a glass: For he beholdeth himself, and goeth his way, and straightway forgetteth what manner of man he was. But whoso looketh into the **perfect law of liberty**, and continueth therein, he being not a forgetful hearer, but a doer of the work, this man shall be blessed in his deed (James 1:21-25).

James also calls this Perfect Law of Liberty "**the engrafted word**," because "engrafted" means "to implant." This is the law which is able to save our souls.

The officers and gifts are all placed in the church by the Lord himself, ***"for the perfecting of the saints."*** The priesthood have to "go through the veil" and themselves become perfect and they are also to offer up the people as an offering without blemish: ***"... that the offering up of the Gentiles might be acceptable, being sanctified by the Holy Ghost"*** (Rom. 15: 16).

While ministering to the Nephites after his resurrection, the Savior gave them the words of the prophet Malachi (because they didn't have them), telling them that they were for future generations (OURS). Malachi is also one of the scriptures quoted to Joseph

Smith Jr., by the angel, pending a future fulfillment. This prophecy then, is a warning to the priesthood of this generation:

> A son honoreth his father, and a servant his master; if then I be a father, where is mine honor? and if I be a master, where is my fear? saith the Lord of hosts unto you, O priests, that despise my name. And ye say, Wherein have we despised thy name? ***Ye offer polluted bread upon mine altar***; and ye say, Wherein have we polluted thee? In that ye say, The table of the Lord is contemptible. And if ye offer the blind for sacrifice, is it not evil? and if ye offer the lame and sick, is it not evil? offer it now unto thy governor; will he be pleased with thee, or accept thy person? saith the Lord of hosts (Mal. 1:6-8).

The "polluted bread" mentioned here, refers to the priesthood offering up the saints in their imperfect condition, which offering is not acceptable to the Lord. Just as those ancient Israelites in Malachi kept offering up the same blemished sacrifices year in and year out, for the same sins, never going on to perfection. The Lord desired to sanctify them; but they refused to enter into His presence. Because of their unbelief they could not enter into "the rest of the Lord" - which rest is the "fullness of His glory" (DC 83:4b/84:24).

> And we did magnify our office unto the Lord, taking upon us the responsibility, **answering the sins of the people upon our own heads, if we did not teach them the word of God with all diligence**;
> **Wherefore, by laboring with our mights, their blood might not come upon our garments;** otherwise, their blood would come upon our garments, and we would not be found spotless at the last day (Jacob 1:19-20/19).

Summary

THE GOD-CENTERED LIFE WORKS. AND IT RESCUES US FROM A LIFE THAT DOESN'T.[123]

For the newly converted, grace is experienced primarily as mercy and forgiveness. As one grows in the faith, grace becomes the imputed desire and power that God gives us to do His will. We have learned that just as Jesus received "grace for grace," that is also God's intent for us. Peter urged believers to "grow in grace" (2 Pet. 3:18) and prayed that grace would be multiplied unto them (2 Pet. 1:2). Each step of the way God rewards our meager responses to His grace with exponentially more grace so that as King Benjamin says: "***And now I ask, Can ye say aught of yourselves? I answer you, Nay***" (Mosiah 1:60/ 2:25). The reality then is that "the closer one is to God, the greater amount of grace they receive." To reassess the words of John Ortberg:

> It is an illusion that saints do not need much grace because they do not sin much. In reality, it's the other way around! SAINTS BURN MORE GRACE THAN ANYBODY ELSE **because** that's what they're living on![124]

We have learned that contrary to what we may have previously thought, there is no scriptural conflict between grace and works. Grace is synonymous with the presence of the Holy Spirit in our lives, and the works spoken of in scripture, those works which are acceptable to God, are in reality works of that self-same Spirit of God - which is by definition, GRACE.

> And he who obeyeth the truth, ***the works which he doeth they are of God*** (John 3:22 IV).

Before leaving the confines of this chapter, we need to add a comment about works. It is often difficult for us to distinguish in others whether their works are of God or man. In all outward appearances, those of who Jesus said, "Depart from me, I never knew you," are Christian leaders much admired and respected (see Matt. 7:21-23). They may have done wonderful things, but by Jesus saying, "I never knew you," he is telling us that they never had a relationship with him. They had impure motives; their works were done for their own glory, not his. The Apostle Paul teaches that without charity, without love in our hearts for God and for our brothers and sisters in Christ, all we do is valueless. This is true even though we may speak with the tongues of angels, have the gift of prophecy and have all knowledge and faith, such that we can remove mountains (see 1 Cor. 13:1-3). All is vain without the love of God in our hearts.

Through the words of Joseph Smith, we have learned that the Other Comforter that the Lord desires to give to those who have demonstrated their faithfulness is none other than the abiding presence of the Lord Jesus Christ himself. **It is this Other Comforter then that lies at the heart of the New Covenant promise wherein we will be taught "face to face."** It is this second Comforter that seals us His and gives us a guarantee of salvation in the celestial kingdom.

While in our present mortal state we cannot abide the fullness of God's glory. But we have learned that unless the words of our Savior be made into a lie (see Matt. 5:48), we can indeed achieve "without sin" perfection in this life; and that realization is in fact the function and purpose of the gospel. It is this state of "without sin" perfection that is required for the redemption of Zion:

> And then cometh the New Jerusalem; and blessed are they who dwell therein, for it is they whose garments are white through the blood of the lamb… (Ether 6:10/13:10).

Per Jesus (Matt. 22:36-40) the greatest two commandments are: one, "to love the Lord thy God with all thy heart, and with all thy soul, and with all thy mind" – this is known as the **Perfect Law of Liberty.** This is the law administered by the Melchizedek priesthood; the law that frees us from sin and brings us into the presence of God. And two, "to love thy neighbor as thyself" – the **Royal Law** which is administered by the priesthood of Aaron. While we cannot be saved by keeping the Royal Law, we must keep it in order to be saved.

In the closing chapter of the Book of Mormon, Moroni, in a very profound verse, encapsulates for us the process of becoming perfect in Christ. The essential steps being to love God with all our might, mind and strength (the Perfect Law of Liberty) and then to rely on the grace of God to complete the work.

> Yea, come unto Christ, and be perfected in him, and deny yourselves of all ungodliness, and if ye shall deny yourselves of all ungodliness, and love God with all your might, mind and strength, then is his grace sufficient for you, that by his grace ye may be perfect in Christ; and if by the grace of God ye are perfect in Christ, ye can in no wise deny the power of God (Moro. 10:29/32).

And finally, we can conclude by saying that our salvation is entirely a work of grace. As Paul says, "not of works, lest any man should boast" (Eph. 2:9). It is God's grace, this infused Spirit of God, that we receive in this life as we grow from "grace to grace," that will have the power to raise us in the resurrection to come.

> **...for that same spirit which doth possess your bodies at the time that ye go out of this life, that same spirit will have power to possess your body in that eternal world** (Alma 16:232/ 34:34).

Postscript

In "The Everlasting Covenant" chapter, we added a postscript because a friend sent a copy of a page from Jonathan Cahn's book, ***The Book of Mysteries***. This page gave us additional enlightenment concerning the New Covenant. Likewise, the second page[125] received from my friend gives us additional New Covenant insight concerning "The Other Comforter and Perfection."

The lesson "the teacher" taught this day stemmed from Cahn's question: "How does one live up to the standards of God? How does one attain such high standards?" The teacher replied by saying, "The only one who can live up to the standards of God…is God. And the only one who can live the life of Messiah is the Messiah." The teacher went on to say, "There's only one way – you let Him live it. You let God meet the standards of God. You let Messiah live the life of Messiah through you."

Cahn replied, "So it's Him and not me."

"It's Him through you. It's Him living His life…through your living your life in Him. In the Book of First Corinthians it is written, 'We are God's fellow workers.' But in the original language the words *fellow workers* are just one word – *sunergos*."

Cahn asks, "And what does it mean?"

"*Ergos*," said the teacher, "means to act, to work, or to do. And *Sun* means with or together. So *sunergos* means to act together, to work with, to move together, or to do as one. That's the key. It's impossible for you to live the life of God. But it's impossible for God not to live the life of God. So the key is not to live up to the standards of God, but to let God live out His life through you. It means to let God live in your living…as, in His living, you live. It means to let God love in your loving…as, in His loving, you love. It is from *sunergos* that we get the word *synergy*. That's the energy of salvation, the energy of God, and the energy of you flowing together as one… one energy, one motion, one life."

Study Guide

1. Joseph Smith addresses for us the very confusing topic of the "Other Comforter." Discuss.

2. Discuss Daniel Muhlenkamp's statement as to how the Other Comforter is God's "secret weapon."

3. What is the difference between "Without Sin" perfection and "Resurrection" perfection?

4. Have your feelings about Matt. 5:48, "Be ye therefore perfect" changed at all?

5. Lastly, discuss the Royal Law and the Perfect Law of Liberty.

CHAPTER 17

The Kingdom Law

"There is only one real law – the law of the universe," said Dorothy Sayers. "It may be fulfilled either by way of judgment or by way of grace, but it must be fulfilled one way or the other."[126]

"A Moment of Grace"

In November 2004, in New York City, a group of teenagers had been to a movie and afterwards they were bored so they decided to break into a car, they stole a credit card and proceeded to a video store where they charged $400 worth of DVDs and video games. While they were at it, they went to a grocery store and bought a few groceries including a 20-pound frozen turkey.

After that they went joyriding and at approximately 12:30 a.m. they were approaching an oncoming car driven by Victoria Ruvolo. Victoria was returning home after attending her 14-year old niece's vocal recital. Just as these two vehicles were preparing to pass in the night, one of the teens leans out the window and throws the frozen turkey through the windshield of the approaching car. The turkey bends the steering wheel backwards and smashes into Victoria's face where it breaks almost every bone.

Victoria remembers almost none of this as she undergoes weeks of surgery and recovery. Her face had been shattered like pottery and is now stapled together by titanium plates; an eye affixed by synthetic film; a wired jaw; a tracheotomy.

The public is outraged as the news media follows every detail of the case. They cry out for justice and suggest what should happen to that teenager who threw the turkey. Finally, nine months later Victoria manages to walk unaided into a courtroom.

A trembling teenager pleads guilty to a lesser charge. The sentence: a trifling six months behind bars, five years of probation, a bit of counseling, a dash of public service. People shake their heads in righteous indignation. Is that it? Why are we so soft on crime? Who's responsible for this plea bargain anyway?

The victim - that's who. The victim requests leniency.

After he makes his plea, the teen turns to face Victoria and he starts weeping. The attorney leads the assailant to Victoria where they embrace. She holds him tight, comforts him, strokes his hair and offers reassuring words. "I forgive you," she whispers. "I want your life to be the best it can be."

It takes quite an event to bring tears to the eyes of New York attorneys and judges. This was such an event. TV and radio reporters file their stories in voices that for once are hushed and respectful. The New York Times calls it "a moment of grace."[127]

Unto Every Kingdom is Given a Law

> **And unto every kingdom is given a law; and unto every law there are certain bounds also, and conditions. All beings who abide not in those conditions, are not justified; for intelligence cleaveth unto intelligence; wisdom receiveth wisdom; truth embraceth truth; virtue loveth virtue; light cleaveth unto light;**
> **mercy hath compassion on mercy, and claimeth her own; justice continueth its course, and claimeth its own; judgment goeth before the face of him who sitteth upon the throne, and governeth and executeth all things** (DC 85:9b-10b / 88:38-40).

> **"...with what measure ye mete, it shall be measured to you again"** (Matt. 7:2).

In our preceding chapters we have primarily discussed grace from the perspective of how God so abundantly bestows unmerited grace upon His people; how God gives us "grace upon grace" until that day we can behold His presence. In this chapter we shall learn that grace is not only God's operative principle in His dealings with His children, but that also, if we are to merit citizenship in the kingdom of God, it also must become our operative principle in our interaction with others (i.e. "...with what measure ye mete, it shall be measured to you again" – Matt. 7:2).

Neil Simmons[t] begins his article on "Justice or Mercy" by analyzing the term: Mercy. He says that it is clear that the ancient Israelites had an example of how mercy is the proper operating law of the kingdom of God. Once a year the high priest would enter the Holy of Holies and sprinkle the blood of the sacrifice upon the Mercy Seat[u]. At each end of the Mercy Seat were cherubim and in between was a space on which rested the cloud or visible symbol of the divine presence. From this place God dispensed mercy to man when the blood of the atonement was sprinkled thereon.

We often make a comparison between the kingdoms of men and the kingdom of God by saying that each kingdom has a ruler, a land, and citizens of the kingdom. Simmons says, however, that such comparisons are clearly inadequate as they do not begin to address the vast gap between these kingdoms.

Simmons makes the point that the word "kingdom" can be used to describe different realms or orders of creation be it mineral, plant, animal or human. Each of these kingdoms are governed by a unique set of laws. He says that in the human realm the fundamental law is the rule of justice**. Justice is the basic rule of all human governance**. All mankind demands fairness. This trait is readily observable even in the lives of very small children. Justice implies that there is a law, therefore transgression of a law must

---

[t] The genesis and much of the content of this chapter comes from a phone conversation with and subsequent receipt of an unpublished article written by Neil Simmons entitled "Justice or Mercy" (2012). My sincere thanks to Brother Neil for his invaluable spiritual insights.

[u] The lid of the Ark of the Covenant. The Ark contained the two stone tablets engraved with the Ten Commandments.

bring some form of negative consequences or it would not be a law, and there would be no such thing as justice.

By way of contrast, the kingdom of God runs not on the rules of justice, but on the rules of grace and mercy.[v] This statement is exemplified by the parable of the unforgiving servant; one who owed a vast sum to his master and had not the money to repay. The master took pity on the servant and forgave his debt in full. The servant then turned to his fellow servant who owed him a small sum of money but could not repay. The unforgiving servant then had him cast into prison until he could pay. Other fellow servants saw what had happened and went and told the master.

> Then his lord, after that he had called him, said unto him, O thou wicked servant, I forgave thee all that debt, because thou desiredst me: Shouldest not thou also have had compassion on thy fellow servant, even as I had pity on thee? And his lord was wroth, and delivered him to the tormentors, till he should pay all that was due unto him.
> So likewise shall my heavenly Father do also unto you, if ye from your hearts forgive not everyone his brother their trespasses (Matt. 18:32-35).

Why are we required to live by the law of grace and mercy? Because God loved us and Christ died for us while we were yet sinners (Rom. 5:8). Because the Book of Mormon says that we are saved by grace "after all we can do" (2 Ne. 11:44/25:23). Because our Lord says, "...with what measure ye mete, it shall be measured again" (Matt. 7:2). Because it is the law of the kingdom, "mercy hath compassion on mercy, and claimeth her own." If we want to receive mercy we must give mercy.

The scripture simply says, "For all have sinned and come short of the Glory of God" (Rom. 3:23). Therefore, can we be saved by

---

[v] Lest it be misunderstood, this statement is directed towards the *modus operandi* of those who would dwell in the kingdom of God.

justice? The answer is an emphatic No! Who has not violated a law of God? None.

For God, who gave the law of justice to rule in the realm or kingdom of mankind, it is impossible for Him to annul the law, or simply delete the consequences of violating the law. God has sent us His Son, Jesus, to solve the problem of sin. As Isaiah declared: "...he was wounded for our transgressions...with his stripes we are healed" (Is. 53:5).

> This being the intent of this last sacrifice, to bring about the bowels of mercy, which overpowereth justice and bringeth about means unto men that they may have faith unto repentance.
> And thus mercy can satisfy the demands of justice, and encircles them in the arms of safety, while he that exercises no faith unto repentance, is exposed to the whole law of the demands of justice; therefore, only unto him that has faith unto repentance, is brought about the great and eternal plan of redemption (Alma 16:216-217/34:15-16).

The requirement is to give unmerited blessings everywhere.

Examples of Grace and Mercy being the operative laws of the kingdom are found throughout scripture. Walk the second mile. Turn the other cheek. Pray for them that despitefully use you. Love one another, and even more difficult, love your enemies; and perhaps most difficult of all for those of the church - cease contention. Forgive others and you might be forgiven. The law of the kingdom of God is to do what is required and then do extra. In each potential instance of grace there is a challenge: to pursue justice or fairness or accept injustice and treat it with an overflow of love and pardon. This is what the celestial law is all about as it requires way more than what is justified. **The requirement is to give unmerited blessings everywhere.**

> One who has been touched by grace will no longer look on those who stray as "those evil people" or "those poor people who need our help." Nor must we search for signs of "love worthiness." Grace teaches us that God loves because of who God is, not because of who we are.[128] – Philip Yancey

If Christ is not seen as the prophecy of a brother's possibilities, he simply is not seen. ***The love of Christ is the love of him in others.*** To the man of faith, the meanest of human creatures has possibilities for divine son-ship through the gospel, and, what is more, the man of faith acts toward the mean man as if that mean man were already a son of God. He does not wait for grace to manifest itself in the life of the sinner. He acts graciously toward the sinner and wins him from his sordidness because he believes in him.[129]

It should be understood that while there is a difference between grace and mercy, they are often confused because in God's realm they are invariably used together. The lines are blurred because usually when God pours out His mercy, He pours out His grace as well. Mercy is God not punishing us as our sins deserve. **While mercy is deliverance from judgment, grace is where God instead substitutes a blessing for the judgment that we deserve.** As someone has said, "grace and mercy are the flip sides of the same coin of God's love.[130]"

- Mercy bandages the wounds of the man beaten by robbers. Grace covers the full cost of his recovery.
- Mercy hears the cry of the thief on the cross. Grace promises paradise that very day.
- Mercy converts Paul on the road to Damascus. Grace calls him to be an apostle.
- Mercy saves John Newton from a life of rebellion and sin. Grace makes him a pastor and author of the timeless hymn, "Amazing Grace."

- Mercy is when the father forgives the prodigal son. Grace is when he throws an extravagant party.[131]

The "Nicholas Effect"

In 1994, a seven year old American boy by the name of Nicholas Green was killed by a highway robber while asleep in the back seat of the family rental car while on vacation in Italy. Italian newspapers talked about their "national shame," that something like that could happen in Italy. The tragedy would have ended there, but instead Nicholas' parents made a decision that changed everything. Without hesitation they made the decision to donate Nicholas' organs to seven Italians, some of who were near death. They received Nicholas' corneas, kidneys, liver, pancreas, and his heart.

What happened subsequently in Italy and around the world was called the "Nicholas Effect." This selfless act of grace won the heart of the Italian people; his name now appears on the walls of schools and hospitals all over the country. In 1998 a made-for-television movie was produced entitled "Nicholas' Gift." Thanks to the donation of Nicholas' organs, organ donations in Italy more than tripled and world-wide countless lives have been saved because of the Green family's act of grace. A foundation has been formed in Nicholas' name that every year offers a grant to an Italian doctor to learn the latest organ transplant techniques in the United States.

Grace is a Way of Life

It is helpful for us to be reminded that the kingdom of God in many respects is like any other realm or order of existence where the laws are immutable and inviolable. To receive the benefit of any kingdom we must operate according to its laws. First and foremost we must understand that grace is the law of the kingdom of God; it is a way of life; not random and occasional acts.

Section 90/93 (2a-b/12-14) of the Doctrine and Covenants tells us that Jesus grew spiritually from "grace to grace." Whenever Jesus was confronted with instances that cried out for justice, he responded within the law of Grace. This then, in the words of Neil Simmons, "raised his spiritual maturity." And then at the next injustice, he responded in grace so that he grew spiritually from a Grace Point to a Grace Point.

Jesus had something unjust happen to him when he was arrested, condemned and killed by man's justice system. Notice however, that he handled all of that with Grace. He did not justify himself. As the scripture said, he was like a lamb, and opened not his mouth to his accusers. His words on the cross illustrate the point: "Father, forgive them, they know not what they do." Per Simmons:

> It is very helpful for us to understand what produces spiritual maturity. When we have something bad happen to us, we desperately want to have justice; we wish to justify ourselves, we wish to put the judgment and blame upon others. We want justice, we feel the need for justice...When was the last time you had the opportunity to grow spiritually? Unexpectedly, that opportunity presents itself every time you have something happen that causes you to want justice; and instead of seeking justice, you turn from that position and assume the Christ-like stance of giving Grace. Remember, spiritual growth occurs from grace to grace: that means from unmerited blessing to unmerited blessing [both as we give and receive]. That is how Jesus' spiritual maturity occurred and that is how your own spiritual maturity develops.

The Father has given us his Only Begotten Son, an unmerited gift. So the Father demonstrates the law of the kingdom of God is actually Grace. The Father did not demand justice on behalf of the

brutal mistreatment of his Son. The Son gives us Mercy, and thus demonstrates that the law of the kingdom of God is Mercy.

> **Oh give thanks unto the Lord; for He is good; for His mercy endureth forever** (Ps. 136:1).

ADMONITION: Coveting the Law and Rejecting Grace

Once again, concerning the law and grace, we will offer an excerpt from the 2008 inspired document given through Jim Hobbs to the Waldo Congregation (see Appendix A).

> *The Gentiles have continued to reject the fullness of My Gospel, the Book of Mormon, because of the vain and foolish traditions of men. Many of you refuse to accept the truth which is in My Word but you accept the false traditions that have been handed down without putting them to the light of My Scriptures. You worship your history not knowing there are errors in it. You read My Second Witness, the Book of Mormon, without understanding it. You fall into the same errors many of the early saints fell into. The Jews have My Law but reject Me because of their vain and foolish traditions. You like the Jews have the fullness of My Gospel but do not understand it. <u>You covet My Law but reject My Grace</u>. My Law does not save you but salvation is through My Sacrifice I gave upon the cross. You were redeemed from the fall by Me. Now you stand responsible for your own actions, that is whether or not you accept Me as your Savior. Laman and Lemuel believed in My Law, but they rejected My Grace, My Love, Me.*
>
> *Many of My Children are as Laman and Lemuel. They want only to accept the traditions and the sweet enticing of some of My Priesthood.*
>
> *Many reject My plain and simple gospel and in that you reject Me because you do not know Me. You have enjoyed the gentle caress of My Spirit from time to time but you do not have an intimate relationship with Me. You have not*

experienced My hurt, My sorrows, My concerns for My Children, your brothers and sisters. You judge each other harshly, with no regard for their soul. You would cast each other off rather than labor with that diamond enmeshed in sin.

A Prayer from Buchenwald

This prayer was found scrawled on a scrap piece of paper by someone killed in the German death camp at Buchenwald:

O, Lord, when I shall come with glory in your kingdom, do not remember only the men of good will, remember also the men of evil. May they be remembered not only for their acts of cruelty in this camp, the evil they have done to us prisoners, but balance against their cruelty the fruits we have reaped under the stress and in the pain; the comradeship, the courage, the greatness of heart, the humility and patience which have been born in us and become part of our lives, because we have suffered at their hands.... May the memory of us not be a nightmare to them when they stand in judgment. May all that we have suffered be acceptable to you as a ransom for them.[132]

Of Perfection

In my conversation with Neil regarding grace as the kingdom law and the concept of growing from "grace to grace" as Jesus did, our conversation turned to Jesus' admonition that we are to be "...perfect, even as your Father which is in heaven is perfect" (Matt. 5:48). As the result of our conversation, I realized that there was more that needed to be said as to what perfection might look like. **Namely, does perfection look the same for everyone?**

In his earthly ministry, Jesus pointed to the little children and said of them, "Of such is the kingdom of God" (Luke 18:16). As a young lad Neil had asked his father about perfection; how he could be perfect. His father wisely asked him if he thought perfection would be the same for a child, as for an adolescent teen, as for an older adult. The obvious answer then as now would be, no, it would not be the same.

From a sermon he once preached, John Moody offers another view of perfection using the example of a perfect rose:

> I mentioned every stage of the life of a rose from sprouting seed to flowering plant. I noted that if as the rose bud was starting to open a bug came along and took a bite out of it, that it was still a perfect rose. And after a rose has bloomed and the petals have fallen and only the seed filled hip remains it is still a perfect rose. While in man's eyes only a rose blossom without spot, bug bite or any malformation is a perfect rose, but in truth the rose was perfect at every stage of its life if it did the best it could do and filled the purpose of its creation. It is not the rose's fault that a bug bit it or it was damaged in a storm or by drought.

As far as perfection is concerned, we all have different starting points. Our New Covenant interaction with God then is to be an individual one; one suited to our needs. The mere mention in scripture of the New Covenant promise that God will teach us personally (see Heb. 8:10-11) implies that, in some sense at least, perfection is an individual process whereupon we grow from grace to grace. To be taught personally by God then does not imply that we are all-knowing or all-powerful and that we won't even have sins of ignorance. But, it does mean that our hearts are right before God; that we love Him with all our might, mind and strength; that we have a hunger and thirst for righteousness; that we are eager to learn those things most pleasing to God where he will write His law upon our hearts rather than tablets of stone.

> **Then one of them, which was a lawyer, asked him a question, tempting him, and saying, Master, which is the great <u>commandment</u> in the law?**

> **Jesus said unto him, Thou shalt love the Lord thy God with all thy heart, and with all thy soul, and with all thy mind. This is the first and great commandment.**
> **And the second is like unto it, Thou shalt love thy neighbour as thyself.**
> **On these two commandments hang all the law and the prophets** (Matt. 22:35-40).

Robert Barclay on Concerning Perfection

Robert Barclay (1648-1690) was an early convert to Quakerism. His book, ***An Apology for the True Christian Divinity***, first published in 1678, has been described as "one of the most impressive theological writings of the [seventeenth] century…"[133] In his book, Barclay undertakes to defend Quakerism, giving full answers to those who would oppose their doctrine. ***An Apology*** is based upon fifteen propositions first published by Barclay in 1675, in a work entitled ***Theses Theologicae***. Here we are concerned with, and offer excerpts from, his "The Eighth Proposition: Concerning Perfection." Without the possibility of perfection in this life, Barclay makes the passionate case then that the gospel, and even the sacrifice of Christ would therefore be deemed ineffectual and useless. Barclay puts forth an extremely logical and comprehensive argument as to God's intent to make us perfect in Christ; to thus provide us through the law of the spirit the work of perfection.

The Eighth Proposition Excerpts

> **In whom** [the person] **this pure and holy birth is fully brought forth, the body of death and sin comes to be crucified and removed, and their hearts united and subjected to the Truth: so as not to obey any suggestions or temptations of the evil one, but to be free from actual sinning and transgressing of the law of God, and in that respect perfect: yet doth this perfection still admit of a growth; and there remaineth always, in some part, a possibility of sinning, where the mind doth not most diligently and watchfully attend unto the Lord.**

[Note: The following bulleted items consist of quoted excerpts from Robert Barclay's ***An Apology for the True Christian Divinity.*** Having originally been translated into English in 1678, Barclay's English is somewhat difficult to understand but well worth the effort.]

• First, we place not this possibility [of perfection] in man's own will and capacity...we attribute it wholly to man as he is born again.

• ...we understand not such a perfection as may not daily admit of a growth, and consequently mean not, as if we were to be as pure, holy, and perfect as God in his divine attributes of wisdom, knowledge and purity; but ***only a perfection proportional and answerable to man's measure,*** whereby we are kept from transgressing the law of God and enabled to answer what he requires of us, even as he that improved his two talents so as to make four of them perfected his work, and was so accepted of his Lord as to be called a "good and faithful servant," nothing less than he that made his five ten. Even as a little gold is perfect gold in its kind, as well as a great mass, and a child hath a perfect body as well as a man, though it daily grow more and more. Thus Christ is said (Luke 2:52) to have "increased in wisdom and stature, and in favour with God and man," though before that time he had *never sinned,* and was (no doubt) perfect, in a true and proper sense.

• Lastly, though I affirm that after a man hath arrived to such a condition in which a man may not sin, he yet may sin; I will nevertheless not deny but there may be a state attainable in this life, in which to do righteousness may become so natural to the regenerate soul, that in the stability of this condition they can not sin. Others may perhaps speak more certainly of this state, as having arrived to it. For me, I shall speak modestly, as acknowledging myself not to have arrived at it; yet I dare not deny it, for that it seems so positively to be asserted by the apostle, in these words (1 John 3:9), "He that is born of God sinneth not, neither can he, because the seed of God remaineth in him."

• And what is this but to attribute to God the height of injustice, to make him require his children to forsake sin, and yet not to afford them sufficient means for so doing? Surely this makes God more unrighteous than wicked men, who if, as Christ saith, "their children require bread of them, will not give them a stone, or instead of a fish a serpent" [Luke 11:12]. But these men confess, we ought to seek of God power to redeem us from sin, and yet believe they are never to receive such a power: such prayers then cannot be in faith, but are all vain.

• … no man is bound to that which is impossible: since then Christ and his apostles have commanded us to keep all the commandments, and to be perfect in this respect, it is possible for us so to do.

• And as this perfection or freedom from sin is attained and made possible where the Gospel and inward law of the Spirit is received and known, so the ignorance hereof has been and is an occasion of opposing this Truth.

• Blessed then are they that believe in him, who is both able and willing to deliver as many as come to him through true repentance, from all sin, and do not resolve, as these men do, to be the devil's servants all their lifetime, but daily go on forsaking unrighteousness, and forgetting those things that are behind, "press forward toward the mark, for the prize of the high calling of God, in Christ Jesus" [Phil. 3:14]; such shall not find their faith and confidence to be in vain, but in due time shall be made conquerors through him in whom they have believed; and so, overcoming, shall be established as "pillars" in the house of God, so as "he shall go no more out" (Rev. 3:12).[134]

Amazing Grace

John Newton calls God's love "Amazing Grace." He was a cruel slave-trader who first called out to God in the midst of a storm that nearly threw him overboard. After his conversion he renounced his profession and eventually became a minister. He never lost sight of the depths from which he had been lifted. When he wrote "...that saved a wretch like me," he meant those words with all his heart.

Bill Moyers made a documentary film on the hymn "Amazing Grace" which includes a scene filmed in Wembley Stadium in London. Various musical groups, mostly rock bands, had gathered together in celebration of the changes in South Africa, and for some reason the promoters scheduled an opera singer, Jessye Norman, as the closing act.

The film cuts back and forth between scenes of the unruly crowd in the stadium and Jessye Norman being interviewed. For twelve hours groups like Guns 'n' Roses have blasted the crowd through banks of speakers, riling up fans already high on booze and dope. The crowd yells for more curtain calls, and the rock groups oblige. Meanwhile, Jessye Norman sits in her dressing room discussing "Amazing Grace" with Moyers.

In the film, she tells Bill Moyers that Newton may have borrowed an old tune sung by the slaves themselves, redeeming the song, just as he had been redeemed.

Finally, the time comes for her to sing. A single circle of light follows Norman, a majestic African-American woman wearing a flowing African dashiki, as she strolls onstage. No backup band, no musical instruments, just Jessye. The crowd stirs, restless. Few recognize the opera diva. A voice yells for more Guns 'n' Roses. Others take up the cry. The scene is getting ugly.

Alone, a capella, Jessye Norman begins to sing, very slowly:

> ***Amazing grace, how sweet the sound***
> ***That saved a wretch like me!***
> ***I once was lost but now am found—***
> ***Was blind, but now I see.***

A remarkable thing happens in Wembley Stadium that night. Seventy thousand raucous fans fall silent before her aria of grace.

By the time Norman reaches the second verse, "'Twas grace that taught my heart to fear, And grace my fears relieved...," the soprano has the crowd in her hands.

By the time she reaches the third verse, "'Tis grace has brought me safe this far, And grace will lead me home," several thousand fans are singing along, digging far back in nearly lost memories for words they heard long ago.

> ***When we've been there ten thousand years,***
> ***Bright shining as the sun,***
> ***We've no less days to sing God's praise***
> ***Than when we first begun.***

Jessye Norman later confessed she had no idea what power descended on Wembley Stadium that night...Truly, when grace descends, the world falls silent before it.[135]

Grace: A Gift from Above

When the world experiences extra-ordinary instances of grace, it is a gift from God's kingdom above; it is a heavenly intrusion into our world of justice that causes all to stop and marvel at what just happened. It is this amazing grace that John Newton wrote of, and of which Jessye Norman sang, that has the power to change us and to reveal the heart of God. Grace is truly a gift from above.

Study Guide

1. Neil Simmons states that the law of human governance is "justice" while the kingdom of God runs on "grace and mercy." Do you agree? Discuss.

2. Discuss the difference between grace and mercy.

3. Simmons says that "spiritual growth occurs from grace to grace." Discuss.

4. Question: Does perfection look the same for everyone?

PART IV:

THE CHURCH

And I saw another angel fly in the midst of heaven, having the everlasting gospel to preach unto them that dwell on the earth, and to every nation, and kindred, and tongue, and people,

Saying with a loud voice, Fear God, and give glory to him; for the hour of his judgment is come: and worship him that made heaven, and earth, and the sea, and the fountains of waters (Rev. 14:6-7).

CHAPTER 18

The Former and Latter Rains

But ye shall receive power, after that the Holy Ghost is come upon you: and ye shall be witnesses unto me both in Jerusalem, and in all Judea, and in Samaria, and unto the uttermost part of the earth (Acts 1:8).

After Jesus' resurrection and prior to his ascension, he told the disciples to tarry in Jerusalem until they received the baptism of the Holy Spirit. Acts 2 records that the Holy Spirit came upon them and had the sound of a mighty rushing wind. Cloven tongues of fire appeared and sat on each one of them. They began to speak other languages as the Spirit gave them voice. The gathered crowd was amazed as each one heard them speak in their own native tongue.

This outpouring of the Spirit occurred on the day of Pentecost. "Pentecost" is an English transliteration of the Greek word ***pentekostos*** which means "fifty." It was a word adopted by Greek-speaking Jews to mark the Jewish holiday, Festival of Weeks, and was originally a harvest festival celebrating the first fruits of the wheat harvest; but in time came to mark the day in which the law was given to Israel on Mt. Sinai. This celebration was to be on the fiftieth day after Passover (Lev. 23:16).

How appropriate that the New Covenant, the law of the Spirit and this perfect law of liberty, was given on the same day which marked the reception of the old law; signifying that the new had now superseded the old. Jesus, in his post-resurrection appearance to the Nephites explains:

> Behold, I say unto you, that the law is fulfilled that was given unto Moses.
> Behold, I am he that gave the law, and I am he who covenanted with my people Israel; therefore, the law in me is fulfilled, for I have come to fulfill the law; therefore, it hath an end…For behold, the covenant which I have made

> with my people, is not all fulfilled; but the law which was given unto Moses, hath an end in me (3 Ne. 7:5-6, 9/15:4-5, 8).

Dreaming dreams and seeing visions

The Day of Pentecost is considered by many to be the event that marked the birth of the Christian church. Before that day, there were followers of Jesus but no movement that could meaningfully be called "the church." Some said of that remarkable outpouring of the Spirit that the disciples were drunk with new wine. Peter responded by saying:

> For these are not drunken, as ye suppose, seeing it is but the third hour of the day. But this is that which was spoken by the prophet Joel;
> And it shall come to pass in the last days, saith God, I will pour out of my Spirit upon all flesh: and your sons and your daughters shall prophesy, and your young men shall see visions, and your old men shall dream dreams:
> And on my servants and on my handmaidens I will pour out in those days of my Spirit; and they shall prophesy (Acts 2:15-18).

Now you might remember that Moroni quoted to Joseph Smith this very scripture from Joel, saying that it had not yet been fulfilled but soon would be. This and several other scriptures indicate that a great spiritual outpouring shall take place in the last days concurrent with the New Covenant. And yet Peter quoted from Joel implying that this was being fulfilled at that time.

The answer was that it was partially fulfilled. The Bible uses the term, "former and latter rains" (see Joel 2:23 and James 5:7), equating that terminology to great outpourings of the spirit. Many scholars equate what happened at Pentecost to the "former rains" while saying that the "latter rains" are yet to come.

> **Be glad then, ye children of Zion**, and rejoice in the Lord your God: for he hath given you the former rain

> moderately, and he will cause to come down for you the rain, the former rain, and the latter rain in the first month (Joel 2:23).

Hopefully, we are among the children of Zion Joel is addressing. This is saying that at Pentecost when the first rain materialized, it came "moderately." In Israel this rain occurs around seeding time in the fall of the year. The first month referred to here is in the spring just before harvest.

So the latter rain falls usually in the first month, Nisan of the Jewish ecclesiastical year, which is our March-April. When the first month arrives, we will not only receive the latter rains which will be much greater than "moderate," but we will also receive an amount equal to the former rains. So, bottom line, what happened at Pentecost was spectacular, but it will not compare to the latter rains.

> Be patient therefore, brethren, unto the coming of the Lord. Behold, the husbandman waiteth for the precious fruit of the earth, and hath long patience for it, until he receive the early and latter rain (James 5:7).

James is telling us to bear our burdens and be patient because the Lord will be coming soon. Soon we will be receiving the latter rain.

The former rain falls at sowing-time. This rain is crucial to moisten the ground and to germinate the seed. Pentecost was essential to the spiritual birth of the church. You and I would not be here otherwise.

As crucial as the former rain is, that alone is not enough. Unless the latter rain comes to ripen the grain, the harvest will not be ready for the sickle and the labor of the sower would have been in vain. This outpouring of the spirit to come is consistent with this revelation given to Joseph Smith in June of 1834:

> Therefore, in consequence of the transgression of my people, it is expedient in me that mine elders should wait for a little season for the redemption of Zion...and this

> cannot be brought to pass until mine elders are endowed with power from on high; for, behold, **I have prepared a great endowment and blessing to be poured out upon them** (DC 102:3c-e/105:9, 11-12).

What was the result of the outpouring of the Spirit on the Day of Pentecost? Thousands were converted on that very day; and the glad tidings of a risen Savior have been carried to the uttermost parts of the earth. And yet, as great of a day as that was, we can say that the best is yet to come. The latter rain will be more abundant than the former rain. The great work of the gospel is not to close with less manifestation of the power of the spirit than marked its beginning.

In the last days, the power of God will be manifested as never before. As we shall see, the Book of Mormon is key to opening up the heavens so that the latter rains might fall. This is what the New Covenant is all about.

The Book of Mormon contains "the truth" that David predicted should "spring out of the earth" in the latter days when "righteousness would look down from heaven," and the Lord should "give that which is good," and Palestine would yield its increase, and glory begin again to dwell in David's land (Ps. 85:11; Isa. 29: 17; Joel 2:21–23; Ezek. 36: 1–8). The book was published to the world in 1830. In 1846 to 1852 the former and latter rains began to be restored to Canaan again, after a drought of eighteen hundred summers. - Saints Herald 1885

ADMONITION: Our Invitation

In the inspired document given through Jim Hobbs (see Appendix A) we see that God has issued us an invitation to "try Him," to "test Him," that we might experience our own Pentecost; that we won't be passed by in the great revival shortly to come:

My apostles had their Pentecost (Acts 2). The Restoration had its Pentecost [1833, 1836]. Will you receive my Pentecost for you? Try Me! Test Me! See if I will pour out My Spirit upon you. Will you lay down your traditions, your preconceived ideas, your agendas and set a date and time for Me to manifest Myself to you and in you? Will you come together with this one purpose in mind, united in heart to receive? I love you My children and desire to do great things through you. But if you cannot all unite in one desire and purpose to receive My Spirit, I cannot give unto you My Pentecost in one body as I desire. I am reaching out to you, will you not reach out to Me?

A great revival is soon to come forth among My children. Will you My Restoration people be a part of it? Or will it pass you by because of preconceived ideas? I call on you to bow down and humble yourselves that I may involve you in My great and marvelous work which is even now in the process of coming forth.

Study Guide

1. What do you think of Peter's assessment that the Day of Pentecost fulfilled that which was prophesied by the prophet Joel? (See Acts 2:15-18).

2. What is meant by the term "Former and Latter Rains"?

3. Discuss this latter day endowment to come (see DC 102:3c-e/ 105:9, 11-12) in light of the "Admonition" experience of Jim Hobbs. What would it mean for us to "lay down our traditions, our preconceived ideas and agendas"? All that we might be united as one in receiving God's Spirit.

CHAPTER 19

Establishing the Church

1 But if they will repent, and hearken unto my words, and harden not their hearts, *I will establish my church among them*, and they shall come in unto the covenant, and be numbered among this the remnant of Jacob, unto whom I have given this land for their inheritance, and they shall assist my people, the remnant of Jacob;
2 And also, as many of the house of Israel as shall come, that they may build a city, which shall be called the New Jerusalem;
3 And then shall they assist my people that they may be gathered in, who are scattered upon all the face of the land, in unto the New Jerusalem.
4 And then shall the power of heaven come down among them; and I also will be in the midst, and then shall the work of the Father commence, at that day even when this gospel shall be preached among the remnant of this people.
5 Verily, I say unto you, At that day shall the work of the Father commence among all the dispersed of my people; yea, even the tribes which have been lost, which the Father hath led away out of Jerusalem.
6 Yea, the work shall commence among all the dispersed of my people, with the Father, to prepare the way whereby they may come unto me, that they may call on the Father in my name;
7 Yea, and then shall the work commence, with the Father, among all nations, in preparing the way whereby his people may be gathered home to the land of their inheritance (3 Ne. 10:1-7/21:22-28).

Because of the way the first verse is phrased above, wherein the Lord says that "if they [the Gentiles] will repent…I will establish my church among them," this would not normally be thought of in terms of one of the covenants of God that must yet be fulfilled. Indeed, perhaps most would skim by this verse with the assumption that the "establishment of the church" would refer to a past event, the restoration of the church in 1830.

Indeed, a cursory examination of the Doctrine and Covenants reveals that even the Lord himself used the word "established" in October, 1830, referring to the recent restoration of the church:

> And verily, verily I say unto you, that this church have I **established** and called forth out of the wilderness (DC 32:2a/33:5).

However, when we examine the context and chronological sequence of the above verse (3 Ne. 10:1/21:22), it becomes apparent that the Lord is using the word "establish" in a different vein, differently from that of initially causing something to come into existence. An examination of various online dictionaries reveals these additional meanings for "establish":

- To achieve permanent acceptance or recognition for
- To make firm or stable
- To cause to grow and multiply or thrive
- To put in a favorable position
- To put beyond doubt
- To show to be valid or true - prove
- To gain full recognition

The Book of Mormon has several precedents of using the word "establish" in a manner other than initial inception. In Alma there are several instances where the existing church becomes more fully established through the repentance of the people; by teaching and declaring the word of God; or, by imposing regulations to establish the order of the church (see Alma 4:3-4; 6:1; 21:24-25; 29:54-56/ 6:3-4; 8:1; 45:21-22; 62:44-47).

- This is my church, and I will ***establish*** it… (Mosiah 11:166/27:13).
- And they began to ***establish*** the church more fully… (Alma 2:4/4:4).
- Therefore Helaman and his brethren went forth to ***establish*** the church again in all the land (Alma 21:25/45:22).

- They did ***establish*** again the church of God… (Alma 29:56/62:46).
- And it shall come to pass that I will ***establish*** my people, O house of Israel. And behold, this people will I ***establish*** in this land (3 Ne. 9:57-58/20:21-22).

Again, the first verse of this chapter is helpful for us to clarify what group of Gentiles "they" is referring to. In the LDS version it is perhaps more clear because of where their chapter break is. Chapter 21 begins with RLDS 3 Nephi 9:86, and then continues mid-verse through 3 Nephi 10:8. Let's begin with 3 Nephi 9:98/21:11:

> Therefore it shall come to pass, that whosoever will not believe in my words, who am Jesus Christ, whom the Father shall cause him to bring forth unto the Gentiles, and shall give unto him power that he shall bring them forth unto the Gentiles, (it shall be done even as Moses said,) **they shall be cut off from among my people who are of the covenant.**

Whosoever will not believe "my words," the words of the "marred servant" (see v. 96/10), whom many believe to be the Book of Mormon, "they shall be cut off from among my people who are of the covenant." This indicates that this initial judgment is among God's people, no doubt a judgment that has been well under way for some time.

Belief in the Book of Mormon will then become a clear dividing line that shall enable God to more fully "establish" His church and allow His work to proceed. Belief in the Book of Mormon will allow God to manifest greater things to the church (see 3 Ne. 12:3/26:9). Belief in the Book of Mormon, the New Covenant, will then cause God to remove the curse, the condemnation pronounced upon the church early in its history (see DC 83:8a-b/84:54-57 below).

Then verses 9:99-104/21:12-18 describe a general judgment, a physical judgment, taking place among the Gentiles. Perhaps this will be a world-wide judgment but certainly it will be in the land of

America because it refers to "the remnant of Jacob" being in their midst. Verses 105-106/19-21 then revert to the covenant people wherein God will move to do away with "the lyings, deceivings, envyings, strifes, whoredoms and priestcrafts." That whosoever will not repent, "Them will I cut off from among My people, O house of Israel, and I will execute vengeance and fury upon them - even as upon the heathen."

Then, we come to the first verse of chapter 10/21:22 and the word "they," which is a reference to the immediately preceding verses 105-106 of chapter 9/21:19-21; God's people, the people of the covenant. For those who are repentant and believe in "My words," the words of Christ, the Book of Mormon, God will "establish" His church among that group of Gentiles.

After the "establishing" of the church, we then see that great things begin to happen wherein the gospel is preached in endowed power to the remnant; and then it goes forth to all the tribes of Israel, even the lost, and then to all nations. This then, verse 10:1/21:22 is a prophecy of when the restored church once again is united with signs and miracles following.

Concerning the condemnation that rests upon the church because we have treated lightly the New Covenant, the Book of Mormon, there is no room for comfort just because we can say, "we believe the Book of Mormon." Let's look a little closer at what God says:

> And your minds in times past have been darkened because of unbelief, and because you have treated lightly the things you have received, which vanity and unbelief hath brought the whole church under condemnation. And this condemnation resteth upon the children of Zion, even all; and they shall remain under this condemnation until they repent and remember <u>the new covenant</u>, even the Book of Mormon and the former commandments which I have given them, <u>not only to say, but to do according to that which I have written</u>, <u>that they may bring forth fruit meet</u>

> for their Father's kingdom, otherwise there remaineth a scourge and a judgment to be poured out upon the children of Zion; for, shall the children of the kingdom pollute my holy land? Verily, I say unto you, Nay (DC 83:8a-c/84:54-59).

"...not only to say, but to do..."

Implied in the mentioning of the Book of Mormon as being the New Covenant is the imperative that we understand what the New Covenant is all about and how it fits into God's overall plan of salvation. It is of the Book of Mormon and the former commandments that God says, knowledge is not enough, "Not only to say, but to do according to that which I have written." "The Lord requireth the heart and a willing mind; and the willing and obedient shall eat the good of the land of Zion in these last days" (DC 64:7a/34).

> But, behold, verily I say unto you, There are many who have been ordained among you, whom I have called, but few of them are chosen: they who are not chosen have sinned a very grievous sin, in that they are walking in darkness at noonday (DC 92:1d-e/95:5-6).

As the sequence in 3 Nephi bears out, judgment is and has begun with God's own people:

> **For the time *is come* that judgment must begin at the house of God...** (1 Peter 4:17).

Joseph Smith received a revelation in 1837 saying the same thing:

> Behold, vengeance cometh speedily upon the inhabitants of the earth...**And upon my house shall it begin, and from my house shall it go forth, saith the Lord. First** among those among you, saith the Lord, who have professed to know my name and have not known me, and have blasphemed against me in the midst of my house, saith the Lord (DC 105:9b-10b/112:24-26).

In *God's Plan of Salvation,* I used the experience of an Evangelist as he was asked for a special blessing by a lady considering which of all the Restoration groups to attend. She was concerned that her children be taught properly. The Evangelist related that God's answer was to the point and somewhat surprising:

> The adversary has moved into the Restoration movement and scattered the sheep as a wolf, tearing them to pieces. All of them now suffer strife and adversity because the adversary is working among them all. This is the fate of the church as revealed to Joseph Smith Jr. long ago that there would be a desolation and abomination starting in His own home. We now are witnessing the fruits of this event. Many in leadership and priesthood serve for their own desires and do not prosper the Kingdom. Consequently many have lost their authority to act for Me. Therefore **a new Restoration must occur** and a new dedication to My Spirit must take place **in order for My Church to unite** and rise up and become what was first intended for the Church from the beginning. Therefore she was not to concern herself with which church, but instead which one still taught the fundamental concepts of the Book of Mormon and the truth of Jesus Christ for her family and children to absorb (emphasis added).[136]

Literally, this is not saying that there will be a new Restoration per se; but, as it says above, **"a new dedication to My Spirit...in order for My Church to unite and to rise up and become what was intended for the Church from the beginning.**"

Also, in *God's Plan of Salvation,* a second Evangelist testimony concerns a group that gathered to pray on the Temple Lot[w] in Independence. The Evangelist said that he heard a voice that said God would soon be bringing all the Restoration groups together along with the Native Americans.[137]

---

[w] A vacant plot of land in the possession of the Church of Christ (Temple Lot) dedicated in 1831 as the spot for a temple in Zion.

We know that priesthood has been restored for the last time (see DC 32:1d/33:3); DC 105:12a/112:30). We, of necessity, will leave to God all of the decisions concerning who has authority and who does not.

> For, verily, I say that the rebellious are not of the blood of Ephraim, wherefore they shall be plucked out. Behold, I, the Lord, have made my church in these last days, like unto a judge sitting on a hill, or in a high place, to judge the nations; **for it shall come to pass, that the inhabitants of Zion shall judge all things pertaining to Zion; and liars, and hypocrites shall be proved by them, and they who are not apostles and prophets shall be known** (DC 64:7b-7d/64:36-39).

"A second Title Page" - Ray Treat

Ray Treat likens 3 Nephi 10:1-7/21:22-28 to a second title page of the Book of Mormon. He cites the four "commences" contained in verses 4, 5, 6 and 7 (see opening scripture). He says that we see virtually the same information as in the title page but in more detail. He says, "You have the covenant in the first verse, and then you have three different groups of Lamanites from 1-4, and then 5 and 6 is the house of Israel, and 7 is the rest of the people." Treat goes on to say:

> The Lord knew we were going to be put on hold in 1834. He knew that beforehand, and arranged to have a second title page, and the work commences again in Third Nephi 10:4/21:25-26. It's an endowment verse, a verse of great power. Jesus Christ himself is there, and He's saying, "I'm going to put this in the context of another title page in saying to you: 'This is what I intended in the first place. This is what you could have had if you had made full use of the Book of Mormon at that time because once you have the [new] covenant established in your life, there is no limit to the spiritual power you can have.'" And so, when that

second title page gets put into action there won't be any more falling away. That will be the final push.[138]

Second Title Page Commentary

I must admit that when I first read what Ray Treat had written concerning 3 Nephi 10:1-7/21:22-28 equating to a second title page, I was not too sure of his interpretation. However, the more I have examined and compared these verses to the Title Page, the more convinced I have become that Brother Ray is correct in his assessment that these verses from 3 Nephi represent a new beginning for the Restoration.

To begin with, the language varies somewhat because Moroni wrote the Title Page while Mormon engraved 3 Nephi. Also, as Treat says, the level of detail appears to be greater in 3 Nephi. The Title Page gives us a succinct purpose for the Book of Mormon while 3 Nephi is a prophecy of how this purpose will come to fruition. As one examines the 3 Nephi verses there appears to be a correspondence not only with the Title Page but also with early revelations in the Doctrine and Covenants that in like manner reveal the purpose of the Restoration Movement.

Areas of correspondence begin with verse 10:1/21:22 where God says, "I will establish My church." As discussed previously in this chapter, the word "establish" should be interpreted as something more than the mere creation of an entity but also to place it on a firm foundation; to cause it to grow, multiply, and thrive; to show to be valid and to gain full recognition. In 1828 the Lord said that "If this generation harden not their hearts, I will establish my church among them" (DC 3:13a/10:53). That generation and succeeding generations have hardened their hearts rejecting the fullness of the gospel. Thus, the church has not yet become fully established.

The Title Page mentions that the purpose of the Book of Mormon is that the remnant may come to know of the covenants of the Lord, that they are a remnant of the house of Israel and "that they are not cast off forever." This knowledge is crucial as this remnant is the key to the subsequent convincing of the house of Israel and all nations that Jesus is the Christ, the Eternal God.

The same sequence appears in 3 Nephi where, as Treat points out, there is a series of "commences" beginning with verse 10:4/21:25-26. This first commence likewise says that the work of the Father begins "at that day even when this gospel shall be preached among the remnant of this people." It was this task of preaching the gospel to the remnant that the Lord gave the church in the early days of its inception, a mere five months after the church was organized (see DC 27:3a/28:8). Third Nephi 10:4/21:25-26 shows that this initial task given to the church will finally be accomplished as the "powers of heaven" will accompany the preaching of the gospel to the remnant. As mentioned in the Title Page above, after the remnant comes unto the covenant, the true purpose of the Restoration begins to be realized with the three following commences wherein the work is taken to the remainder of the house of Israel and then to all nations.

While the level of correspondence between the Title Page and those 3 Nephi verses may be debatable, there is no doubt that our 3 Nephi verses (10:1-7/21:22-28) represent a time when indeed the church is "established" and thus is enabled, with the accompanying "power of heaven" in its midst, to fulfill the purpose for which the church was established.

Hosea, Ephraim and the Church

Hosea was a prophet sent primarily to the northern kingdom of Israel [a.k.a. Ephraim] shortly before her demise. Already at this time the northern kingdom had been losing people and territory as the Lord delivered them into the hands of her enemies (2 Kings 10:32). Hosea was not speaking into a vacuum when he warned the Israelites of the coming disaster at the hands of Assyria.

Hosea was told to name his first child Jezreel or Sowing. This signified that Israel would no longer be a nation and would be sown among the nations. This is what was already happening piecemeal and would be concluded by the Assyrian Empire.

He was told to name his second child Lo-ruhamah, which means No Mercy. By this Israel was to understand that the Lord's patience with them was at an end and He would no longer extend mercy to them as a nation.

Finally he was told to name his last child Lo-ammi, Not a People. In this name, the Lord declared that they were no longer to be counted as His Covenant People. This means that they would become Gentiles, as no longer having a Covenant with the Lord.

All of this is in the first chapter of his prophecy. Then the chapter ends with a promise that this condition would not continue forever, that they would in time [the last days] be restored to their former status and also be reunited with Judah.[139]

> Yet the number of the children of Israel shall be as the sand of the sea, which cannot be measured nor numbered; and it shall come to pass, that in the place where it was said unto them, Ye are not my people, there it shall be said unto them, Ye are the sons of the living God (Hosea 1:10).
>
> And I will sow her unto me in the earth; and I will have mercy upon her that had not obtained mercy; and I will say to them which were not my people, Thou art my people; and they shall say, Thou art my God (Hosea 2:23).
>
> Afterward shall the children of Israel return, and seek the Lord their God, and David their king; and shall fear the Lord and his goodness in the latter days (Hosea 3:5).
>
> O Israel, return unto the Lord thy God; for thou hast fallen by thine iniquity. Take with you words, and turn to the Lord: say unto him, Take away all iniquity....
> I will heal their backsliding, I will love them freely: for mine anger is turned away from him. I will be as the dew unto Israel: he shall grow as the lily, and cast forth his roots as Lebanon. His branches shall spread, and his beauty shall be as the olive tree, and his smell as Lebanon. They that dwell

> under his shadow shall return....**Ephraim** shall say, What have I to do any more with idols? (Hosea 14:1-2, 4-8).

What does Hosea's prophecy have to do with us today? Remember that the fate of Israel and Ephraim are intertwined. Ephraim was the youngest son of Joseph and the recipient of the birthright at the hands of Jacob. Ephraim became the principal tribe of the northern kingdom of Israel and in time become synonymous with it. In approximately 930 BC Assyria overran Israel and carried them away to eventually become scattered throughout the world where they would no longer be a covenant people, and thus became Gentiles. Their tribal identities became lost and thus they were known as the lost ten tribes of Israel.

The connection of Ephraim specifically to the Restoration Church is made in Section 64 (b-c/36-37) where Ephraim is equated to "my church." Section 83 tells us that the purpose of the church concerns the restoration of God's people (1b/84:2). Section 108 then talks of a great gathering where the borders of Zion will be enlarged and its stakes strengthened, a time when the fullness of the gospel will be "preached unto every nation, and kindred, and tongue, and people" (7b/133:37). A time when "they shall fall down and be crowned with glory, even in Zion, by the hands of the servants of the Lord, **even the children of Ephraim**; and they shall be filled with songs of everlasting joy" (6d/133:32-33).

The bottom line concerning the church is that God has decreed that it shall fulfill the purpose for which it has been appointed. There will be repentant Gentiles and the church will become established as never before. There is no doubt that the disparate groups of the Restoration will come together as one before the houses of Israel and Judah can come together as one. It is God's purpose to "gather together in one all things in Christ, both which are in heaven, and which are on earth" (Eph. 1:10). The church has a vital function that must be and will be fulfilled.

The experience of the evangelist we've cited indicates that God has a collective view of the Restoration Movement and looks to the time when we shall once again become one body, the church God intended from the beginning. This view is bolstered by an experience of Bill Leutzinger published by Patrick McKay in his book, *Healing the Breach.*

The Same Woman

I attended the Zarahemla Branch on October 23, 2012, to hear an evangelist from The Church of Jesus Christ preach. That night after going to bed, I had the following dream: I saw a woman tall and stately, and she had the word "LAW" written over her chest. I immediately understood she represented the Reorganized Church of Jesus Christ of Latter Day Saints [Josephites].

I looked and again saw a woman clothed in gray clothes, somewhat bent over and humble. She had written across her chest the word "CUSTODIAN." I understood she represented the Church of Christ [Temple Lot].

I again looked and saw a woman, with the word "LOYALTY" written across her chest and realized she represented The Church of Jesus Christ of Latter-day Saints [Mormon Church].

Once again I looked and beheld a woman, and she had the words "MANY GIFTS" written over her chest. I was made to understand she represented The Church of Jesus Christ [Bickertonites].

When I awoke, I shared the dream with my wife who responded, "Oh, it is like the pieces of a puzzle. All of these different women will get together."

I said, "No, they all represented the same woman with different characteristics."[140]

Study Guide

1. Review and discuss the various meanings given for "establish." In light of that discussion and the material presented in this chapter, how would you then interpret 3 Ne. 10:1/21:22 where God says, "I will establish My church."

2. The author quotes the Apostle Peter and Joseph Smith as saying that the latter-day judgment will begin at God's own house (see 1 Peter 4:17; DC 105:9b-10b/112:24-26). Do you feel this prophesied judgment has begun? If so, how has it manifested itself?

3. Ray Treat has likened 3 Ne. 10:1-7/21:22-28 to a second title page for the Restoration. What are your thoughts?

4. Discuss Hosea's prophecy and Bill Leutzinger's experience in light of their implications for us today.

PART V:

THE BOOK AND THE LOVE OF GOD

And righteousness will I send down out of heaven; and truth will I send forth out of the earth, to bear testimony of mine Only Begotten.

And righteousness and truth will I cause to sweep the earth as with a flood, to gather out mine own elect from the four quarters of the earth, unto a place which I shall prepare; an holy city, that my people may gird up their loins, and be looking forth for the time of my coming; for there shall be my tabernacle, and it shall be called Zion; a New Jerusalem *(Gen. 7:69-70/Moses 7:62)*.

CHAPTER 20

The Unsearchable Riches of Christ

"Lord I crawled across the barrenness to you with my empty cup uncertain in asking any small drop of refreshment. If only I had known you better I'd have come running with a bucket."[141] -Nancy Spiegelberg

"I do not understand the mystery of grace -- only that it meets us where we are and does not leave us where it found us."[142] – Anne Lamott

In the preface, I wrote of the inadequacy I felt in trying to describe God's intention for us in the New Covenant; that in the final analysis, it is a concept and way of life so stupendous that it must be revealed by God's Spirit. I have come to realize that my inadequacy stems from my very human efforts to comprehend the grace of God, which grace lies not only at the heart of the New Covenant, but ultimately is an infinite and divine attribute resident in God Himself. To fully understand grace is to comprehend even God. Hence the difficulty and yet the necessity of saying even more about grace, even if it is from our limited human perspective. I am convinced that even though we can't fully comprehend God's grace, God has made us for the express purpose of being the grateful recipients of His grace for time and eternity – His Amazing Grace.

My frustration in trying to describe the grace of God was somewhat alleviated as I happened across the following words attributed to A.T. Pierson (1837-1911). Alleviated because he was a noted minister who had an international ministry, preached thousands of sermons and wrote over fifty books. Yet, in spite of his impeccable credentials, he arrived at the very same dead end as he tried in vain to describe the grace of God for his congregation – "**the unsearchable riches of Christ**" (Eph. 3:8).

> A. T. Pierson was a powerful preacher, educator, and missionary statesman at the turn of the 20th Century. He

once tried to preach on God's blessings as described in Ephesians 1-3, a section of scripture that continually talks about our unsearchable wealth and riches in Christ. Pierson said:

> In the words of the text, "**the unsearchable riches of Christ**," "unsearchable" literally means riches that can never be explored. You not only cannot count or measure them, but you can form no estimate of them; and you not only can form no estimate of them, but you never can get to the end of your investigation. There is a boundless continent, a world, a universe of riches that still lies before you when you have carried your search to the limits of possibility. I feel as though I had a theme, about which no man ought to speak. An archangel's tongue could do no justice to it.

Pierson nevertheless tried to point out the truths about the believer's wealth as described in these three chapters (Eph. 1-3). Then he told his congregation:

> I sink back exhausted, in the vain attempt to set before this congregation the greatest mystery of grace that I ever grappled with. I cannot remember, in thirty years of Gospel preaching, ever to have been confronted with a theme that more baffled every outreach of thought and every possibility of utterance than the theme that I have now attempted in the name of God to present.[143]

I am grateful for the words of Pierson as he has given voice to my inadequacy - riches that can never be explored; that cannot be counted or measured, and no estimate formed; an investigation that knows no end. In the words of John Newton, after ten thousand years we will have only begun to sing God's praises - His Grace will be ever new.

Karl Barth made the comment that Jesus' gift of forgiveness, of grace, was to him more astonishing than Jesus' miracles. Miracles broke the physical laws of the universe; forgiveness broke the moral rules. "**The beginning of good is perceived in the midst of bad....The simplicity and comprehensiveness of grace - who shall measure it**?"[144]

> The call of our day is the call of love...The real purpose of life can be understood only in the love of God. No human life is adequately nor intelligently motivated until it responds in the aura of this grace. It is not possible for us fully to understand the selfless love which is inherent in the incarnation. In our most prayerful and intellectually alert moments, when our minds and hearts are reaching to the uttermost, we find ourselves at the threshold of this reality. We are so overcome by the glory of it that we cannot adequately articulate our experiences. **In these moments we begin to comprehend the truth that God is not an object which we may observe from a distance, but an absolute reality who draws us to his bosom.**[145] – Arthur Oakman

In my memory in the church, I cannot ever remember that grace has been a significant topic of conversation. Others I have queried have pushed back on my recollection and have recalled that it has been spoken about and taught in the church, albeit perhaps not emphasized the way it might be in a Protestant church. I suspect that to a certain extent at least, what we think about grace has been influenced by the flawed Protestant concept (speaking generally) where salvation comes at no cost and one is saved by grace from that moment on, regardless of what type of life you might live.

In our consideration of grace, the Restoration concept of the three glories (see DC 76 and 1 Cor. 15:40-42) **is a crucial difference-maker**. Nevertheless, I find that, concerning grace, we have much we can learn from our Protestant friends. The bottom line is that regardless of how much grace was or was not taught in the church, the grace of God is not intended to be an abstract concept but a way of life that yields the fruit of the kingdom of God – a way of life that as of yet we have failed to realize.

> For sin shall not have dominion over you: for ye are not under the law, but under grace (Rom. 6:14).

Grace is a world we're not used to.

Grace is a world we're not used to – it is unmerited and unearned favor freely given by God. With the incarnation of Christ we entered into a new era, a new realm, an entirely new way of thinking and living. Every other religion is predicated upon what we can do for God. Christianity is based upon what God can do for us – an amazing and foreign thought to us.

In the movie ***The Last Emperor,*** the young child anointed as the last emperor of China lives a magical life of luxury with a thousand eunuch servants at his command. "What happens when you do wrong?" his brother asks. "When I do wrong, someone else is punished," the boy emperor replies. To demonstrate, he breaks a jar, and one of the servants is beaten. In Christian theology, Jesus reversed that ancient pattern: when the servants erred, the King was punished. Grace is free only because the giver himself has borne the cost.[146]

> **The LORD is merciful and gracious,**
> **slow to anger, and plenteous in mercy....**
> **He hath not dealt with us after our sins;**
> **nor rewarded us according to our iniquities.**
> **For as the heaven is high above the earth,**
> **so great is his mercy toward them that fear him.**
> **As far as the east is from the west,**
> **so far hath he removed our transgressions from us**
> (Ps. 103:8, 10-12).

In the New Testament, "the law" refers back to the Old Testament where people looked at obedience to the commandments as the way to acceptance with God. With the law, God's promises were conditional; with the law, God says: "Obey my voice, and I will be your God, and ye shall be my people" (Jer. 7:23). The problem as we previously found was that the law did not come "with batteries," it provided no power to produce obedience and yet proscribed severe penalties for disobedience. The purpose of the law was to reveal the problem; to show us how helpless we are so that we will turn to Christ. The law functions like a mirror – it reveals our flaws but has no power to help us. "The sting of death is sin; and the strength of sin is the law" (1 Cor. 15:56). The law reveals our need for grace.

With the law there is no leeway. Under the law we are obligated to keep the whole law; we cannot pick and choose; we must keep all the laws all the time. Even if we stumble in just one point, we become equally guilty as if we broke all the laws (see James 2:10). However, with the New Covenant, with the grace way of living, "IF" has been changed to "SINCE" and "HAVE TO" has been changed to "THANK YOU" because, in the words of the Apostle Paul, God has already blessed us: "Blessed be the God and Father of our Lord Jesus Christ, who hath blessed us with all spiritual blessings in heavenly places in Christ" (Eph. 1:3).

In Paul's letter to the Galatians, he marveled that those who had been made free from the yoke of bondage in the law were once again considering returning to the tenets of the Mosaic Law. Paul told the Galatians, "I do not frustrate the grace of God, for if righteousness come by the law, then Christ is dead in vain" (Gal. 2:21).

> This only would I learn of you, Received ye the Spirit by the works of the law, or by the hearing of faith? Are ye so foolish? having begun in the Spirit, are ye now made perfect by the flesh? (Gal. 3:2-3).

LEGALISTS TRUST IN CHRIST A LOT. BUT THEY DON'T TRUST IN CHRIST ALONE.[147]

Paul's words to the Galatians ring true in many of our lives today. The law can be equated to legalism. Legalism is not the presence of rules per se, but the wrong attitude toward the rules. Legalism assigns to the rules a power to produce obedience that God never gave them. Legalism puts people under an impossible load. Legalism puts us on a leash. Legalism is a guilt-driven system; always living under a threat, "thou shalt not." Legalism is the joyless bondage of continuing to "try harder." As Paul says, if we are operating under the wrong system Christ is of no benefit (see Gal. 2:21 above). In the words of William Kynes:

> For those who put all their stress on the rigors of following Jesus, the Christian life becomes spiritually dysfunctional and deadening, resulting in a frustrating return to the works of the law as the means to please God.[148]

Grace is a Person

Today, many Christians are willing to accept Christ as their Savior by grace, but then soon seek to live the Christian life by their own efforts. That's because they are confused about grace; it's because they are not taught the truth about grace in their churches. **The truth is that grace is a person. Grace is a relationship not just a theology. The dispenser of God's Grace is Jesus Christ. The more we have of him the more we experience of grace.**

> For the law was given by Moses, but grace and truth came by Jesus Christ (John 1:17).

> For the grace of God that bringeth salvation hath appeared to all men (Titus 2:11).

Abide in Me

It was in the early 1990s, while living in Atlanta, Georgia, that I remember being especially discouraged about the situation in my life, being overwhelmed by the responsibilities I had. I was on my way somewhere one evening when I happened to hear a portion of a sermon by Dr. Charles Stanley. He was talking about a similar period in his life when he happened to read from John 15:

> Abide in me, and I in you. As the branch cannot bear fruit of itself, except it abide in the vine; no more can ye, except ye abide in me. ***I am the vine, ye are the branches: He that abideth in me, and I in him, the same bringeth forth much fruit: for without me ye can do nothing....***

> If ye abide in me, and my words abide in you, ye shall ask what ye will, and it shall be done unto you.
> Herein is my Father glorified, that ye bear much fruit; so shall ye be my disciples (John 15:4-5, 7-8).

Dr. Stanley testified that for a long time there was something missing from his life. Finally, it dawned upon him that he had been like a branch trying to produce fruit on its own. He realized that branches were not designed to produce fruit - they were designed to have fruit produced through them!

Prior to John 15, Jesus and his disciples had just left the upper room where he had led them through the last supper; where he had wrapped a towel around himself as a household servant would and washed their feet, modeling for them Christ-like love and servanthood; where he had announced the betrayal; where Peter had proudly promised that he would never leave or forsake Jesus; where they had shared communion. In the upper room Jesus endeavored to explain to his non-comprehending disciples that while he would be leaving them, that they would not be left alone, that he would send them another comforter, even the spirit of truth.

At the end of John 14, Jesus said, "Arise, let us go hence." Jesus and his disciples then began their walk towards the Garden of Gethsemane, where Jesus would soon pray and then be arrested. Time is of the essence. Jesus knew the timeline, and the time was growing very short. He took care with every word. He would begin with the parable of the vine and the branches.

While Jesus, in the time remaining, could not possibly tell them everything they needed to know, he nevertheless revealed to them the secret that would allow their communion to continue unabated. In fact, this would be much, much better as Jesus then would abide within them instead of merely being an external presence in their lives.

In fact, "abide" (Greek, *meno*) means to remain, or stay, or continue. For example, in John 1:38-39, two of the disciples who first encountered Jesus asked him "Where are you staying?" They wanted to know where Jesus made his residence. The word "staying" is the same word translated "abide" in John 15. To *abide* is to *reside*. To abide is to continue, to stay, to remain.[149]

By saying that "without me ye can do nothing," Jesus is saying that nothing of any spiritual significance can be accomplished apart from this abiding in the vine. A vine and its branches is the ideal allegory because a vine must remain connected or it will wither and die.

When a father walks with his small child in a crowded city market or on a street teeming with traffic, he gives the child one and only one responsibility, "Keep hold of my hand." Our goal therefore is not to know every detail of the future; but to hold the hand of the one who does.

> "Jesus is the solution to every problem in our lives. We don't have marital problems, financial problems, parenting problems, leadership problems, relationship problems, we have **abiding** problems."[150] – John Bruce

Interestingly, the principles presented in AA[x] as a means to getting clean and sober are all about connection to God and connection to another human being. When a person is trying to get sober they turn their will over to God and find another person, a sponsor who has successfully made the journey themselves, to come alongside them, to guide them, encourage them, and hold them up when they are too weak to stand on their own. It is the law of AA that you must cling to your sponsor and if you lose touch or choose not to stay "connected" to that person you will quickly fall back into destruction.

In his book, *What's So Amazing About Grace?,* Philip Yancey quotes from Nancy Mairs' memoir *Ordinary Time*[151]. Mairs tells of her years of mutiny against childhood images of a "Daddy God," who could

---

[x] Alcoholics Anonymous

only be pleased if she followed a list of onerous prescriptions and prohibitions:

> The fact that these took their most basic form as commandments suggested that human nature had to be forced into goodness; left to its own devices, it would prefer idols, profanity, leisurely Sunday mornings with bagels and the New York Times, disrespect for authority, murder, adultery, theft, lies, and everything belonging to the guy next door….I was forever on the perilous verge of doing a don't, to atone for which I had to beg forgiveness from the very being who had set me up for trespass, by forbidding behaviors He clearly expected me to commit in the first place: the God of the Gotcha, you might say.[152]

Mairs broke a lot of those rules, felt constantly guilty, and then, in her words, "learned to thrive in the care of" a God who "asks for the single act that will make transgression impossible: love."[153]

The best reason to be good is to want to be good. Internal change requires relationship. It requires love. "Who can be good, if not made to by loving?" asked Augustine. When Augustine made the famous statement, "If you but love God you may do as you incline," he was perfectly serious. A person who truly loves God will be inclined to please God, which is why Jesus and Paul both summed up the entire law in the simple command, "Love God."[154]

Our relationship with Christ does not mean the absence of rules.

We should be clear that our relationship with Christ does not mean the absence of rules. It means that rules do not form the basis of the relationship, but instead are an outgrowth or a byproduct of that relationship. Dr. Tony Evans tells a wonderful story that illustrates this very point.

> Upon their marriage, the husband made a list of twenty five rules, things that the wife must do. He told her that if she wants him to love her she's going to have to do it this way. At the end of each week he would go over the list with her and verify that each item was accomplished, and

accomplished on time. She did her best but was miserable. She came to hate him and his list. A few years later he died. She was not sad he died. Then she went on a trip and met a man named Bill. She fell in love with Bill and a few months later they were married. She was cleaning the house one day and she came upon the old list she had from her first husband. The list of twenty five things she saw and she began to laugh. What made her laugh was that she was now doing all twenty five things on the list and loving it; but when she was doing it for the old husband she was hating it, all because she had a relationship over here that she didn't have over there and still the law was being fulfilled because of the relationship.[155]

When we heed the call to begin afresh a life of obedience, we may think that by more study and self-scrutiny we will grow into it…obedience will gradually come. That's a mistake. Jeremiah learned this lesson when the Lord said to him, "Return…I will cure you" (Jer. 3:22). God pointed to Himself as the cure. In the Lord's eyes, the truly obedient person is the one who truly longs to know Him.

God doesn't want our achievements, He wants us. God doesn't want our rule keeping, He desires us. But remember, Jesus will never force you or coerce you into obeying. He will never insist on being your Master. Instead, He insists on loving you.

Father, I know now that the life of continual obedience is impossible without continual fellowship with You.[156]

\- Joni Eareckson Tada

In the words of Tony Evans: "Grace-based Christians obey because it's their delight. Law-based Christians obey because it's their duty. Grace-based Christians obey and love it. Law-based Christians obey and resent it. To grace-based Christians, the spiritual life is the lifting of a burden (see Matt. 11:30); but to legalistic Christians, living for God feels like carrying a heavy load."[157]

God's grace is to be our motivator. The more we come to understand His Grace the more we want to do what God asks us to do; no act of love or sacrifice becomes too great. The Apostle Peter, speaking of Christ said "Whom having not seen, ye love; in whom, though now ye see him not, yet believing, ye rejoice with joy unspeakable…" (1 Peter 1:8). **Unspeakable joy is the outgrowth of our relationship with Christ. Joy such that it must find an outlet in praise. Jesus endured the cross for the joy set before him** (Heb. 12:2).

William Kynes calls our attention to Matt. 11:28-30 to illustrate how the two sides of grace and discipleship come together in our union with Christ: "Come unto me, all ye that labour and are heavy laden, and I will give you rest. Take my yoke upon you, and learn of me; for I am meek and lowly in heart: and ye shall find rest unto your souls. ***For my yoke is easy, and my burden is light.***"[158]

In the chapter "Living An Amazing Life," we read that the impetus for receiving the revelation of Section 76 concerning the three glories, was when Joseph Smith became aware from revelations that had previously been received that many important points concerning salvation had been lost from the Bible. He said that it became evident that if man was to be rewarded according to the deeds done in the body, the term "Heaven" must include more kingdoms than one.

To further prepare for writing this chapter, I listened to a twelve CD series of sermons by Dr. Tony Evans called ***The Magnificent Grace of God***.[159] Also, I was particularly attracted to comments by Dr. William Kynes entitled "Discipleship or Grace: Must it be One or the Other?" I found these men had so many things to say which were both compelling and enlightening. The fatal flaw or the missing link comes down to that very thing Joseph Smith perceived: that to truly make sense of the scriptures and ultimately to comprehend the grace of God, there must be more kingdoms than one.

Houston: there's a problem!

In Dr. Evans' treatment of "works and grace" he made it clear that they are "mutually exclusive" when it comes to salvation, "but they have an important relationship in a Christian's life."[160] Dr. Evans extolled the myriad benefits of discipleship (and properly so) and what difference it makes in a person's life – IN THIS LIFE! **However, when it came to what difference it may or may not make in the next life, he had little to say.**

Just as was stressed in "The Other Comforter and Perfection," Evans mentioned all requisite scriptures about how we "grow in grace" (see 2 Peter 1:2, 3:18; John 1:16); saying, "the more you access grace the more you grow in grace." **Again however, to what end?** From an eternal point of view, if our growth is optional, wouldn't one be tempted to take the easy way out? After all, "just being in heaven is what counts" they would say. Dr. Kynes refers to this category of Christians as "carnal Christians" – those who are justified[y] but not sanctified[z], believers without obedience. He calls this distortion of the gospel "cheap grace." Dr. Kynes says many laudable things:

> God's saving purpose extends to our restoration from our fallen nature and our conformity to the image of Christ who is the image of God (Rom. 8:29). Nothing less will do.
>
> The gospel is a work of God's grace from first to last, and it promises us a full salvation – not from the penalty of our sin only, but also from its power in our lives, and ultimately even from its presence in the world. Consequently our justification cannot be separated from our sanctification or from our final glorification with Christ (Rom. 8:30). They are all of a piece, aspects of the one saving gospel.

---

[y] **Justified**: the action of declaring or being made righteous in the sight of God.

[z] **Sanctified**: the acting out of our discipleship; the process of becoming holy or without sin.

Dr. Kynes quotes 19th century Anglican Bishop J. C. Ryle:

> He who supposes that Jesus Christ only lived and died and rose again in order to provide justification and forgiveness of sins for His people, has yet much to learn. Whether he knows it or not, he is dishonouring our blessed Lord, and making Him only a half Saviour. The Lord Jesus has undertaken everything that His people's souls require not only to deliver them from the guilt of their sins by His atoning death, but from the dominion of their sin, by placing in their hearts the Holy Spirit; not only to justify them, but also to sanctify them.

Dr. Kynes says that "this profound work of the Spirit" is what the prophets in the Old Testament such as Jeremiah have spoken of, a New Covenant where God will put His laws into their minds and write them on their hearts (Jer. 31:31-34).

I like how theologian Sam Storms expresses the eternal value of our experiences in this life:

> To think that everyone in heaven is equally knowledgeable, equally holy, equally capable of enjoying God, is to argue that the progress we make now on earth is irrelevant to our heavenly state. What we do and know and achieve now, by God's grace, will have eternal consequences.
>
> Your capacity for happiness in heaven is shaped by the development and refinement and depth of your capacity on earth. What we experience in joy and understanding and insight now is not destroyed, but is the foundation on which all our eternal experience and growth is based.[161]

Christianity is not a self-help religion, but a relationship with God through Jesus Christ that brings new life by the Spirit that will ultimately result in the restoration of the divine image in us.[162]

I was heartened that both Evans and Kynes seem to define "saving works" as being the works of God and not of man. Kynes even defines "faith" as a work of God and not our own:

> Most will acknowledge the central role of the Holy Spirit in conversion. Only by the convicting and regenerating work of the Spirit is saving faith even possible. Our faith is itself a gift of God. Sadly, however, many restrict the Spirit's work to this initial entry point of the Christian life and assume that they are on their own from that point. They leave the gospel of grace behind. They hear the imperatives of Scripture—the call of discipleship and the demands of holiness—and consider that success depends entirely on human effort. They feel the force of Paul's admonition to "work out your salvation with fear and trembling" (Phil. 2:12), but they forget to read to the end of the sentence. There Paul grounds his imperative on an essential indicative: **"for it is God who works in you to will and to act according to his good purpose"** (2:13). The Holy Spirit is not only graciously involved in our conversion but also in the ongoing work of sanctification in our lives.

Kynes offers this from John Owen:

> Let us consider what regard we ought to have to our own duty and to the grace of God. Some would separate these things as inconsistent. If holiness be our duty, they would say, there is no room for grace; and if it be the result of grace there is no place for duty. But our duty and God's grace are nowhere opposed in the matter of sanctification; for one absolutely supposes the other. We cannot perform our duty without the grace of God; nor does God give his grace for any other purpose than that we may perform our duty.[163]

Of grace and works, Dr. Evans says:

- Grace enables what God expects.
- The only reason we can work out our salvation is that God is working in us.

- Everything we do is simply an expression of His work.
- When grace is at work, the works we do for the Lord are inspired and enabled by grace. It's not that we're working to gain God's favor, but we're working out what He has already worked in.[164]

How We Can Tell It's Working

Adam fell, that men might be; and men are, that they might have joy (2 Ne. 1:115).

A Case Study

Dr. Evans shares the testimony of a good friend of his who used to attend his church, who is now a coach for the Cleveland Browns football team. The Browns did not win a game the entire 2017 season and have been the worst team in NFL history for that three year period[aa]. The coach related how miserable and depressed everyone was coming into their facility each day, spending up to twenty two hours a day trying to figure out what all is wrong. When the news media called wanting to know why they couldn't win a football game, they didn't answer their phones. He said that he was as tired and frustrated as everybody else; but, as tired as he was, he said he's had this joy inside him; that while he was singing songs and praising God, all the other coaches were cussing all the while he had peace inside. He said that he prayed for a win but God has not yet answered his prayers – but at least he was winning on the inside while the team was losing on the outside.[165]

As with the coach, you can tell you are living by grace when you experience calm in the midst of the storm; you have a peace that surpasses understanding (Phil. 4:7); you have learned that God's grace is sufficient for every situation (2 Cor. 12:9); you not only experience joy, but joy unspeakable (1 Peter 1:8); like Paul, you no longer boast of what you have done, but instead delight in boasting

---

[aa] P.S. "Won, won and won!" (The headline read). The drought ended on September 23, 2018, as the Cleveland Browns beat the New York Jets for their first win since 2016.

in what God has done. You find yourself doing things you never thought you could do – "Not that we are sufficient of ourselves… but our sufficiency is of God" (2 Cor. 3:5). You find it easier to say no to sin and you now find yourself loving people you couldn't stand before. In summary, you find that you are not the same person you used to be – that you are being transformed into the image of Christ.

> But we all, with open face beholding as in a glass [mirror] the glory of the Lord, are changed into the same image from glory to glory, even as by the Spirit of the Lord (2 Cor. 3:18).

Last but not least, you might remember from "The Other Comforter and Perfection – Part I," the Greek word for grace, ***charis***, Strong's #5485, includes this phrase in its definition: **"...especially the divine influence upon the heart, and its reflection in life; including gratitude..."** By definition then, gratitude is part and parcel of living by grace. You know you are living by grace when your gratitude to God for what He has done in your life knows no bounds. In the words of Philip Yancey:

> If I had to summarize the primary New Testament motivation for "being good" in one word, I would choose ***gratitude***. Paul begins most of his letters with a summary of the riches we possess in Christ. If we comprehend what Christ has done for us, then surely out of gratitude we will strive to live "worthy" of such great love. We will strive for holiness not to make God love us but because he already does. As Paul told Titus, it is the grace of God that "teaches us to say 'No' to ungodliness and worldly passions, and to live self-controlled, upright and godly lives."[166]

The Book of Mormon wonderfully describes for us how this transformation into the image of Christ can come about. In Alma's ministry to the Zoramites, he told them that "…even if you can no more than desire to believe, let this desire work in you even until you can give place for a portion of my words" (Alma 16:151/32:27).

He told them that the word can be compared to a seed, and that if it is a good seed and they nourish it and do not cast it out by unbelief; that they would begin to feel swelling motions within; that their very souls would begin to be enlarged, their understanding would be enlightened. That through their diligence, faith and patience in nourishing the word, that by and by they would reap the rewards of their faith; even to pluck the fruit of the tree of life, "...which is most precious, which is sweet above all that is sweet... white above all that is white; yea, and pure above all that is pure" (Alma 16:171/32:42).

What Alma taught the Zoramites is applicable to us as we experience the grace of God. We begin to feel this swelling in our breasts, our souls enlarged and our understanding enlightened. We know that we are being changed from grace to grace and that "Praise God - it's working."

Isaiah (2:2-3) tells us that in the last days the nations of the world will come to Zion to learn of her ways. I am convinced that the "grace of God" resident in "the unsearchable riches of Christ" will be primary in the lessons to be taught and learned by the nations. Only through God's grace can the rich and poor be reconciled; only grace can resolve ethnic and cultural differences and break the vicious cycles of lust, greed, poverty, war and revenge.

Grace with an Exclamation Point!

On Friday, August 3, 2018, as I was writing this chapter, I had an experience like never before in my lifetime, where heaven intervened to provide its own exclamation point on the grace of God.

I debated with myself about the wisdom of including this testimony because my desire is not to make this book or even this event about me. In the end I chose to include it precisely because it is not about me. I hope this experience will strengthen the faith of others as it has mine.

It was approaching the end of the day when I walked outside in my house slippers to turn off the water for our sprinkler. The faucet is located on the west side of the house. I walked out the front door, turned left and proceeded to walk toward the west in front of the house. At the corner of the house is a small retaining wall about a foot high. On the other side of the wall was rock landscaping material. As I stepped off the wall facing west my feet suddenly slipped out from under me and I began to slide and fall backwards.

I believe that if everything had taken its natural course, the back of my head would have hit the corner of the retaining wall. But instead, my next memory was one of being literally suspended in air, now turned around and facing eastward back towards the house.

There was no panic as somehow I knew exactly what to do. Very deliberately I reached out with my right hand and firmly grasped the downspout. Then, with my left hand, I reached in behind the downspout and braced myself at the corner of the foundation. Then, in slow motion, I felt my body gradually settle onto the landscape rock. It was so gentle, like one laying a new-born baby in its crib. I laid there for several minutes, dazed, trying to make sense out of what just happened. Finally, I came to the inescapable conclusion that heaven had intervened to save me from serious injury or worse.

The recurring thought, since that time, is that when judgment comes upon the earth God has in numerous places promised to protect His people. I have no doubt now that in whatever circumstances to come, God, by whatever means necessary, can and will intervene to protect His people. Our job then, is to continue to prepare our hearts and minds for that which is to come. Praise God! May the glory be His!

"Grace is but glory begun, and glory is but grace perfected."[167] –Jonathan Edwards

Study Guide

1. Discuss the following statements:

"To fully understand grace is to comprehend even God."

"God is not an object which we may observe from a distance, but an absolute reality who draws us to his bosom." - Arthur Oakman

"Grace is not intended to be an abstract concept but a way of life that yields the fruit of the Kingdom of God."

"We don't have marital problems, financial problems, parenting problems… we have abiding problems."

2. Read and discuss the implications of Dr. Tony Evans' illustration about the husband with his list of twenty-five rules.

3. Discuss "justification" and "sanctification" and what difference they make, not only in this life, but the life to come.

4. What indicators do we have that tell us that we are living by grace? How we can tell that "it's working."

CHAPTER 21

The Love of God

He doeth not anything save it be for the benefit of the world; for he loveth the world, even that he layeth down his own life, that he may draw all men unto him (2 Ne. 11:96/26:24).

In the mid-1980s, Tina Turner recorded a song called, "What's Love Got to Do with It?" One verse of her song goes like this:

What's love got to do, got to do with it
What's love but a second hand emotion
What's love got to do, got to do with it
Who needs a heart when a heart can be broken[168]

That turned out to be a hit song that won the Grammy in 1985 for best song of the year. The person who wrote those lyrics apparently had some difficulty with love; so much so that it caused him to question whether or not love was really worth the effort. So, "What's love got to do with it?" The answer to such a question of course is, EVERYTHING! Love is the first and the last, and love is everything in between. God's love for us goes farther than even time itself, into the deep recesses of eternity past. God's love for us extends from eternity to the cross; and then from the cross to eternity again. In the beginning was God. In the beginning was love.

As our New Covenant journey is drawing to a close we hearken back to the very beginning; to the love in God's own heart when He called creation forth. Love is the attribute that most describes God; it provides His motivation and undergirds all He does. The New Covenant mercy and grace of which we have studied, and of which we are in awe, are but outgrowths of that love.

"The real purpose of life can be understood only in the love of God." - Arthur Oakman

In "The Unsearchable Riches of Christ" chapter we quoted Arthur Oakman as saying: "**God is not an object of which we may observe from a distance, but an absolute reality who draws us to his bosom.**[169]" In the context of his quote, he was saying that it is impossible through study and scholarship to adequately describe in finite words God's infinite grace. That being true of grace, it is also most certainly true of God's love. Nevertheless, as this is a chapter describing the love of God, I must acknowledge that "fools often go where angels fear to tread." Again, using the words of Arthur Oakman: "The real purpose of life can be understood only in the love of God."[170] However, we begin our discussion of God's love by acknowledging that all do not think that God is so good.

The Heresy of Marcion

Marcion (85-160 AD) was a second-century bishop who believed that the Old Testament god was an inferior god who created the world and its accompanying evil. He believed that Jesus was a savior sent by God, but he rejected the Old Testament and the God of Israel. He believed that the wrathful Hebrew God was a separate and lower entity than the all-forgiving God of the New Testament. He not only rejected the Old Testament but also much of the new, leaving the writings of Paul and part of Luke. The premise of Marcionism is that many of the teachings of Christ are incompatible with the actions of the God of the Old Testament. Christ came to reveal a loving, compassionate and gracious God, while the God of the Old Testament was vengeful, harsh and judgmental.

Although the heresy of Marcion was eventually rejected by the church there are vestiges extant today. Many who say, "I like the Jesus of the New Testament, however it's the God of the Old Testament I can't stand." Per Bill Muehlenberg, Marcionism has not disappeared, but can be found in many of our churches today – even in so-called Bible-believing churches:

> Many contemporary Christians act as if they are in fact closet Marcionites. They too have a very low view of the Old Testament, and tend to somehow think that the God of the Old Testament is much different than the God of the New. They seldom even read the Old Testament, and they tend to shrink away from what they find there when they do read it.
>
> Indeed, we have many believers today trying to resurrect Marcionism. The emergent church often moves along these lines. Many of them assure us that God is not a God of judgement, he is simply into love and acceptance, and probably everyone will be saved anyway. Indeed, according to some popular emergent leaders, hell almost certainly does not even exist.[171]

In addition to "closet Marcionism" today, many seem to echo the sentiments of Albert Einstein who believed in a "deist god." A God who invented physics and mathematics and started the universe into motion, and then wandered off to deal with "other more important matters." This is the only way they can explain the existence of evil in the world.

Recently I happened to watch a television program[172] that featured an astrophysicist by the name of Dr. Hugh Ross. I wasn't real sure what an astrophysicist was, so I had to look it up.

> **Astrophysics** is a branch of space science that applies the laws of physics and chemistry to explain the birth, life and death of stars, planets, galaxies, nebulae and other objects in the universe. It has two sibling sciences, astronomy and cosmology, and the lines between them blur.[173]

The interesting thing about Hugh Ross is that he is a Christian. His studies over the years have served to convince him that the Bible is true. Dr. Ross' insights that follow come from this television program however he is the author of a book entitled ***Beyond the Cosmos***[174] that discusses many of the same topics.

Dr. Ross says that because of the powerful new telescopes we have, we have been able to determine that our universe is still expanding. With these telescopes we can literally see the history of our universe. Scientists have determined that only an expanding universe model would permit the existence of life.

So because of these telescopes that reveal an expanding universe, even atheist astronomers have pretty much now admitted that there must be a god. That some force or cause outside of our universe intervened to start everything into motion. In their own words they now say, "We are stuck with some kind of deity." **They are forced to admit that if this deity intervened once with the miracle of creation; that it is possible for this deity to intervene again.**

"We are stuck with some kind of deity."

Ross says that the debate now has shifted to "what kind of god is it that we have?" – Not whether God exists at all.[175] The debate now concerns whether or not we have a personal God; a God that loves us and cares for us; or, whether it is a deist God that Albert Einstein believed in. One who created the universe; and then lost interest and went off to do something else more interesting.

Sometimes, because of the difficulties of life, we have a hard time recognizing the love of God. It's always there but sometimes we can't see it. When we lose our job, when our finances are a mess, when we're struggling to achieve our goals, when we lose a loved one, when our health is failing, when our children don't respond to our love; and even when God doesn't seem to be answering our prayers; in all of these things, we can question the love of God.

One of the major problems we have in understanding God's love is that often we have conflicting agendas. We focus on today. We become impatient because we want our situation changed right now. We want a miracle – and the sooner the better. However, we need to recognize that **God is focused on eternity**. He is not interested in quick fixes that teach us nothing. Whenever we encounter trials of any kind, we need to first take a step back, pause and then ask God what He would have us learn from this particular trial we are facing. **God is interested in transforming our lives into the image of His Son. He is interested in deep, lasting and profound changes in our lives.**

> **It is in appreciation of the divine self-emptying love – literally being swept up in it – that a man is transformed. He begins to see that most of what is termed noble and good in himself is but the muddy reflection of what he must become.[176] – Arthur Oakman**

Unfortunately, transformation seems to come about because of the trials we face in life. It is through the difficulties of life and encountering God along the way that we come to know the love of God. Christian journalist Malcolm Muggeridge underscored this when he said:

> Contrary to what might be expected, I look back on experiences that at the time seemed especially desolating and painful with particular satisfaction. Indeed, I can say with complete truthfulness that everything I have learned in my seventy-five years in this world, everything that has truly enhanced and enlightened my existence, has been through affliction and not through happiness.[177]

The good news is this: God promises NEVER to leave us alone; we don't need to face our problems by ourselves.

> But they that wait upon the Lord shall renew their strength; they shall mount up with wings as eagles; they shall run, and not be weary; and they shall walk, and not faint (Is. 40:31).

> Who shall separate us from the love of Christ? Shall tribulation, or distress, or persecution, or famine, or nakedness, or peril, or sword? ...Nay, in all these things we are more than conquerors through him that loved us (Rom. 8:35, 37).

One of my favorite passages of scripture is this from Romans 8:28: **"...we know that all things work together for good to them that love God**." Paul was absolutely certain that **if we love God**; that ultimately everything that happens in our lives will work together for good. The key here is "work together." That means the sum total of everything that happens in our lives, whether in our view they are good or bad, that God will take all of these things and weave them together to produce what He knows is the very best for us.

> Does that include the worst that happens to us? Yes.
> Does that include the things that hurt us deeply? Yes.
> Does that include the times when we are heartbroken? Yes.
> Does that include the times when we sin? Yes.
> Does that include the times when we doubt God? Yes, yes and yes.
> All things are all things!

Once we learn to trust God and to accept His will for us we can say, "I can't understand why this is happening, but I'm sure there's a reason for it. I may find out tomorrow. I may find out twenty-five years from now. Or I may not find out until I die. But one day this will all make sense. Until it does, I'm going to relax and give this problem to God."

I BELIEVE

I believe in the sun
even when it isn't shining.
I believe in love
even when I am alone.
I believe in God
even when he is silent.[178]

(These words were found scrawled on a cellar wall where Jews had hidden during World War II in Cologne, Germany.)

God's Ultimate Purpose

The love of God can best be understood in light of God's ultimate purpose:

...for this is my work and my glory, to bring to pass the immortality, and eternal life of man (DC 22:23b/Moses 1:39).

In *The End for which God Created the World,* Jonathan Edwards writes:

> God has a disposition to communicate himself, to spread abroad His own fullness. **His purpose was for his goodness to over-spill his own Being, as it were.** He chose to create the heavens and the earth so that His glory could come pouring out from Himself in abundance. He brought a physical reality into existence in order that it might experience His glory and be filled with it and reflect it – every atom, every second, every part and moment of creation. He made human beings in His own image to reflect His glory.[179]

God's aim is not just to return us to our former estate in heaven, but to return us conforming to His image and likeness. R.C. Sproul suggests that many Christians have the tendency to think that through the obedience and sacrifice of Christ alone, that we are restored to Paradise. He says that if Christ's justification alone puts us back into the condition Adam and Eve were before the fall, that we still would not have the "positive righteousness" necessary for eternal life. While Adam and Eve were innocent, we know that God had not yet given them permission to partake of the Tree of Life. This indicates that they were not yet in the fullest state of life they could potentially enjoy; they were in need of a time of testing.[180]

As Lehi was preparing for death, he felt it imperative that his sons come to an understanding of God's plan (see 2 Ne. 1/1-2). These were the important points made by Lehi:

- Redemption comes through the Messiah. No flesh can dwell in the presence of God, save it be through the merits and mercy and grace of the Holy Messiah.
- There MUST BE an opposition in all things, both good and evil. God created things both to act and to be acted upon. Man could not act for himself without being enticed by one or the other. If not so, righteousness could not be brought to pass - neither wickedness, neither holiness, nor misery, neither good, nor bad.
- Without the fall, our first parents would have remained innocent forever; having no joy, for they knew no misery, doing no good, for they knew no sin. They would have had no children and all things would have remained the way they were forever and ever.
- Lehi testifies to his children that he has chosen the good part, and implores them to do likewise. He then beautifully sums up God's purpose in our creation by saying "**Adam fell, that men might be; and men are, that they might have joy**" (v. 115/2:25). This tells me that God is good and His intentions toward us are good. Joy is not to be dependent upon our day to day circumstances. True joy is being in God's presence. Lehi's teaching shows how love is behind the giving of all the covenants.

"ADAM FELL THAT MEN MIGHT BE
AND
MEN ARE THAT THEY MIGHT HAVE JOY"

I love this statement of Andrew Murray: "**When God created man in His image and likeness, it was that he might have a life as like His own as it was possible for a creature to live**."[181] And yet, consider this, in spite of being created in His image and thus having a life as like His own as it is possible for us to have; in spite of that:

> **There will always be more to see when we look at God, because His infinite character can never be exhausted. We could - and will - spend countless millennia exploring the depths of God's being and be no closer to seeing it all than**

when we first started. This is the magnificence of God and the wonder of Heaven.[182]

Theologian Sam Storms writes:

> We will constantly be more amazed with God, more in love with God, and thus ever more relishing His presence and our relationship with Him. Our experience of God will never reach its consummation. We will never finally arrive, as if upon reaching a peak we discover there is nothing beyond. Our experience of God will never become stale. It will deepen and develop, intensify and amplify, unfold and increase, broaden and balloon.[183]

We are most fortunate that we have in the Restoration unique scriptures that tell us how much God cares for us. One is from the Inspired Version where God is talking with Enoch. Enoch's city of Zion had been taken up into heaven and Enoch saw that the remainder of the people, except for the family of Noah, would perish in the great flood. Enoch saw God weeping and he marveled at that. He said, "...How is it that thou canst weep, seeing thou art holy, and from all eternity to all eternity?" God replied, "Behold these thy brethren, they are the workmanship of mine own hands, and I gave unto them their knowledge in the day that I created them" (see Gen. 7:35, 39 IV/Moses 7:28-32).

Another is from 3 Nephi (see 8:16-24/17:15-23) when Christ appeared to the Nephites in the new world. Jesus knelt on the ground and prayed unto the Father for them. The account says "no tongue can speak, neither can there be written by any man, neither can the hearts of men conceive so great and marvelous things... [which they] heard Jesus speak" (3 Ne. 8:18/17:27). After he prayed, he told them to arise and he said:

> Blessed are ye because of your faith. And now **behold my joy is full**.
> And when he had said these words, **he wept**, and the multitude bear record of it, and he took their little children, one by one, and blessed them, and prayed unto the Father

> for them. And when he had done this **he wept again**, and he spake unto the multitude, and saith unto them, Behold your little ones (3 Ne. 8:22-24/17:20-23).

These two scriptures reveal the love, the depth of feeling that God has for each one of us. We learn that our response to God can cause God, the creator of all things, to suffer pain and agony, or to experience great joy.

In this writing we have studied the Everlasting Covenant, also called the Covenant of Redemption or the Covenant of the Father and Son. We've learned that this covenant was from the very beginning, even from before the foundation of the world. We have learned that this plan of redemption, this New Covenant of love, grace and mercy, was fully agreed upon by the Godhead, and that the Father sent His Son, and the Son willingly agreed to this mission of redemption with all the glory to be given to the Father (see "The Everlasting Covenant").

> Then answered Jesus and said unto them, Verily, verily, I say unto you, The Son can do nothing of himself, but what he seeth the Father do: for what things soever he doeth, these also doeth the Son likewise (John 5:19).

> Jesus saith unto him, I am the way, the truth, and the life: no man cometh unto the Father, but by me. If ye had known me, ye should have known my Father also: and from henceforth ye know him, and have seen him. Philip saith unto him, Lord, shew us the Father, and it sufficeth us. Jesus saith unto him, Have I been so long time with you, and yet hast thou not known me, Philip? **he that hath seen me hath seen the Father...** (John 14:6-9).

To say that the God of the Old Testament is "wrathful and judgmental" while the God of the New Testament is "loving and kind" is at the very least misleading. We must remember that the Bible Jesus read was the Old Testament, and that he and the church worshipped that God. In its pages, God is frequently depicted as a God who does not anger easily and whose forgiveness, love and mercy endure forever (see Ps. 136). Both the New Testament and the Book of Mormon depict a God who is the same today, yesterday and forever.

> Every good gift and every perfect gift is from above, and cometh down from the Father of lights, with whom is no variableness, neither shadow of turning (James 1:17).

> For do we not read that God is the same yesterday, today, and for ever; and in him there is no variableness neither shadow of changing (Morm. 4:68/9:9).

The New Testament church saw no separation between Christ and God, and in fact, recognized them as the same God. John is very explicit that Christ is the Creator God of the Old Testament (John 1:1-3, 10). The Apostle Paul portrayed Jesus as that God that led Israel out of Egypt to the Promised Land saying: "[They] did all eat the same spiritual meat; and did all drink the same spiritual drink: for they drank of that spiritual Rock that followed them: and that Rock was Christ" (1 Cor. 10:3-4).

Study Guide

1. Discuss this Arthur Oakman statement: "The real purpose of life can be understood only in the love of God."

2. What is Marcionism and do we still see vestiges of that today?

3. Per scientist Hugh Ross, even atheist astronomers have now admitted that there must be a God. They say, "We are stuck with some kind of deity." How can we know what kind of God it is we have?

4. Christian journalist Malcolm Muggeridge says that everything he has learned, everything that has enhanced and enlightened his existence, has been through affliction and not through happiness. Has that been your experience?

5. Discuss God's ultimate purpose in our lives.

CHAPTER 22

The Love of God: A Testimony

And this is life eternal, that they might know thee the only true God, and Jesus Christ, whom thou hast sent (John 17:3).

In March of 2015, I was to give a sermon with the theme, "We Are Forgiven." In my preparation, I naively (very much so) had decided that I would try to describe for that congregation the "love of God." I don't know what I was thinking, but perhaps I said to myself, "It's so obvious. How hard could it be?" I soon learned a great lesson, a humbling lesson, that it is easier said than done.

The first thing that came to my mind is that we often compare a mother's love for their child to the love of God. There's this Jewish proverb that says, "God could not be everywhere so He made mothers." I found this really cute saying about a mother's love that I think says it all:

> **A mother is a person who seeing there are only four pieces of pie for five people, promptly announces she never did care for pie.**

Next I thought of the hymn, "My God How Wonderful Thou Art." We find in this hymn that even a mother's love cannot compare to God's love:

> **No earthly father loves like you,**
> **no mother half so mild**
> **bears and forbears as you have done**
> **with me, your sinful child.**[184]

Lastly I thought of the words of this Swedish hymn:

> **The love of God is broad like beach and meadow,**
> **wide as the wind, and an eternal home.**[185]

After contemplating how to describe the love of God, I was disappointed with myself. I wasn't satisfied with what I had come up with. I told God that I wanted to find some words to share with that congregation that would more adequately describe His love. I believe He helped me find these words:

Could we with ink the ocean fill,
And were the skies of parchment made,
Were every stalk on earth a quill,
And every man a scribe by trade,
To write the love of God above,
Would drain the ocean dry.
Nor could the scroll contain the whole,
Though stretched from sky to sky.[186]

These words were found scrawled on the wall of an insane asylum after the occupant had been found dead in his room and carried to his grave. In the ensuing years these lines were often quoted, and many hearts were touched. In 1917 Frederick Lehman incorporated these words as the third stanza into his hymn entitled "The Love of God is Greater Far."

The love of God is greater far
Than tongue or pen can ever tell.
It goes beyond the highest star
And reaches to the lowest hell.[187]

There continued to be great interest in those words scrawled on that asylum wall. Many felt that the language of those lines indicated a source beyond that person, somewhere in the dim past. They felt that the lines had only been quoted by the inmate in the story. After endless searching in libraries someone decided to ask a Jewish rabbi—perhaps he would have a clue. The rabbi listened intently to the words, and quietly replied, "Yes, I can tell you who the author of those lines is. Rabbi Hertz, chief rabbi in the British Empire at one time, wrote a book entitled ***A Book of Jewish Thought*** (published in 1920). Go to a Jewish bookstore, and on page 213 you will find that this poem was written in A.D. 1050 by a Jewish poet, Meir Ben Isaac Nehorai." It is in the hymnology of the synagogue used for the Feast of Weeks (Pentecost).[188]

How appropriate for our discussion as to whether the God of the Old Testament is a God of love or not. Those words, so movingly describing the love of God, were penned by a Jewish Rabbi whose God was the God of the Old Testament.

As many before us have found, the love of God is far greater than we can ever tell. God's love is to be experienced and enjoyed and most of all it is to be given away. It's when we freely give away this love that God has so freely given us that others come to experience that love; and out of that love, desire to have a relationship with Him. **We may not be able to describe God's love but by our actions we can reveal God's love**.

"The Heart Can Grasp What the Mind Can't Comprehend"

I will briefly delay relating what my ultimate experience was as I endeavored to tell that congregation about God's love, in lieu of expanding on the statement above that says, "**by our actions we can reveal God's love.**" Just recently, on Facebook of all places, Matt Frizzell made the statement that I believe is key to approaching the topic of God's love: **THE HEART CAN GRASP WHAT THE MIND CAN'T COMPREHEND**! To illustrate that point I want to share a story, an experience of popular Christian writer Max Lucado from his book, ***It's Not About Me***.

Max and the Rabbi

Max found himself seated on a plane next to an orthodox Jewish Rabbi. Lucado had his Bible open upon his lap, studying the Ten Commandments. The rabbi, seeing this, leaned over and said, "I see you like Jewish authors." So began a wonderful conversation. Lucado told the rabbi he was puzzling over the commandment, "You shall not take the name of the Lord your God in vain."

The rabbi thought about that for a moment, and then said to him, "Don't think language; think lifestyle." Lucado asked what he meant by that.

The rabbi then went on to explain what the commandment really means. "The command calls us to elevate the name or reputation of God to the highest place. We exist to give honor to his name."

He proceeded to create a story involving a Manhattan skyscraper. Everyone in the building works for the CEO, whose office is on the top floor. Most have not seen him but they have seen his daughter. She works in the building for her father. She exploits her family position for her benefit.

One morning she approaches Bert, the guard, "I'm hungry, Bert. Go down the street and buy me a Danish."

The demand places Bert in a quandary. He's on duty. Leaving his post puts the building at risk. But the boss' daughter insists, "Come on, now; hurry up."

What option does he have? As he leaves, he says nothing but thinks something like, ***"if the daughter is so bossy, what does that say about her father?"***

She's only getting started. Munching on her muffin, she bumps into a paper-laden secretary, "Where are you going with all those papers?"

"To have them bound for an afternoon meeting."
"Forget the meeting. Come to my office and vacuum the carpet."

"But I was told that I had to get this done."
"And I'm telling you to do something else."

The woman has no choice. After all, this is the boss' daughter speaking. All of this causes the secretary to question the wisdom of the boss.

And the boss' daughter goes on making demands of others and interrupting schedules. She never invoked the name of her dad. She never says, "My dad said..," there was no need to.

Isn't she the boss' child? Doesn't the child speak for the father? And so Bert abandons his post. A secretary fails to finish a task. And more than one employee questions the wisdom of the man upstairs. Does he really know what he is doing? They wonder.

The rabbi then paused. His point was clear: the girl dishonored the name of her father, not with vulgar language, but with insensitive living. If she keeps this up the whole building will be second-guessing the CEO.

The rabbi then scratched his chin and then proposed another scenario, "But, what if the daughter acted differently?" and then proceeded to recast the story.

Rather than demand a muffin from Bert, she brings a muffin to Bert. "I thought of you this morning," she explains. "You arrive so early. Do you have time to eat?" And she hands him the muffin.

In route to the elevator she bumps into a woman with an armful of documents. She says, "My, I'm sorry. Can I help?" The secretary smiles, and the two carry the stacks down the hallway.

And so the daughter engages the employees. She asks about their families, offers to bring them coffee. New workers are welcomed, and hard workers are applauded. She, through her kindness and concern, raises the happiness level of the entire company.

She does so not even mentioning her father's name. Never does she declare, "My father says...," there is no need to. Is she not his child? Does she not speak on his behalf? Reflect his heart? When she speaks, they assume she speaks for him. And because they think highly of her, they think highly of her father.

They've not seen him.
They've not met him.
But they know his child, so they know his heart.[189]

The Printer's Daughter

At the time Martin Luther was having his Bible printed in Germany, a printer's daughter encountered God's love. No one had told her about Jesus. Toward God she felt no emotion but fear. One day she gathered pieces of fallen scripture from the floor. On one paper she found the words "For God so loved the world, that he gave…" The rest of the verse had not yet been printed. Still, what she saw was enough to move her. The thought that God would give anything moved her from fear to joy. Her mother noticed the change of attitude. When asked the cause of her happiness, the daughter produced the crumpled piece of partial verse from her pocket. The mother read it and asked, "What did he give?" The child was perplexed for a moment and then answered, "I do not know. But if He loved us well enough to give us anything, we should not be afraid of Him."[190]

> **For God so loved the world, that he gave his only begotten Son, that whosoever believeth in him should not perish, but have everlasting life (John 3:16).**

Bill and the Deacon

Bill was a wild-haired, T-shirt-wearing, barefoot college student. He was esoteric and brilliant, and while attending college, he became a Christian.

Across the street from the campus was a well-dressed, very conservative church that wanted to develop a ministry to the students at the college, but they were not sure how to go about it.

One day Bill decided to go into that church. He walked in with no shoes, jeans, a T-shirt, **and wild hair**. The service had already started, so Bill started down the aisle, looking for a seat. But the church was packed, and he couldn't find one. By now people were looking a bit uncomfortable, but no one said anything.

Bill got closer and closer to the pulpit, and when he realized there were no seats, he just sat down right in the aisle on the carpet.

By now the congregation was really uncomfortable, and the tension in the air was thick. About this time, from way at the back of the large church, a deacon was slowly making his way toward Bill. The deacon was in his eighties, with silver-gray hair and a pocket watch, a godly man who was very elegant, dignified, and walked with a cane.

It took a long time for the man to reach the boy. The church fell utterly silent, except for the clicking of the man's cane. All eyes were focused on him; you couldn't hear anyone breathing. The people were thinking, ***The minister can't even preach the sermon until the deacon does what he has to do.***

The elderly man reached Bill and paused. Then he dropped his cane to the floor, and, with great difficulty, lowered himself and sat down next to Bill to worship with him.

The church was silent with emotion. When the minister gained control, he said, "What I am about to preach, you will never remember. What you have just seen, you will never forget."[191]

To believe in the redemptive love of God through Jesus is to believe in a reordering of life, to believe that things are not as they seem. It is to believe in transformation of the whole person; it is to believe that beyond the ugly is beauty; beyond the broken is wholeness; beyond dementia is a sound mind; beyond sorrow is joy; beyond insanity is sanity; and beyond death is life.[192]

The Story of Tokichi Ishii

In a similar vein, I want to share with you the modern-day story of a Japanese criminal by the name of Tokichi Ishii. He had murdered men, women and children – anyone who stood in his way was eliminated without pity. Now he was … [on death-row awaiting execution.] [There] he was visited by two Canadian women who tried to talk to him through the bars, but he only glowered at them like the caged, savage animal that he was. In the end they abandoned the attempt; but they gave him a Bible, hoping that it might succeed where they had failed. He began to read it, and, having started, could not stop. He read on until he came to the story of the Crucifixion. He came to the words: "Father, forgive them, for they know not what they do," and these words broke him. "I stopped," he said. "I was stabbed to the heart, as if pierced by a five-inch nail. **Shall I call it the love of Christ?** Shall I call it his compassion? I do not know what to call it. I only know that I believed, and my hardness of heart was changed." Later, when he went to the scaffold, he was no longer the hardened criminal he once had been, but a gentle, smiling radiant man. The murderer had been [literally] born again; Christ had brought Tokichi Ishii back to life.[193] Ishii's last words were in the form of a poem:

> **My name is defiled,**
> **My body dies in prison,**
> **But my soul purified**
> **Today returns to the City of God.**[194]

God's love is most revealing and shines brightest when we see His love, grace and mercy expressed in the lives of those among us whom we deem least worthy. Truly, "the heart can grasp what the mind can't comprehend."

> **"Come now, and let us reason together, saith the Lord: though your sins be as scarlet, they shall be as white as snow…"** (Is. 1:18).

> **Jesus says that "even if a man is dead in sin and has lost everything that makes life worth living, I can make him alive again."**[195] – William Barclay

> **The people that walked in darkness have seen a great light: they that dwell in the land of the shadow of death, upon them hath the light shined** (Is. 9:2).

Now, I'd like to share with you a testimony, which is in fact the concluding two paragraphs of the sermon I delivered to that congregation where I attempted to describe for them the love of God. As Paul Harvey used to say, this is the rest of the story.

> You recall that I began this message by talking about the difficulty I had in describing God's love. I then expressed some satisfaction that God led me to some very beautiful and profound words scrawled on the wall of that insane asylum. Well, right after that, I attended a service at the Highlands congregation. I don't usually attend the contemporary service but a member of my First People Congregation was speaking and I wanted to go and offer the support of my presence.
>
> During one of the praise hymns, there was a line flashed on the screen that said this:
>
> **JESUS IS THE LOVE OF GOD**
>
> It's hard for me to describe, but as the congregation sang those words, what I heard was the voice of the spirit. What I heard was the answer to my prayer; that I might be given words for you this morning, that would describe the love of God; that would describe the love that He has for each one of you. I had tried to make it so difficult; I was trying to describe the indescribable. The answer is so simple and yet so profound. "**Jesus is the love of God**."

Jesus is the answer to those who would say that God has lost interest and doesn't care about us. In Luke 4:18 Jesus says:

> *The Spirit of the Lord is upon me, because he hath anointed me to preach the gospel to the poor; he hath sent me to heal the* **brokenhearted,** *to preach deliverance to the captives, and recovering of sight to the blind, to set at liberty them that are* **bruised.**

Jesus answered by demonstrating his love for the marginalized and dispossessed of the world. Jesus answered by saying that not a sparrow falls to the ground without His Father knowing it. He answered by saying that the very hairs on our heads are numbered to God and that our thoughts and prayers ascend to God on high. Jesus testified that he revealed the true nature of God by saying and doing only those things commanded him of the Father. Jesus came to answer this very question as to what kind of God we have, He said to those around him, ***"he who has seen me has seen the father**."* In the words of William Barclay:

> **Jesus, through his life and death** was demonstrating to men that God is the Father whose love is eternal and unending. When Jesus entered the world, when he healed the sick, comforted the sad, fed the hungry, forgave his enemies, he was saying to men: "God loves you like that." **When he died upon the cross, he was saying: "Nothing that men can ever do to God will stop God from loving them. There is no limit to the love of God. There is no end beyond which that love will not go. God loves you like that."**
>
> **That is why nothing less than death on the Cross would do**. If Jesus had refused or escaped the Cross, if he had not died, it would have meant that there was some point in suffering and sorrow at which the love of God stopped, that there was some point beyond which forgiveness was impossible. But the Cross is God saying in Jesus: "There is no limit to which…and no sin which my love cannot forgive."
>
> **The work of Christ is not something about which a man must know; it is something which he must experience in his own heart and mind and life. It is not so much to be understood as it is to be appropriated. For that reason it is not enough to know how others have interpreted it.**
>
> One thing I know – that because of Jesus Christ and because of what he is and did and does my whole relationship to God is changed. Because of Jesus Christ I know that God is

> my father and friend. Daily and hourly I experience the fact that I can enter into His presence with confidence and with boldness. He is no longer my enemy; He is no longer even my judge; there is no longer any unbridgeable gulf between Him and me; I am more at home with God than I am with any human being in the human world. And all this is so because of Jesus Christ, and it could not possibly have happened without him.[196]

Yes, the answer I was seeking in trying to describe the love of God was so simple and yet so profound, "**Jesus** is the love of God." One word. That's how you describe God's love: **JESUS**. That's how it is with the love of God. We don't have the words to describe it, but we recognize it when we both see and experience it. When we see Jesus walking among us we have seen the Father. We know therefore what God is like. Those who saw that deacon slowly limp down the aisle with his cane clicking every step of the way, they saw the love of God. "The heart can grasp what the mind can't comprehend."

My God, How Wonderful Thou Art

Yet I may love Thee too, O LORD,
Almighty as Thou art;
for Thou hast stooped to ask of me
the love of my poor heart.

No earthly father loves like Thee,
no mother e'er so mild,
bears and forbears, as Thou hast done
with me, Thy sinful child.[197]

As I read those words, they touched my heart. A mental picture filled my mind of the Lord coming to me personally, stooping down before me, and asking me to give him my love. I was literally amazed. How could this be? How could the Lord of glory have such humility to do such a thing? To desire the love of me, a sinner. As I read those words early one morning, I wept. I came in that moment to realize the meaning of "Amazing Grace."

Some have called Karl Barth the greatest theologian of the 20th century. When he was asked in 1962 (on his one visit to America) how he would summarize the essence of the millions of words he had published; he replied:

"Jesus loves me this I know, for the Bible tells me so."

Study Guide

1. The author shares his stumbling attempt in a sermon to describe the love of God. How would you have approached that assignment?

2. Discuss this: "The heart can grasp what the mind can't comprehend."

3. What ultimate answer did the author arrive at in his attempt to describe the love of God?

4. According to William Barclay's logic, why was it necessary that Christ die on the cross?

CHAPTER 23

THE BOOK OF MORMON:

Christ in Print

> And now, my beloved brethren, and also Jew, and all ye ends of the earth, hearken unto these words, and believe in Christ; and if ye believe not in these words, believe in Christ. **And if ye shall believe in Christ, ye will believe in these words; for they are the words of Christ** (2 Ne. 15:11-12/33:10).

In 2016, Patrick McKay[bb] made a presentation at The Book of Mormon Conference in Independence, Missouri, entitled, "The Marred Servant and the Restoration of the House of Israel." In that presentation Patrick makes the case that the Book of Mormon is the "marred servant," whose ministry will be pivotal in "that day" when judgment shall come upon the earth[cc]. In a later conversation with Patrick, he referred to the Book of Mormon as "Christ in Print," an appealing moniker that says volumes about the equivalency of Christ and his Word. The point of this chapter is not to make the assertion that the Book of Mormon is the marred servant, but instead to make the larger point that the Book of Mormon is Christ in Print.

"You have heard my voice..."

In an article written by John Moody entitled, "Priesthood in the Book of Mormon,"[198] he quotes the Lord in a February, 1835, revelation to Joseph Smith, Oliver Cowdery and David Whitmer concerning the selection of the first members of the Quorum of Twelve in the Restoration. The Lord begins by speaking to Oliver. For over two months he had been intensely engaged in writing the Book of Mormon manuscript under Joseph Smith's dictation, and now this work was almost finished. The Lord continues by

---

[bb] Apostle, Joint Conference of Restoration Branches
[cc] See 3 Ne. 9:81-106/20:43-21:21.

including others who will also share in the responsibility of organizing the church, telling them they are to baptize and ordain "according to that which is written; and you have that which is written before you" [the Book of Mormon manuscript] (see DC 16:5c/18:34-36):

> *These words* **[Book of Mormon]** *are not of men, nor of man; but of me...for it is my voice which speaketh them...for they are given by my Spirit unto you and by my power you can read them...and save it were by my power, you could not have them; wherefore you can testify that you have heard my voice and know my words"* (DC 16:5f-g/18:34-36).

Of this Moody says, "**Thus it is affirmed that the Book of Mormon is literally the voice and words of Christ**." To reiterate, Christ affirms that the words of the Book of Mormon are not of men, but his words as he initially spoke them. Because his words were subsequently translated by the "gift and power of God' we can therefore read his very words. Wherefore, when we read the words of the book, as Christ says, we can testify that "we have heard the voice of Christ and know his words."

In 2 Nephi the Lord spoke to Nephi and said that he would remember the promises which he has made to him and his father that he would remember their seed and that through the Book of Mormon his very words would proceed forth unto their seed in the last days.

> And also, that I may remember the promises which I have made unto thee, Nephi, and also unto thy father, that I would remember your seed; **and that the words of your seed should proceed forth out of my mouth unto your seed**.
>
> And my words shall hiss forth unto the ends of the earth, for a standard unto my people, which are of the house of Israel (2 Ne. 12:43-44/29:2).

And then we have this from the Doctrine and Covenant asserting that his word, either uttered by his own voice or the voice of his servants is the same:

> What I, the Lord, have spoken I have spoken, and I excuse not myself; and though the heavens and the earth pass away, my word shall not pass away, but shall all be fulfilled, **whether by mine own voice, or by the voice of my servants, it is the same**; for behold, and lo, the Lord is God, and the Spirit beareth record, and the record is true, and the truth abideth for ever and ever. Amen (DC 1:8a-c/1:38-39).

To say that the Book of Mormon can be equated to or to be literally considered to be the voice of Christ is to speak of a concept called personification.

PERSONIFICATION

As for equating Christ to his word, Patrick McKay points out that there is a literary tool called "personification." It is not unusual for scripture and for secular writings to personify non-human or inanimate entities by giving them human attributes. For example:

> The whole earth is at rest, and is quiet: they break forth into singing. Yea, the fir-trees rejoice at thee, and the cedars of Lebanon, saying, Since thou art laid down, no feller is come up against us (Is. 14:7-8).

> For ye shall go out with joy, and be led forth with peace: the mountains and the hills shall break forth before you into singing, and all the trees of the field shall clap their hands (Is. 55:12).

> Wisdom crieth without; she uttereth her voice in the streets (Prov. 1:20).

> When it comes, the Landscape listens,
> Shadows hold their breath[199] – Emily Dickinson

The most directly applicable example of personifying a book of scripture comes from Ezekiel 37:19 where the Bible, the stick of Judah, is referred to as "him" (KJV). The Orthodox Jewish Bible in English also has "with him."

> Say unto them, Thus saith the Lord God; Behold, I will take the stick of Joseph, which is in the hand of Ephraim, and the tribes of Israel his fellows, and will put them **with him, even with the stick of Judah**, and make them one stick, and they shall be one in mine hand (Ezek. 37:19).

"You have heard my voice..." – A Testimony

Faye Shaw has shared with me the testimony of her husband Gaylord. Occasionally as he studied his scriptures, he would hear the written words actually being spoken. Once, in the 1908 edition [RLDS], his Book of Mormon fell open to Moroni chapter 10, and when he started at the top of the right-hand page and read to the end, he heard Moroni himself speaking his very last words, which he understood in English. Gaylord then turned back to the first two verses he had missed. Moroni knew of the resident Power in the book, for he wrote, "And I seal up these records after that I have SPOKEN a few words by way of exhortation unto you" (vs. 2). Another time, after reading where the Lord commanded Moroni to write what the Brother of Jared had seen and seal it up, Gaylord then heard the same profound words for our day coming from the very mouth of the Lord as He shared with Moroni (Ether 1:100-117/ 4:6-19). Although the tone of His voice and the intonations were of the Christ, Gaylord somehow heard them in English. He was amazed that He spoke rather fast. The Living Word is available in the Book of Mormon, and the book IS Christ in print.[200]

A Book Like No Other

What's so special about the Book of Mormon that it could be called Christ in Print? Unlike the provenance of the Bible, which to scholars at least, seem to be shrouded in the ancient mists of history, the origins of the Book of Mormon are thoroughly documented. And not only its origins, but we know who wrote every word along the way. We do not need to worry about analyzing writing styles to identify the authors. There are not myriads of transcripts and literally thousands of fragments that we need to piece together to come up with "the most accurate translation" like when new Bible translations come out frequently based upon the latest translations or manuscripts.

By way of contrast, the Book of Mormon, as it were, just suddenly appeared out of nowhere. It came forth whole in that there was only one original manuscript, translated and dictated one time through by a poorly educated New York farm boy in a compressed period of time from April through June 1829. That accomplishment by him in such a short time span is highly unusual, of course; but not so much when we consider that this miraculous process fittingly bears witness to the Title Page statement that says it was translated "by the gift and power of God." No other book can make that claim.

The Book of Mormon is called the New Covenant and as such is a book envisioned by God from the very beginning. It was written by servants of the Lord at His command. The Lord was involved every step of the way; from the creation of the plates, throughout Nephite history, and until at last they were deposited in the Hill Cumorah in New York. The three major prophet/authors of the Book of Mormon, Nephi, Mormon and Moroni, have all left record of how the Lord directed those things they wrote. Besides Nephi, Mormon and Moroni, Jacob also saw Christ and had a personal relationship with him (see "A Covenant of Love"). Ray Treat postulates that everything in the Book of Mormon is there for a purpose.[201] He has cited several references[dd] wherein writers are directed what to "put in" or what to "leave out."

[dd] **Nephi**: 1 Ne. 3:252/14:28; 5:223/19:3. **Mormon**: W of M 1:9-10/1:6-7; 3 Ne. 12:5/26:12. **Moroni**: Ether 1:98/4:4; 2:1/5:1; 3:80-102/8:9-26; 6:14/13:13.

Susan Ward Easton has written a very comprehensive article entitled "Names of Christ in the Book of Mormon."[202] She has found that statistically Christ is its dominant figure; that our Savior is referred to by one hundred different names from "Lord" in its very first verse (1 Ne. 1:1) to "Eternal Judge" in its very last verse (Moro. 10:31/34). She has found that the various names for Christ are mentioned an average of every 1.7 verses in the Book of Mormon.

Very early on (c. 559-545 BC), the messiah to come was identified as Jesus Christ by an angel of God:

> And according to the words of the prophets, and also the word of the angel of God, his name shall be Jesus Christ, the Son of God (2 Ne. 11:36/25:19).

The title page of the Book of Mormon states that its purpose is to convince "Jew and Gentile that Jesus is the Christ, the Eternal God." The prophets knew their writings were to bear witness that Jesus is the Christ. Therefore, it would not be an exaggeration to say that the Book of Mormon is "Christ in Print."

Recognizing then how we got the book and its internal character, we can fully understand how the Book of Mormon could be personified as "the servant of Christ." It is a worthy servant because it is his creation. In his closing words, Nephi appeals to the future readers of the Book of Mormon:

It is a worthy servant because it is his creation.

> And now, my beloved brethren, and also Jew, and all ye ends of the earth, hearken unto these words, and believe in Christ; and if ye believe not in these words, believe in Christ. **And if ye shall believe in Christ, ye will believe in these words; for they are the words of Christ** (2 Ne. 15:11-12/33:10).

Jesus answered the temptations of the devil by saying that "man shall not live by bread alone but by every word of God" (Luke 4:4). We are told in Alma that the word can be compared to a seed. If by faith, we plant the word in our hearts and nourish that word; that it will begin to grow until that day in which we can harvest the fruit thereof (Alma 16:152-173/32:28-43). Dwight Burford says about that seed:

> Like all seeds, God's Word has life contained within itself (John 5 & 12). God's Word contains all of the information needed to bring forth a new life from within us...**God's Word contains the DNA, if you will, of the body of Christ** (Romans 1)...Thus, those who hear the word of God, and receive His word such that they allow it to grow within their very souls, are spiritually conceived; and if they continue in the same word of truth, in time they will bring forth an abundance of fruit to the honor and glory of our Heavenly Father (Luke 8 with Galatians 6:7-10).[203]

"Him shall ye hear..."

On that second day of Jesus' ministry to the Nephites he said:

> Behold, I am he of whom Moses spake, saying, A prophet shall the Lord your God raise up unto you of your brethren, like unto me, him shall ye hear in all things whatsoever he shall say unto you. And it shall come to pass that every soul who will not hear **that prophet,** shall be **cut off** from among the people (3 Ne. 9:60-61/20:23).

Then, thirty-eight verses later, he says "...whosoever will not believe in **my words**...shall be **cut off** from among my people which are of the covenant" (3 Ne. 9:98/21:11).

<u>These verses relate Christ to his personified word. Christ and his word are the same.</u>

In Conclusion

Many say that the Book of Mormon is a "good book," while some even say it is scripture; however, some go on to say it is not "real history" and thus not essential since we already acknowledge

Christ and have a Bible. Our dilemma is that Christ has not given us the option of choosing which words he has spoken. We are told that we are to live by his every word, "My sheep hear my voice, and I know them, and they follow me" (John 10:27). The Book of Mormon has been given to the Gentiles as their test. Christ has said that "I will try the faith of My people" (3 Ne. 12:52/26:11). The relationship between Christ and his word is such that if we reject his word, we reject him. He gives us his word for a reason. If we ignore his word, we ignore him and thus our end is less than it could have been. John Moody invites us to consider the consequences.

> If we do not believe the Book of Mormon is a literal historical record: for us its laws and commandments would then be invalid for they were never given - its covenants meaningless since they were never entered into - the promises and prophecies, having never been made, are void - and any good examples or teachings we find in the book would have little weight since, if these things never really happened, we'd have no reason to expect the same results from our own efforts. Indeed, the Book of Mormon's confirmation of the resurrection of Christ, now widely denied by scholars, is also gone. Its assurance that God still speaks today, that the day of miracles isn't past, and the truth of the biblical record - all is lost. And of course its value as a foundation for Church organization and government, as well as the greatest missionary tool of all time, goes right out the window.[204]

What can be said at this point is that it is as Nephi said of his writings and hence of the Book of Mormon, "these are Christ's words." For that and for other reasons mentioned, I believe that the Book of Mormon is in reality, "Christ in Print."

Study Guide

1. In regards to the Book of Mormon being Christ in Print, discuss the concept of personification.

2. Discuss DC 16:5f-g/18:34-36 (see also 2 Ne. 15:11-13/33:10-11) where the Lord equates the Book of Mormon to his literal voice and words. Is this not "Christ in Print"?

3. The author makes the statement that the Book of Mormon is a book like no other. Discuss.

4. In the section "Him shall ye hear..." discuss how Jesus relates himself to his word (see 3 Ne. 9:60-61/20:23; 9:98/21:22; and 9:106/21:20).

CHAPTER 24

THE BOOK OF MORMON:

A Covenant of Love

> **Sing, O heavens; and be joyful, O earth; and break forth into singing, O mountains: for the Lord hath comforted his people, and will have mercy upon his afflicted. But Zion said, The Lord hath forsaken me, and my Lord hath forgotten me.**
> **Can a woman forget her sucking child, that she should not have compassion on the son of her womb? yea, they may forget, yet will I not forget thee. Behold, I have graven thee upon the palms of my hands** (Is. 49:13-16).

Covenants are the avenue through which the God of Love works; they are far more profound than mere contracts; they are sacred, intimate and respectful. To go deeper into the nature of Covenant we must appreciate how precious and costly it is - how giving and self-sacrificing. It was from out of Himself that Christ took that which was formed into all creation. And it was by the blood of the Lamb slain from the foundation of the world that the Everlasting Covenant works, and is brought to its fulfillment.

Bradley Artson[ee] shares with us this Jewish concept of covenantal love.

> Jewish love is covenantal. Covenants are not necessarily restricted to equal parties. Kings and vassals are not equal, yet they provide the sociopolitical context for the biblical covenant. God and the Jewish People do not claim to be equal. But they do insist on the ability to bridge the chasm of disparity with relationship, and in relationship one may stand as a partner even with someone who is not your equal. Love…spans that gulf, and un-equals are able to stand in partnership and in dignity together, despite their

---

[ee] Dean of the Ziegler School of Rabbinic Studies at American University in Los Angeles, California.

> differences. Our entire tradition is a recurrent outpouring of covenantal love, so that God creates the world, we are told, in order to have an object to love.[205]

"The Everlasting Covenant of Love"

It is interesting to note speculation concerning the etymology or source of the word Mormon. Benjamin Urrutia[ff] says "This word could easily have been formed by combining two ancient Egyptian words, *mor* ("love") and *mon* ("established forever"). This would render a meaning of "love established forever"[206] [or, "The Everlasting Covenant of Love"].

This rendering of Mormon above, while speculative, would seem to be consistent with how the Book of Mormon acquired its name. Although most people associate the naming of the Book of Mormon to be for its principal editor and prophet, Mormon; however, Mormon himself seems to indicate that is not the case. According to the text of the Book of Mormon, the word Mormon stems from the Land of Mormon, the land where Alma established the church and introduced the rite of baptism (about 150 BC).

> And behold, I am called Mormon, **being called after the land of Mormon,** the land in the which Alma did establish the church among this people; yea, the first church which was established among them after their transgression (3 Ne. 2:96/5:12).

As David Lamb says, "Why would God's holy word be named after a man? The Holy Scriptures were not named after any one author nor was the Doctrine and Covenants called the 'Book of Joseph Smith.' Why then would the Book of Mormon be the exception to the rule and bear the name of a man?"[207] In addition Lamb says:

> A study of the title page of the Book of Mormon tells us its main purpose is to restore a knowledge of the covenants to the house of Israel. This adds weight to the understanding

---

[ff] Urrutia (1950 -) is an author and scholar born in Ecuador and a convert to the Church of Jesus Christ of Latter-day Saints.

> that the name Mormon was always associated with the place of the restoration of the covenant to the Nephites. In fact, the name Mormon became synonymous with the concept of restoring the covenants.
>
> In light of this understanding, the Book of Mormon is not named for a man. It is named for the place where the covenant was restored. Symbolically, the Book of Mormon bears the name "Book of the Restoration of the Covenant."[208]

The Book of Mormon then is a book of covenantal love, even a New and Everlasting Covenant made with Israel for the express purpose of spanning that gulf separating Israel from their God. It is a harbinger of redemption signaling to Israel that the time of their exile has come to an end.

> For a small moment have I forsaken thee; but with great mercies will I gather thee. In a little wrath I hid my face from thee for a moment; but with *everlasting* ***kindness*** will I have mercy on thee, saith the Lord thy Redeemer (Is. 54:7-8).

As I mentioned in the Preface, when I began writing this book I had certain ideas in mind about how I would approach the subject of covenants. Much to my surprise I soon began to be captivated by the concept of what it would be like to live a New Covenant life wherein we would have such a close, intimate relationship with God that we would no longer need anyone to teach us about Him. I ended up writing several chapters I did not intend.

If, as we have attested, the Book of Mormon is indeed the New Covenant, then it follows that it should have much to teach us about the New Covenant life itself. This is a subject to which we will shortly turn. However, before that I want to call your attention to the Isaiah quote above, to the phrase "everlasting kindness," and more specifically to the word "kindness." The actual Hebrew word used in the original is ***chesed*** (kheh'-sed).

Fairly late in writing this book, I came across an article[209] written by Norman H. Snaith posted by Michael D. Marlowe on his website bible-researcher.com. Marlowe begins his foreword by saying that biblical scholars have often complained that the word ***chesed*** (חֶסֶד) in the Hebrew Bible is difficult to translate into English, because it really has no precise equivalent in our language. English versions usually try to represent it with such words as "loving-kindness," "mercy," "steadfast love," and sometimes "loyalty," but the full meaning of the word cannot be adequately conveyed without an explanation; an explanation provided by Snaith in his article.

Chesed **(kheh'-sed) (חֶסֶד)**

This section consists entirely of quoted or paraphrased excerpts from the Snaith article. In some cases emphasis will be added.

Snaith begins by saying that "loving-kindness" is a word invented by Miles Coverdale[gg] to translate the Hebrew *chesed* when it refers to God's love for his people Israel. **The word is used only in cases where there is some recognized tie between the parties concerned**....The theological importance of the word *chesed* is that it stands more than any other word for the attitude which both parties to a covenant ought to maintain towards each other....

Chesed conveys the idea of the steadfastness and persistence of God's sure love for His covenant people. Man's steadfastness is like the wild flowers, here today and gone tomorrow, while the Word of the Lord is steady and sure, firm and reliable.

God's loving-kindness is that sure love which will not let Israel go. Not all Israel's persistent waywardness could ever destroy it. Though Israel be faithless, yet God remains faithful still. This

[gg] The English Puritan Miles Coverdale (1488-1569) was the first to translate the complete Bible into English. The Coverdale Bible was published in 1535. - Wikipedia.org

steady, persistent refusal of God to wash his hands of wayward Israel is the essential meaning of the Hebrew word which is translated loving-kindness....

The widening of the meaning of the Hebrew ***chesed,*** used as the covenant word and especially of the covenant between God and Israel, is due to the history of God's dealings with his covenant-people. **The continual waywardness of Israel has made it inevitable that, if God is never going to let Israel go, then his relation to his people must in the main be one of loving-kindness, mercy, and goodness, all of it entirely undeserved.** For this reason, the predominant use of the word comes to include mercy and forgiveness as a main constituent in God's determined faithfulness to his part of the bargain. **It is obvious, time and again, from the context that if God is to maintain the covenant he must exercise mercy to an unexampled degree....**

If Israel received the proper treatment for her stubborn refusal to walk in God's way, there would be no prospect for her of anything but destruction, since God's demand for right action never wavers one whit. **Strict, however, as the demands for righteousness are, the prophets were sure that God's yearnings for the people of his choice are stronger still....**His passion for righteousness is so strong that he could not be more insistent in his demand for it, but God's persistent love for his people is more insistent still.

The story of God's people throughout the centuries is that her waywardness has been so persistent that, if even a remnant is to be preserved, God has had to show mercy more than anything else. **It is important to realize that though the Hebrew *chesed* can be translated by loving-kindness and mercy without doing violence to the context, yet we must always beware lest we think that God is content with less than righteousness. There is no reference to any sentimental kindness, and no suggestion of mercy apart from repentance, in any case where the Hebrew original is *chesed*. His demand for righteousness is insistent, and it is always at the maximum intensity. The loving-kindness of God means that his mercy is greater even than that.** The word stands for the wonder of his unfailing love for the people of his choice, and the solving of the problem of the relation between his righteousness and his loving-kindness passes beyond human comprehension.

How the Book of Mormon Epitomizes New Covenant Life

We will approach this section of how the Book of Mormon epitomizes New Covenant life both from the perspective of what it says and what its pages enact in the life of a believer. In order to fully appreciate what we have in the Book of Mormon, we must begin by taking a brief look at traditional attitudes towards the subject of revelation.

Terryl Givens in his book *By the Hand of Mormon* documents that there has been three models of revelation that have been historically significant. The first being "revelation as doctrine" wherein the Bible is viewed as a collection of inspired and inerrant teachings. In "revelation as history," the Bible witnesses to the primary revelation wherein "God reveals Himself…in His great deeds." Finally, in "revelation as inner experience," we find a "privileged interior experience of grace or communion with God," such as the mystics have known.[210]

Givens remarks that the first two models have been normative for Christians while being emphatically resistant to the implications of the third. These two models reject the notion that revelation consists of particular truths or information revealed to individuals outside the channels of scripture itself or of God's historically significant activity. The idea being that through the incarnation of Christ, which shows us the Father, and through the pages of the Bible we now have revealed to us "all we need to know."

As a young man, I personally encountered this train of thought as, with my wife-to-be, we had pre-martial counselling with a Protestant minister who was aware of my RLDS faith and its belief in modern-day revelation. The minister acknowledged that in the New Testament there were many miraculous experiences;

however, he said, now that we have the New Testament and the canon of scripture is complete, "we have all we need to know."

In Charles Thompson's 1841 defense of the Book of Mormon, five of the six objections he listed as directed at the new revelation were really five variations on the same theme: "the Bible is full and complete" [i.e. a closed canon].[211] None of the six criticisms had to do with what the Book of Mormon said.[212]

Some theologians have even suggested that explicit directives from above would compromise individual agency. In presenting these two normative Christian views of revelation as non-particularized, I do not mean to imply that these views are held by all. However, there is no doubt that these are prevalent views.

These views of revelation have even determined the ways in which God is said to answer our prayers. Givens quotes Edward Gee as saying, "There are four ways of God's answering prayers. [1] By giving the things prayed for presently…[2] or by suspending the answer for a time, and giving it afterwards…[3] or by withholding from you that mercy which you ask, and giving you a much better mercy in the room of it…[4] or lastly, by giving you patience to bear the loss or want of it."[213] It is pointed out that such a model entirely exempts God from the responsibility to speak.

Dialogic Revelation

Now we turn to the Book of Mormon model of personal or dialogic revelation. Dialogic revelation (which some refer to as Direct revelation) is, as it implies, two-way communication through dialogue with God which may be expressed in words, impression, visions, dreams, etc.

Givens points out that in 1 Nephi alone we read of eight visions, various angelic visitations, several occasions on which Nephi is "visited" by the Lord, "constrained by the Spirit," "led by the Spirit," "commanded" by the Lord and so forth. But more to the point Nephi and his father describe several occasions that cannot be interpreted as mere dreams, spiritual promptings, or heaven-sent impressions. Givens says that the expression "the voice of the Lord came" occurs more than two dozen times.[214]

These examples of personal revelation are repeated time and time again throughout the pages of the Book of Mormon. Givens says that in the Bible, "Prophecy was preeminently the privilege of the prophets";[215] while, "By way of contrast...the Book of Mormon hammers home the insistent message that revelation is the province of everyman."[216]

While we will not attempt to cite all of the particulars, of those eight visions in 1 Nephi, the vision of Nephi is one we can cite that is illustrative of the Book of Mormon's model of personal revelation (see 1 Ne. 3/10-14).

Nephi's Vision

While in the wilderness, Nephi's father, Lehi, had a vision in which he was taken to a large and spacious field where he saw a tree "whose fruit was desirable to make one happy" (1 Ne. 2:49/8:10). Lehi partook of the fruit and it filled his soul with joy. Other features of the allegorical dream include a large and spacious building, a rod of iron, a spacious field and a fountain of waters, Lehi's family and multitudes of people.[217]

After Lehi related his experience, Nephi was desirous that he also could know of these things for himself. He expressed his faith in the "power of the Holy Ghost" which he says "is the gift of God unto all those who diligently seek Him" (1 Ne. 3:26/10:17):

> For he is the same yesterday, to-day, and forever....For he that diligently seeketh shall find, And the mysteries of God shall be unfolded unto them by the power of the Holy Ghost, as well in this time as in times of old (1 Ne. 3:27, 29-30/10:18-19).

As Nephi sat pondering the things his father had seen, "believing that the Lord was able to make them known unto me," the Spirit of the Lord appeared to him in the form of a man and he was carried away to an exceedingly high mountain. Here a conversation ensued as the Spirit asked, "Behold, what desirest thou?" Nephi replied, "I desire to behold the things which my father saw" (see 1 Ne. 3:39-40/11:2-3).

The Spirit first asked him if he believed that his father actually saw the tree of which he had spoken. Nephi replied in the affirmative: "Yea, thou knowest that I believe all the words of my father." The Spirit then shouted Hosanna praising God and blessed Nephi because of his faith and said, "Wherefore, thou shalt behold the things which thou has desired" (see 1 Ne. 3:41-44/11:4-6).

After Nephi saw the tree he said unto the Spirit, "I behold Thou has shown unto me the tree which is most precious above all." The Spirit said, "What desirest thou?" and Nephi replied, "To know the interpretation thereof."

> For I spake unto him as a man speaketh; for I beheld that he was in the form of a man; yet, nevertheless, I knew that it was the Spirit of the Lord: and he spake unto me as a man speaketh with another (1 Ne. 3:50/11:11).

Instead of a verbal explanation, by way of response Nephi is shown the Virgin Mary, bearing the young Christ in her arms. The angel then asked Nephi if he knew the meaning of the tree which his father saw. Nephi said, "Yea, it is the love of God which sheddeth itself abroad in the hearts of the children of men; wherefore it is the most desirable above all things" (1 Ne. 3:64/11:22). He apprehended that the fruit of the tree signifies the love of God, concretized in the gift of His Son.[218]

With the angel as his personal guide, Nephi not only received an interpretation of his father's vision in much greater detail, but also was shown Christ and his earthly ministry along with significant events in the Land of Promise and even all things until the end of the world. He was not allowed to write all he saw as he was told that the Apostle John would write of the end of the world.

The Revelation *of* the Book of Mormon

It is hard to talk about revelation ***in*** the Book of Mormon, without talking about the revelation ***of*** the Book of Mormon. Suffice it for now to say that the process by which the Book of Mormon itself came into existence enacts and epitomizes the principle of revelation that the record itself is at such pains to foster and promote.[219]

The lack of conspicuously distinctive doctrine…mean[s] that the book's primary claim to the reader's attention will be as a pointer to meaning, rather than an embodiment of meaning.…And the way this sign becomes operative in the experience of the convert is through the exercise of the kind of revelation it both enacts and invites.[220]

> And when ye shall receive these things, I would exhort you that ye would ask God, the eternal Father, in the name of Christ, if these things are not true;
> And if ye shall ask with a sincere heart, with real intent, having faith in Christ, he will manifest the truth of it unto you, by the power of the Holy Ghost; and by the power of the Holy Ghost, ye may know the truth of all things (Moro. 10:4-5).

It is no secret that the Restoration faith consists of many different groups with varying opinions about almost every aspect of the gospel. However, the one operative principle, the tie that binds in every case is the Book of Mormon. The above invitation by Moroni has been validated time and time again across church boundaries that extend to the Christian world at large, even to those who otherwise think of Joseph Smith as a charlatan or fraud and who would never think of abandoning their current faith.

The witness of the Book of Mormon is such that in many cases the testimony "just comes" without any conscious effort or even any awareness of Moroni's challenge. My own testimony would be a case in point. As a teenager, even though having been baptized as a young boy, I was almost completely unchurched and certainly not aware of Moroni's invitation at book's end. I remember retiring one night and out of curiosity beginning to read the Book of Mormon. I remember distinctly this "burning in my bosom" and having the certain feeling that this book was true. I was not even aware that this wonderful feeling I had was called the Holy Spirit. I would learn that much later.

As a young man, after having been married and starting to attend church regularly, one of the first pastors we had was George Vaughan. George was a physicist at Midwest Research Institute in Kansas City and a convert to the church. George worked with a church member and lunched with a group that would often discuss the topic of religion. One day during lunch, the church member happened to mention the Book of Mormon. George made an offhand comment that he'd like to read the book "sometime." However, the very next day, the church member brought in a copy and gave it to George. That night after dinner, George sat down to relax, picked up the Book of Mormon and began casually to leaf through its pages. Almost immediately he heard a voice saying, ***"This is not a book to be taken lightly!"*** Shaken, George turned to the beginning and started to read again. By the light of morning, George had read the entire book, and as a consequence, the whole direction of his life had suddenly and miraculously changed.

Thomas B. Marsh (an early church apostle) and his wife were converted to the church after reading only the first sixteen pages of the Book of Mormon which Martin Harris had given him right off the press as the book was being printed.[221]

For Southern Baptist minister Lynn Ridenhour, it took much less than sixteen pages to convince him that he was reading God's word:

> Reared in a small conservative Baptist church back in the Missouri hills of the Ozarks, I was taught with strong convictions that Mormons were no different from Jehovah Witnesses, Christian Scientists, or Armstrong followers. They all sooner or later knocked on your door. We were instructed by our parents to "...let none of them in the house. And don't buy their materials." All were cults. Certainly, the Mormons were not within mainstream Christianity.
>
> I was taught that the Book of Mormon was a lie. We have the Bible and no man was to add to the scriptures lest his soul be damned. And I was taught that the rapture could occur any minute.
>
> Establishing a literal kingdom on this earth was pure nonsense. I was also taught that Joseph Smith was the founder of a cult, and we Baptists considered him to be an imposter, egotist, plagiarist, or fanatic. He certainly was not a man sent from God. And I believe my convictions were typical. Most Protestant Christians today share similar sentiments. All this changed one day when I was handed a Book of Mormon by my neighbor.
>
> I took the book and began reading it to prove how wrong my neighbor was for believing in this book. I did not get out of the first page. When I read, "I, Nephi, having been born of goodly parents..." I knew! I knew I was reading God's Word.

And to my surprise, I discovered—the Book of Mormon is filled with Protestant cardinal doctrines, believe it or not. In fact, I discovered, the Book of Mormon is more "Baptist" than the Baptist hymnal in places. I know that's hard to believe, but it's so. I read the Book from cover to cover and found as a Baptist minister, there is absolutely nothing in it that contradicts the Bible. In fact, it actively supports the doctrines of the Bible.

For example, the book lifts up the blood of Christ (Mosiah 1:118/3:18), declares that salvation is only by God's grace (2 Ne. 7:42/10:24), defends the grand theme of salvation (Mosiah 1:108/3:12), and proclaims that salvation comes only through faith on the Lord Jesus Christ (Mosiah 3:8-9/5:7). Other themes such as repentance, atonement by Christ's blood, redemption, and forgiveness run like a scarlet thread through the book as well (Alma 3:87/5:50; Hel. 2:71/5:9; Alma 13:13/21:9; Mosiah 2:3-4/4:2).

Yes, the grand themes of Protestantism are found recorded through and through. From cover to cover. This Baptist preacher had just discovered the restoration gospel.[222]

Ezra Thayre heard Hyrum Smith preach at a meeting in the yard of the Smith home, regarding the Book of Mormon. Following the meeting, Ezra said to Hyrum, "Let me see it," referring to the Book of Mormon. Hyrum handed him a copy of the book and Ezra declared, *"I opened the book and I received a shock with such exquisite joy that no pen can write and no tongue can express."* This transpired without Ezra Thayre reading a single word. When he opened the book again, he felt *"...a double portion of the Spirit....I did not know whether I was in the world or not. I felt as though I was truly in heaven."*[223]

In 1835 Hyrum Smith and David Whitmer, missionaries of the Church of the Latter Day Saints visited the Huntington home. When Zina Huntington, in her early teens, returned from school one day she found the Book of Mormon on the windowsill of the family's sitting room. As she picked it up, she felt the "*Influence of the Holy Spirit*" and pressed the book to her bosom, whispering, "*This is the truth, truth, truth*!"[224]

Following is the conversion experience of Parley P. Pratt, an early convert to the church who became one of the first members of the Quorum of Twelve Apostles in 1835.

> In 1830, then 23, Parley felt a call to abandon his farm and preach the gospel, believing that God would provide financially for him and Thankful [his wife]. After selling their property at "great sacrifice," the young couple, with $10 in their pockets, took a boat from Cleveland, Ohio, to Buffalo, New York. At Buffalo they took passage on the Erie Canal, headed for Albany. But Parley followed a prompting to disembark prematurely at Newark, while Thankful traveled on to their final destination. As a result, Parley was introduced to the Book of Mormon, an experience that forever changed his life. He later recalled:[225]
>
> I felt a strange interest in the book [The Book of Mormon]. ...I opened it with eagerness, and read its title page. I then read the testimony of several witnesses in relation to the manner of its being found and translated. After this I commenced its contents by course. I read all day; eating was a burden, I had no desire for food; sleep was a burden when the night came, for I preferred reading to sleep. As I read, the spirit of the Lord was upon me, and I knew and comprehended that the book was true, as plainly and manifestly as a man comprehends and knows that he exists. My joy was now full, as it were, and I rejoiced sufficiently to more than pay me for all the sorrows, sacrifices and toils of my life.[226]

In her autobiography *Finding My Way Home*, Theresa Moody (1950-2017) of Lakota and Cherokee heritage, shares her testimony of her first encounter with the Book of Mormon. Theresa relates that while living in Horton, Kansas, she had gone to a Little League game to see her youngest brother playing. There, by chance, she happened to meet one of the umpires; who, upon learning that she was Native American, asked to come by for a visit because he had a book he wanted to give her. About a week later he came by her house, giving her a copy of the Book of Mormon, saying it was a record of her ancestors and the things that Jesus taught them, and if she prayed the Lord would reveal its truth to her.[227] Theresa then says:

> He slid the Book of Mormon across the table to me and the moment I touched it I heard a voice in my right ear saying: ***This is true. It belongs to you***. That night I took it to bed with me to begin reading it, praying the Lord would show me the truth. I didn't jump around but began reading at the very first page. **As I began to read the words pulled me along like a current that carried me towards that place where Love dwells.** For most of my life I'd been searching in the flesh for my way back Home to the One whose face continues to fill my mind, who was and is the source of this Love. I yearned for Him to find me and bring me Home. I mourned for this place so many times like a deep hunger that has never been filled or a thirst that never abates but grows till you feel you will never drink sweet water again. I had been thirsty for so long and now I was drawing water from His well; and the more I drank the more I was restored and the more I wanted.
>
> I felt no weariness or sleepiness as the hours passed, and suddenly it was dawn. In these pages I had encountered my ancestors, and the emotional impact caught me off guard. It affected me as if the events in this record were happening right now to those nearest and dearest to me. The next day was a blur, and that night as I finished reading I realized

> this was the account of my native family's history with Jesus at a time when Europeans were still savages.[228]

Theresa writes that while some small efforts have been made to take the Book of Mormon to the Indian People, the actions and focus of many [most?] indicate that they assume Zion can be built without Manasseh.[229] Theresa then goes on to say this about the crucial importance of taking the Book of Mormon to the Indian People:

> Our identity is in Christ, with whom our ancestors walked and talked. Scientists recently discovered that the effect of powerful experiences can alter DNA and be passed down to later generations. The visitation of Christ to our ancient ancestors planted in our DNA a spirituality that transformed us. If this *spiritual seed* planted in us so long ago is left unnourished, empty, and unfulfilled, it leads our people into alcoholism and many other destructive behaviors - but if brought into the light and nourished it will blossom into Zion.[230]

Born Clara B. Nicholas (1913-1995), Little Pigeon was a noted Native American lecturer and author. She authored three books: ***Cry of the Ancients, Children of the Ancient Ones*** and ***The Lovely World of Little Pigeon***. She was married to Oneida Chief Grey Owl (1913-1959). As recounted by Faye Shaw, one day at her home, Little Pigeon shared the story of her first encounter with the Book of Mormon:

> We were sitting at my kitchen table when Little Pigeon began sharing a life-changing event in two ways. A neighbor had invited her to church to hear another Native American speak. Afterwards she was sitting alone at the back when he approached and told her he had a book about her ancestors. He would have his son deliver it. The next day when the young man handed her a Book of Mormon, she immediately opened it and began to read: "I, Nephi,

> being born of goodly parents..." Her ancestors were goodly parents! Her whole life she had been called derogatory names because of her heritage. That had been a heavy burden to her, but now her heart leaped! She affirmed to herself, "I came from goodly parents!" Only when it got too dark to read further did she remember she had left the young man standing at the door. The speaker, Grey Owl, later became her husband.[231]

As demonstrated by every testimony cited, the significance of the Book of Mormon to the truly converted individual rests not only in what it says but also in what it represents and implies. The Book of Mormon is the sudden intrusion into the life of an individual that changes everything; that brings inspiration, guidance and new direction. The mere existence of the Book of Mormon says that God is real; that He is the same yesterday, today and forever; that He is still a God of miracles; that He has not forsaken us; that He is a God of love.

This principle, this invitation by Moroni to "ask and receive" in the closing pages of the Book of Mormon, then became the operative principle in the early church. The following is an excerpt from an open letter "To the Honorable Men of the World" published in a church newspaper in 1832:

> Search the scriptures...and ask your heavenly Father, in the name of his Son Jesus Christ, to manifest the truth unto you, and if you do it with an eye single to his glory, nothing doubting, he will answer you by the power of his Holy Spirit: **You will then know for yourselves and not for another: You will not then be dependent on man for the knowledge of God.**[232]

"You will know for yourselves and... not then be dependent on man for the knowledge of God." This principle established in the Book of Mormon, by what it says and what it enacts in the lives of believers, then is the essence of the New Covenant which has been the subject of this book. No wonder the Lord says of the Book of Mormon, that it is the New Covenant.

As our journey together draws to a close, I want to include the farewell of Moroni. Due to the uncertainty of his situation, Moroni, the last prophet in the Book of Mormon, wrote three farewells. In addition to his final one in Moroni 10, his first farewell was when, after his father Mormon was slain in battle, he finished his father's book of Mormon (Morm. 4/8-9). Next, his father had commanded him to abridge the Book of Ether, a record of the Jaredites, the first of three groups recorded in the Book of Mormon led to this land. Toward the end of that record, again thinking that this was the last he would write, he penned the following:

> And now I, Moroni, bid farewell unto the Gentiles, yea, and also unto my brethren whom I love, until we shall meet before the judgment seat of Christ, where all men shall know that my garments are not spotted with your blood;
> **And then shall ye know that I have seen Jesus, and that he hath talked with me face to face, and that he told me in plain humility, even as a man telleth another in mine own language, concerning these things; and only a few have I written, because of my weakness in writing.**
> And now I would commend you to seek this Jesus of whom the prophets and apostles have written, that the grace of God the Father, and also the Lord Jesus Christ, and the Holy Ghost, which beareth record of them, may be, and abide in you for ever. Amen. (Ether 5:39-41/12:38-41).

These words of Moroni exemplify the nature of the New Covenant experience wherein the Lord will converse with us and teach us face to face. Moroni is not alone in his experience as others including Lehi (1 Ne. 1:8/1:9), Nephi (2 Ne. 8:3/11:2), Jacob (2 Ne. 8:4/11:3), Lamoni (Alma 12:142-143/19:12-13), Mormon (Morm. 1:16/1:15) and the brother of Jared (Ether 1:76-77/3:13-14) saw Christ as well as the multitude and disciples in 3 Nephi at his resurrection appearance. Thus, their teachings and testimonies of Jesus are based on firsthand knowledge.

My personal New Covenant journey has made a profound difference in my life as I hope it will yours. I find that I now look at the gospel with new eyes; that I look at myself and others differently and even perceive God differently. It is having discovered the purpose of life, of creation, and being allowed to peer into the very heart of God. It is the experience of being set free to enjoy God's bounty.

As I said in the Preface, I started this work with the intention of writing about the covenants of God, which hopefully was accomplished; however, I ended up in a place entirely unexpected – the grace, mercy and love of God.

We live in perilous times. We are told that this land is a land of promise and that those who possess this land must serve the God of the land, which is Jesus Christ, or they will be swept off when they are ripe in iniquity (see Ether 1:31, 35/2:9,12). Regardless of one's political beliefs, it has become self-evident that the disarray and division in our land is such that what was once unimaginable is now imaginable. Regardless of what peril may come, God makes a promise to protect His people:

> And the day shall come that the earth shall rest. But before that day the heavens shall be darkened, and a veil of darkness shall cover the earth; and the heavens shall shake, and also the earth.
> And great tribulations shall be among the children of men, but my people will I preserve (Gen. 7:68-69 IV/Moses 7:61).

> And I will shew wonders in the heavens and in the earth, blood, and fire, and pillars of smoke.
> The sun shall be turned into darkness, and the moon into blood, before the great and the terrible day of the Lord come.

> And it shall come to pass, that whosoever shall call on the name of the Lord shall be delivered: for in mount Zion and in Jerusalem shall be deliverance, as the Lord hath said, and in the remnant whom the Lord shall call (Joel 2:30-32).

While the Book of Mormon was written by a branch of the house of Israel to their descendants, it is by the providence of God that He has allowed this book to come to their posterity by way of the Gentiles. God, by temporarily giving to the Gentiles care for the house of Israel (Morm. 2:37/5:10), is showing them grace and mercy so that they will have the opportunity to share in the blessings God has in store for His people – that none might be excluded. By making a covenant and being baptized and receiving a remission of sins and being filled with the Holy Ghost, they become numbered with God's covenant people who are of the house of Israel.

This opportunity for the Gentiles to respond is about to slip away as shortly the fullness of the gospel will be shifted to the house of Israel (see 3 Ne. 7:34-37/16:10-12). This is not only a-once-in-a-lifetime opportunity to respond, but, a unique opportunity out of all creation. There will be only one closing age in history where all the covenants of God are fulfilled and the kingdom of God comes on earth. Heaven awaits our choice.

O My people…

O my people, time is fleeting,
Draw ye nigh and hear my voice.
Hosts of angels still are waiting,
Till you consecrate your choice.
Hosts of angels at your bidding
Wait to rid the earth of sin.
For ye soon must build a place
Where mine elect can enter in.

O ye have the choice before you,
One way life – the other – death,

Worlds unending lie between them,
Heed ye well, your Father sayeth.
Choose ye me and I will choose you,
Be not weary of the pace;
Then when I make up my jewels,
Ye shall find a resting place.[233]
-- Dorothy Wells

Study Guide

1. Do you believe that the Book of Mormon is named after its principal editor, Mormon, or for the Land of Mormon, the place where Alma established the covenant?

2. Discuss Norman Snaith's article on the Hebrew word ***chesed*** and explain the difficulty of translating this word into English.

3. Terryl Givens lists the three models of revelation that have been historically significant in Christianity. Discuss.

4. In light of these models of revelation, Givens quotes Edward Gee as saying that there are four ways that God answers prayers. Do you agree? What has been your experience?

5. What is dialogic revelation and how is that exemplified in Nephi's vision?

6. If as stated, the Book of Mormon lacks a conspicuously distinctive doctrine, then why do you suppose it is so controversial?

7. Discuss the Book of Mormon testimonies listed. Are any of these similar to your own experiences or someone you know?

8. In this, our final chapter, the author states that his New Covenant journey has made a profound difference in his life. Likewise, express your thoughts about how your thinking has evolved as you have completed this part of your journey.

APPENDICES

APPENDIX A

ADMONITION OF THE LORD
Counsel to the Children of the Lord

(Given through Jim Hobbs at the Waldo Congregation, July 13, 2008)

Preface

I listened to Mike Sanders preach Sunday evening, June the 22nd. The Lord used him to bring out some things that I have been concerned about for several months. As I mowed my yard on Monday, I told the Lord we have been called to repentance over and over, now would He give us something positive that we could do to get out from under this curse upon the Restoration. The Lord began to reveal some things to my mind. As I came in and began to write them down, He gave me the following:

Mine Erring Children Whom I Love

My Children: In the beginning of the coming forth of the Restoration I restored My Authority, the fullness of My Gospel and My gifts of the Spirit to the earth.

My sons lost sight of My Purpose for the Restoration. I established My Covenant with them. They took My Covenant lightly and broke it. I removed Mine erring children from the land of Zion that they not pollute their inheritance. I gave them the gifts of the Spirit in 1833. I endowed them in Kirtland in 1836 and again they took My Word lightly and had to leave Kirtland in 1837. They came to Far West and brought their errors with them. I allowed them to be removed from the state of Missouri. The wicked punishing the wicked. My Children had the greater light and rejected it. In Nauvoo many of the errors were brought to light and My Children separated.

In D&C 45:4 My Word says they, the early saints, rejected the fullness of My Gospel and the ripening of the Gentile times began.

Most today are not even aware that the Gentiles, the early Restoration saints, rejected My Gospel and that is why I scattered them.

Although many did respond to My Word and sought to keep it and did have My Spirit to direct them; there were those who sought for self-aggrandizement and were lifted up in pride, especially among some of the leadership which brought My Judgment upon My Children.

Those who allowed My Spirit to direct them did much good and the church grew because of their dedication. They have received their reward. But just as with Israel, one family took the idols and gold and hid them under their tent floor and Israel began to be defeated by their enemies. Many suffered because one broke My Commandments. So many of the saints suffered because of those who would not obey My Words.

You here who have received and responded to My Gospel have also accepted many false traditions that have been perpetuated by the Restoration.

The Gentiles have continued to reject the fullness of My Gospel, The Book of Mormon, because of the vain and foolish traditions of men. Many of you refuse to accept the truth which is in My Word but you accept the false traditions that have been handed down without putting them to the light of My Scriptures. You worship your history not knowing there are errors in it. You read My Second Witness, the Book of Mormon, without understanding it. You fall into the same errors many of the early saints fell into. The Jews have My Law but reject Me because of their vain and foolish traditions. You like the Jews have the fullness of My Gospel but do not understand it. You covet My Law but reject My Grace. My Law does not save you but salvation is through My Sacrifice I gave upon the cross. You were redeemed from the fall by Me. Now you stand responsible for your own actions, that is whether or not you accept Me as your Savior. Laman and Lemuel believed in My Law, but they rejected My Grace, My Love, Me.

Many of My Children are as Laman and Lemuel. They want only to accept the traditions and the sweet enticing of some of My Priesthood.

Many reject My plain and simple gospel and in that you reject Me because you do not know Me. You have enjoyed the gentle caress of My Spirit from time to time but you do not have an intimate relationship with Me. You have not experienced My hurt, My sorrows, My concerns for My Children, your brothers and sisters. You judge each other harshly, with no regard for their soul. You would cast each other off rather than labor with that diamond enmeshed in sin.

When you shake the hand of a red person the red does not rub off on you, or the black of a black person or the yellow of a yellow person. Neither will the sin of a sinner rub off on you when you put your arm around a hurting sinner. I forgave an unclean woman in the temple. I allowed an unclean woman, Mary, to anoint Me with costly oil and spices and to wash My feet with her tears. She, a sinner, saved by My Grace, knew Me and My love and that love shown in her response to My Word and My Love. Simon and those setting around would have cast her out and ridiculed her and would make it hard for her to come into My Fellowship. Some of your brothers and sisters have been changed by My Love as was Mary, yet like Simon some of you would cast them out, not caring for their souls. You are jealous of them like the brother of the prodigal son. You are jealous because they receive many spiritual blessings you covet but do not receive.

I am the vine and you are the branches. You cannot bear fruit unless My Sap, My Spirit, moves through you and lives in you.

I would bless you beyond measure if you would allow My Spirit to live in you. That is, My Father and I will come and live in you, that which My Apostle Paul calls a mystery, Christ in you (Col. 1:27). I want to perform My Works, My Strange Acts through you. For that to happen My Spirit must live in you. You must accept My Love and My Grace for yourselves that My Love may radiate through you to others.

All of you sitting in this congregation have the ability and the authority to heal the sick, raise the dead, open the eyes of the blind, unstop the ears of the deaf, and raise the lame were you willing to submit yourselves to My Spirit, that is let Me live in you. You can be a blessing to this community, to this city and to those hurting and enmeshed in sin – desiring to be delivered. I can lead you to those who will respond. You know not the hearts of men so you cannot choose wisely. The scriptures say, "I added to My Church daily such as should be saved." You cannot add such to My Church unless My Spirit, I and My Father live in you and direct you.

My apostles had their Pentecost (Acts 2). The Restoration had its Pentecost [1833, 1836]. Will you receive my Pentecost for you? Try Me! Test Me! See if I will pour out My Spirit upon you. Will you lay down your traditions, your preconceived ideas, your agendas and set a date and time for Me to manifest Myself to you and in you? Will you come together with this one purpose in mind, united in heart to receive? I love you My children and desire to do great things through you. But if you cannot all unite in one desire and purpose to receive My Spirit, I cannot give unto you My Pentecost in one body as I desire.

I am reaching out to you, will you not reach out to Me? I reached out to the Jews and they rejected Me and were scattered. Will you reach out to Me or like the Jews be cursed and scattered.

I tell you before it happens, the economy of this nation is in the process of failing and civil strife will shortly be throughout the land. I will be your protection during this time. But more importantly, you will be a strength and support for others.

A great revival is soon to come forth among My Children. Will you My Restoration people be a part of it? Or will it pass you by because of preconceived ideas? I call on you to bow down and humble yourselves that I may involve you in My great and marvelous work which is even now in the process of coming forth. Soon you will be compelled to choose Me or mammon.

I poured out My Heart in prayer for My Disciples because they perceived not the great work I had for them. And I promised them another comforter to help them accomplish My Work. You too perceive not the great work I have for you to do. And now I offer to you the same comforter I gave to My Disciples if you will gather together as one, as My disciples did in the upper room. They were of one heart and mind in desiring My Comforter. So you must come together in prayer and supplication as one, with one purpose, that is to receive My Spirit.

Acts 1:8, 14
Acts 1:8 But ye shall receive power, after that the Holy Spirit is come upon you; and ye shall be witnesses unto me both in Jerusalem, and in all Judea, and in Samaria, and unto the uttermost part of the earth.
Acts 1:14 These all continued with one accord in prayer and supplication, with the women, and Mary the mother of Jesus, and with his brethren.

PREFACE
[1] Sayers, Dorothy L., *Christian Letters to a Post-Christian World* (Grand Rapids: Erdmans, 1969), 45, cited in Yancey, *What's So Amazing About Grace* (Grand Rapids: Zondervan, 1997), 59.
[2] Black Elk. "The Great Vision." *First People of America and Canada – Turtle Island,* www.firstpeople.us/articles/Black-Elk-Speaks/Black-Elk-Speaks-The-Great-Vision.html

CHAPTER 1: MAKING A NEW COVENANT
[3] Burford, Dwight. *Why the Book of Mormon is the New Covenant: Part 4: The Melchizedek Priesthood* (self-published, 2018), 19.
[4] Nunn, T. Royal. *Covenants of the Lord: Bonded in Blood* (self-published: 2013), 136.
[5] Sproul, R.C. *The Promises of God* (Colorado Springs: David C. Cook, 2013), 211, 213.
[6] Ibid., 182-186.
[7] "History of the Church of Jesus Christ of Latter-day Saints." *BYU Studies Quarterly,* byustudies.byu.edu/content/volume-4-chapter-27

CHAPTER 2: THE TWO COVENANTS
[8] Murray, Andrew. *The Two Covenants and The Second Blessing* (New York, Chicago, etc.: Fleming H. Revell Company, 1898), 12-13. Retrieved from the Library of Congress,
//archive.org/details/twocovenantsseco00murr
[9] ibid., 16
[10] ibid., 17-18
[11] ibid., 18-19
[12] ibid., 20
[13] ibid., 21-22
[14] ibid., 22-24
[15] ibid., 26
[16] ibid., 27
[17] ibid., 29-30
[18] ibid., 30-32
[19] ibid., 33
[20] ibid., 34
[21] ibid., 41-42
[22] ibid., 42-43

CHAPTER 3: THE HIGHER AND LESSER LAWS

[23] Tvedtnes, John A. "The Higher and Lesser Laws." Ed. Donald W. Parry, Daniel C. Peterson, Stephen D. Ricks. *Revelation, Reason and Faith, Essays in Honor of Truman G. Madsen*. (BYU Maxwell Institute; 2002). //publications.mi.byu.edu/fullscreen/?pub=1122&index=16
[24] Sperling, Harry. *The Zohar* (New York: Bennet, 1958), 5:330–31. Cited in Tvedtnes, "The Higher and Lesser Laws." (BYU Maxwell Institute, 2002).
The version of the *Zohar* that Tvedtnes cites has various translators for the five volumes: vol. 1, Harry Sperling and Maurice Simon; vols. 2 and 3, Harry Sperling, Maurice Simon, and Paul P. Levertoff; vol. 4, Maurice Simon and Paul P. Levertoff; and vol. 5, Maurice Simon and Harry Sperling. They were all published by Bennet in New York.
[25] The tree of life in the *Zohar* usually refers to the Torah or law of Moses. See *Zohar* Genesis 131b, 193a, 199a, 202b; Exodus 17b; Leviticus 53b; Numbers 148b; Deuteronomy 260a, 261a.
[26] Sperling, *The Zohar,* 3:339.
[27] ibid., 1:366–67.
[28] ibid., 4:16–17.

CHAPTER 4: THE TWO ROADS

[29] *History of the Church (LDS),* 4:461

CHAPTER 5: THE SONG OF ZACHARIAS

[30] Barclay, William. "William Barclay's Daily Study Bible, Luke 1"; StudyLight.org, www.studylight.org/commentaries/dsb/luke-1.html
[31] Davey, Stephen. "The Song of Zacharias: Prelude to Bethlehem – Part II," 3-4. Wisdom for the Heart, wisdomonline.org.
[32] MacArthur, John. "Zachariah's Song of Salvation: Introduction." 18 April 1999. www.gty.org/library/sermons-library/42-16/zachariahs-song-of-salvation-introduction
[33] ibid.
[34] MacArthur, John. "Zachariah's Song of Salvation: The Abrahamic Covenant." 2 May 1999. www.gty.org/library/sermons-library/42-18/zachariahs-song-of-salvation-the-abrahamic-covenant
[35] MacArthur, John. "Zachariah's Song of Salvation: The New Covenant, Part 1." 42-19. 16 May 1999. www.gty.org/library/sermons-library/42-19/zachariahs-song-of-salvation-the-new-covenant-part-1
[36] MacArthur, John. "Zachariah's Song of Salvation: The New Covenant, Part 2." 42-20. 23 May 1999. www.gty.org/library/sermons-library/42-20/zachariahs-song-of-salvation-the-new-covenant-part-2

[37] ibid.

CHAPTER 6: COVENANTS OF THE LORD

[38] Oakman, Arthur A. *The Call of Christ in an Age of Dilemma: Six Studies Based Upon The Apostolic Epistle of 1964* (Independence, MO: Herald Publishing House, 1964), 57.
[39] Treat, Raymond C. "Lessons on the Covenant Relationship: Lesson 2." *Zarahemla Research Foundation*, www.restoredcovenant.org/Default.asp?CAT=Covenant
[40] Treat, "The Hidden Principle: Come Unto Christ."
[41] Oakman, *The Call of Christ*, 45.
[42] ibid., 46.

CHAPTER 7: THE EVERLASTING COVENANT

[43] Barclay, William. *The Letters to the Galatians and Ephesians* (Westminster John Knox Press, 1976), 83-84.
[44] Sproul, R.C. "What Is the Covenant of Redemption?" *Ligonier Ministries*, //www.ligonier.org/blog/what-covenant-redemption/
[45] Nunn, T. Royal. *Covenants of the Lord: Bonded in Blood*, 5.
[46] ibid., 7.
[47] "The Mediator of the Covenant." *Present Truth Magazine*, Volume 28, Part 1, Article 9. www.presenttruthmag.com/archive/XXVIII/28p1-9.htm
[48] Sproul. *The Promises of God*, 28.
[49] "Hebrew Roots," *Wikibooks*, July 9, 2009, en.wikibooks.org/wiki/Hebrew_Roots/The_Law_and_the_Covenants/Covenants:The_Everlasting_Covenant
[50] Moody, John. "Priesthood in the Book of Mormon," 5. Unpublished paper emailed to author 26 March 2018.
[51] Moody, John. *The Inspired Version – Stick of Judah*, 50. 30 September 2012.
[52] Moody, John. "Priesthood in the Book of Mormon," 3.
[53] ibid., 3-4.
[54] Cahn, Jonathan. *The Book of Mysteries* (Lake Mary, FL: FrontLine, 2016), Day 225.

CHAPTER 8: THE PATRIARCHAL COVENANTS

[55] Read, Lenet Hadley. "The Golden Plates and the Feast of Trumpets." *Ensign*, January 2000. https://www.lds.org/ensign/
[56] Bloch, Abraham P. *The Biblical and Historical Background of the Jewish Holy Days* (New York: Ktav Pub House, 1978), 18-19, cited in Read.
[57] *Times and Seasons*, Vol. 3, 707. //www.centerplace.org/history/ts/v3n09.htm

[58] ibid.
[59] Joseph Smith History 1:39. www.lds.org/scriptures/pgp/js-h/1?lang=eng
[60] Read, "The Golden Plates." See Philip Goodman, ed., *The Rosh Hashanah Anthology* (Philadelphia: The Jewish Publication Society of America, 1970), 42; Leo Trepp, *The Complete Book of Jewish Observance* (New York: Behrman House Publishing, 1980), 95.
[61] "Religion: Three Religions, One God." Public Broadcasting System/ Global Connections/ Middle East, www.pbs.org/wgbh/globalconnections/mideast/themes/religion/index.html
[62] Nunn. *Covenants of the Lord,* 74.
[63] Sproul. *The Promises of God,* 119-120.
[64] Reynolds, Noel B. "Understanding the Abrahamic Covenant through the Book of Mormon," 4-5. *BYU ScholarsArchive,* 01 March 2017, //hdl.lib.byu.edu/1877/3771
[65] ibid., 7-8.
[66] ibid., 33-34.
[67] ibid., 32.
[68] ibid., 51.
[69] ibid., 43.
[70] ibid., 45.

CHAPTER 9: THE HOREB COVENANT

[71] "Horeb": *Bible Study Tools* (citing Easton's Bible Dictionary), https://www.biblestudytools.com/dictionary/horeb/
[72] "Mount Horeb": *Wikipedia.* //en.wikipedia.org/wiki/Mount_Horeb
[73] Jacobs, Joseph; Seligsohn, M.; Bacher, Wilhelm. "Sinai, Mount." *Jewish Encyclopedia.* http://www.jewishencyclopedia.com/articles/13766-sinai-mount
[74] Nunn. *Covenants of the Lord,* 96-97.

CHAPTER 10: THE COVENANT TO RESTORE ISRAEL

[75] Moody, John. *Search for the Sacred Record,* 32. (Self-published, 2013).
[76] Moody, John. *The Failure of the Gentiles and the Restoration of Israel,* (Self-published, 2006), 1-2.
[77] Edwards, F. Henry. *A New Commentary on the Doctrine and Covenants* (Independence, MO: Herald Publishing House, 1977), 368.
[78] Moody, John. Email to author dated 12-14-2018.
[79] Millett, Robert L. "The Plates of Brass," *Ensign,* January 1988. The Church of Jesus Christ of Latter-day Saints, Salt Lake City, UT. https://www.lds.org/ensign/1988/01/the-plates-of-brass-a-witness-of-christ?lang=eng#

[80] Sperry, Sidney B. *Answers to Book of Mormon Questions* (Salt Lake City: Bookcraft, 1967), 43-44. Cited in Millett, "The Plates of Brass."
[81] Sperry, *Answers*, 43. Cited in Millett, "The Plates of Brass."
[82] Hardy, Grant R. "Book of Mormon Plates and Records," *Encyclopedia of Mormonism.*
http://eom.byu.edu/index.php/Book_of_Mormon_Plates_and_Records
[83] "Judaism," *Encyclopedia Britannica,*
www.britannica.com/topic/Judaism
[84] Meservy, Keith. "Ezekiel's Sticks and the Gathering of Israel," *Ensign,* February 1987. www.lds.org/ensign/1987/02?lang=eng

CHAPTER 11: OTHER COVENANTS OF THE LORD

[85] Nunn. *Covenants of the Lord,* 7.
[86] Drummond, Henry. "The Founding of The Society." *Henry Drummond page, Cornerstone Books,*
//henrydrummond.wwwhubs.com/programme.htm#founding
[87] ibid.
[88] Smith, Joseph Jr., "An Epitome of Faith and Doctrine." *Times and Seasons* 3:710, 1842
[89] Yancey. *What's So Amazing About Grace?* 238.
[90] Drummond, Henry. "I SAW THE CITY OF GOD," *Henry Drummond page, Cornerstone Books.* //henrydrummond.wwwhubs.com/city.htm

CHAPTER 12: INVITATION TO AN AMAZING LIFE

[91] "Against All Odds Israel Survives, Episode 7, 1967." *Amazon Instant Video,* Questar, Inc. release date: October 10, 2006.
[92] Pumphrey, Clint. "How the Greatest Generation Works," *howstuffworks,* //people.howstuffworks.com/culture-traditions/generation-gaps/greatest-generation1.htm
[93] Oakman. *The Call of Christ,* 7.
[94] Luff, Joseph. "Concerning Our Whereabouts: Watchman, What of the Night." February 10, 1930. *LatterDayTruth.org,*
//www.latterdaytruth.org/pdf/100036.pdf, accessed February 5, 2018.
[95] Merrill, William Pierson. "Rise up, O Men of God." 1911. *Hymnary.org,*
//hymnary.org/text/rise_up_o_men_of_god

CHAPTER 13: LIVING AN AMAZING LIFE

[96] Medinger, Alan P. "Be Ye Perfect: What Does That Mean?" *Exodus Global Alliance,* 1992.
www.exodusglobalalliance.org/beyeperfectwhatdoesthatmeanp43.php
[97] Lewis, C.S. *Mere Christianity* (New York: MacMillan, 1952), 172.
[98] Holland, Jeffrey R. "Be Ye Therefore Perfect - Eventually." *General Conference, The Church of Jesus Christ of Latter-day Saints,* October 2017.

www.lds.org/general-conference/2017/10/be-ye-therefore-perfect-eventually?lang=eng
[99] Bolton, Andrew. *SERMON ON THE MOUNT: Foundations for an International Peace Church* (Independence, MO: Herald Publishing House, 1999), 13-14.
[100] Murray. *The Two Covenants,* 56.
[101] ibid., 61.
[102] ibid., 62.
[103] ibid., 57.
[104] Nunn. *Covenants of the Lord,* 21.
[105] ibid., 23.
[106] ibid., 44.
[107] ibid., 152.
[108] Lucado, Max. *It's Not About Me* (Nashville: Integrity Publishers, 2004), 17.
[109] Hobbs, Jim. Email to author dated November 30, 2018.

CHAPTER 14: HAVING A FORM OF GODLINESS
[110] Nunn, *Covenants of the Lord,* 44.
[111] "Constantine: First Christian Emperor." *Christianity Today,* n.d. www.christianitytoday.com/history/people/rulers/constantine.html
[112] Smith, Heman C. *History of the Reorganized Church of Jesus Christ of Latter Day Saints,* Vol. 1, Chapter 2:9-10, RestoredGospel.com
[113] Cole, Steven J. "Lesson 10: Judged by Your Deeds (Rom. 2:6-11)," *Bible.org,* 2013. //bible.org/seriespage/lesson-10-judged-your-deeds-romans-26-11

CHAPTER 15: THE OTHER COMFORTER AND PERFECTION - I
[114] Merriam-Webster Online Dictionary, https://www.merriam-webster.com/
[115] THOUGHTS FROM GOD MINISTRIES, BIBLICAL GRACE, website no longer valid as of 1/27/19.
[116] Piper, John. "Grace is Pardon – And Power!" *desiringGod,* n.d. https://www.desiringgod.org/articles/grace-is-pardon-and-power
[117] Fenske, Jeff. "The Meaning of Grace." *One Can Happen,* February 19, 2010 (website no longer available).
[118] ibid.
[119] Ortberg, John. *FLOW* (audio CD). Oasis Audio, Carol Stream, IL, March 1, 2005.

CHAPTER 16: THE OTHER COMFORTER AND PERFECTION - II
[120] History of the Church (LDS), Vol. 3, Ch. 25, 381
[121] ibid., 380-381.

[122] "Holy Spirit of Promise," 651. *Encyclopedia of Mormonism* (online)
[123] Lucado. *It's Not About Me*, 8.
[124] Ortberg, John. *FLOW* (audio CD).
[125] Cahn. *The Book of Mysteries*, Day 230.

CHAPTER 17: THE KINGDOM LAW

[126] Sayers, Dorothy L., *Christian Letters to a Post-Christian World* (Grand Rapids: Erdmans, 1969), 45, cited in Yancey, 59.
[127] "A Moment of Grace," *New York Times*, 2005/08/17, //www.nytimes.com/2005/08/17/opinion/a-moment-of-grace.html. Cited in Jeremiah, *Captured by Grace*, 9-11.
[128] Yancey, Philip D. What's So Amazing About Grace? 254.
[129] Oakman, Arthur A. *The Call of Christ*, 62.
[130] Altrogge, Mark. "The Glorious, Life Altering Difference Between Grace and Mercy."
[131] Fowler, James W. *Becoming Adult, Becoming Christian* (San Francisco: Harper and Row, 1984), 121-122. Cited in Jeremiah, *Captured by Grace*, 23.
[132] Shoemaker, H. Stephen. *Finding Jesus in His Prayers* (Nashville: Abingdon Press, 2004), 75.
[133] *An Apology for the True Christian Divinity: Being an Explanation and Vindication of the Principles and Doctrines of the People Called Quakers. Wyethepedia: W&M Law Library,* //lawlibrary.wm.edu/wythepedia/index.php/Apology_for_the_True_Christian_Divinity
[134] Barclay, Robert. *An Apology for the True Christian Divinity* (Farmington, ME: Quaker Heritage Press, 2002 (originally published in 1678)), 205-222. //www.qhpress.org/texts/barclay/apology/
[135] Yancey, Philip D. *What's So Amazing About Grace?* 255-256.

CHAPTER 18: THE FORMER AND LATTER RAINS
CHAPTER 19: ESTABLISHING THE CHURCH

[136] Rupe, Richard. *God's Plan of Salvation* (Self-published, 2016), 238.
[137] ibid., 238-239.
[138] Treat, Ray. "What is the Lord's Purpose for the Book of Mormon?" A Power Point presentation in possession of author.
[139] Nunn. *Covenants of the Lord*, 192-193.
[140] McKay, Patrick S. Sr. *Healing the Breach* (Independence, MO: Lulu Publishing Services, 2008), 148-149. Citing the relating of this experience to the First Quorum of Restoration Seventy, Independence, MO, April, 2014.

CHAPTER 20: THE UNSEARCHABLE RICHES OF CHRIST

[141] Spiegelberg, Nancy. "Precious Grace." *Tentmaker,* www.tentmaker.org/Quotes/grace_quotes.html

[142] ibid.

[143] Pierson, A.T. "Ephesians 3:8-9 Commentary." *Precept Austin,* 15 May 2018. www.preceptaustin.org/ephesians_38-9

[144] Barth, Karl. *The Word of God and the Word of Man* (New York: Harper & Row, 1957), 92. Cited in Yancey, *What's So Amazing About Grace?* 247.

[145] Oakman. *The Call of Christ,* 8-9.

[146] Yancey. *What's So Amazing About Grace?* 60.

[147] Lucado. *It's Not About Me,* 101.

[148] Kynes, William L., "Discipleship or Grace: Must it be One or the Other?" *Knowing and Doing* (C.S. Lewis Institute: Fall 2011). www.cslewisinstitute.org/Discipleship_or_Grace_Kynes_Page_1

[149] Hedges, Brian. "What Does It Mean to Abide in Christ?" *Christianity.com,* March 3, 2014, www.christianity.com/bible/bible-study/what-does-it-mean-to-abide-in-christ.html.

[150] Bruce, John. "Abide in Me - Sermon 2, Lessons from the Vineyard, John 15:4-5." *Vimeo,* 25 September 2016, //vimeo.com/184283720

[151] Mairs, Nancy. *Ordinary Time* (Boston: Beacon Press, 1993), 138. Cited in Yancey, 174.

[152] ibid.

[153] ibid.

[154] Yancey, *What's So Amazing About Grace?* 174.

[155] Evans, Tony. *The Magnificent Grace of God,* CD5 "Liberated by Grace." (Dallas: Urban Alternative).

[156] Tada, Joni Eareckson. *Diamonds in the Dust - 366 Sparkling Devotions* (Zondervan, November 1993), quoted from entry for Oct. 14.

[157] Evans, Tony. *The Grace of God* (Chicago: Moody Publishers, 2004), 12.

[158] Kynes

[159] Evans. *The Magnificent Grace of God.*

[160] Evans. *The Grace of God,* 57.

[161] Storms, Sam. "Joy's Eternal Increase: Edwards on the Beauty of Heaven." *desiringGod,* 2003, www.desiringgod.org/messages/joys-eternal-increase-edwards-on-the-beauty-of-heaven.

[162] Kynes.

[163] ibid.

[164] ibid., 42, 56, 57.

[165] Evans, *Magnificent Grace,* CD 9 "Assisted By Grace"

[166] Yancey, *What's So Amazing,* 174.

[167] Edwards, Jonathan. "Precious Grace." *Tentmaker,* www.tentmaker.org/Quotes/grace_quotes.html

CHAPTER 21: THE LOVE OF GOD

[168] Turner, Tina. "What's Love Got to Do with It?" Lyrics by Terry Britten and Graham Lyle. Album: Private Dancer, 1984. //genius.com/Tina-turner-whats-love-got-to-do-with-it-lyrics
[169] Oakman. *The Call of Christ,* 9.
[170] ibid.
[171] Muehlenberg, Bill. "Modern-Day Marcionism." *CultureWatch,* 27 February 2012, //billmuehlenberg.com/?s=modern-day+marcionism
[172] Ross, Hugh. "Bringing Every Thought Captive."
[173] Balter, Ariel. "What is Astrophysics?" Space.com, 21 December 2017, //www.space.com/26218-astrophysics.html
[174] Ross, Hugh. *Beyond the Cosmos: The Transdimensionality of God, Third Edition* (Covina: RTB Press, 2017).
[175] Ross, "Bringing Every Thought Captive."
[176] Oakman, *The Call of Christ,* 10
[177] Zacharias, Ravi. *Jesus Among Other Gods* (W Publishing Group, 2002), 153. Cited in Muggeridge, "Quote by Malcolm Muggeridge," *Quoty,* www.quoty.org/quote/5688
[178] "I Believe" Anonymous. These words were found scrawled on a cellar wall where Jews had hidden in World War II in Cologne, Germany. //www.outbackpatrol.com.au/god_silent.php
[179] Edwards, Jonathan. *The End for which God Created the World* (Edinburgh: Banner of Truth, 1974), 2:210. Cited in Alcorn, *Heaven,* (Wheaton: Tyndale House Publishers, Inc., 2004), 218.
[180] Sproul. *The Promises of God,* 62, 66.
[181] Murray. *The Two Covenants and The Second Blessing,* 12.
[182] Alcorn. *Heaven,* 172
[183] Storms, Sam. "Joy's Eternal Increase." *desiringGod,* 2003 (an unpublished manuscript on Jonathan Edward's view of heaven). www.desiringgod.org/messages/joys-eternal-increase-edwards-on-the-beauty-of-heaven. Cited in Alcorn, *Heaven,* 172-173.

CHAPTER 22: THE LOVE OF GOD: A TESTIMONY

[184] Faber, Frederick W. "My God How Wonderful Thou Art." 1849, *Hymnary.org.*
[185] Frostenson, Anders. "The Love of God is Broad Like Beach and Meadow." 1968, *Hymnary.org.*
[186] Ruffin, Mike. "Verse of Favorite Hymn Found on Wall In Insane Asylum." *Devotions.com,* 22 February 2003, www.devotions.com/2003/02
[187] ibid.
[188] Glanzer, Ben. MUSIC OF THE MESSAGE: The Story of "The Love of God." *Ministry,* September 1950,

www.ministrymagazine.org/archive/1950/09/the-story-of-the-love-of-god
[189] Lucado. *It's Not About Me*, 141-145.
[190] Bishop, John. *1041 Sermon Illustrations, Ideas and Expositions* (Grand Rapids: Baker Book House, 1952), 213. Cited in Lucado, 71-72.
[191] Jeremiah, David. *A Life Beyond Amazing* (Nashville: W Publishing Group, 2017), 103-104.
[192] Gardner, Marilyn R. "Scratched on the Walls of an Insane Asylum: The Love of God." *communicating.across.boundaries*, 9 September 2012, //communicatingacrossboundariesblog.com/2012/09/09/scratched-on-the-walls-of-an-insane-asylum-the-love-of-god/
[193] Barclay, William. *The Gospel of John Volume 2 (Chapters 8 to 21).* (Philadelphia: The Westminster Press, 1975). See John 11:20-27.
[194] MacDonald, Caroline. *A Gentleman in Prison, The Story of Tokichi Ishii* (George H. Doran Company: New York, 1922), 97. *Archive.org*, www.archive.org/stream/gentlemaninpriso00ishiuoft/gentlemaninpriso00ishiuoft_djvu.txt
[195] Barclay. "Bible Commentaries," John 11.
[196] Barclay, William. *The Mind of Jesus* (HarperSanFrancisco, 1961), 280-281.
[197] Faber, vv. 5-6.

CHAPTER 23: CHRIST IN PRINT
[198] Moody, John. "Priesthood in the Book of Mormon" emailed to author 26 March 2018.
[199] Dickinson, Emily. *The Poems of Emily Dickinson*, (Harvard University Press, 1999), Poem 320. Cited in "There's a Certain Slant of Light, (320)", POETRY FOUNDATION, //www.poetryfoundation.org/poems/45723/theres-a-certain-slant-of-light-320
[200] Shaw, Faye. Email to author dated 2-6-2019.
[201] Treat, Ray. "What is in the Book of Mormon is There for a Purpose," *Recent Book of Mormon Developments, Volume 2*. (Independence, MO: Zarahemla Research Foundation, 1992), 172-3.
[202] Easton, Susan Ward. "Names of Christ in the Book of Mormon." *Ensign*, July 1978. The Church of Jesus Christ of Latter-day Saints, //www.lds.org/ensign/1978/07?lang=eng
[203] Burford, Dwight. *Prayers of Blessing for the Healing and the Gathering of the House of Israel.* (Self-published, 2017), 94.
[204] Moody, John. Email to author dated 2-3-2019.

CHAPTER 24: A COVENANT OF LOVE

[205] Artson, Bradley. "The Jewish Covenant of Love." *HUFFPOST,* 27 February 2012, www.huffingtonpost.com/rabbi-bradley-shavit-artson/jewish-love-covenant_b_1130513.html
[206] Urrutia, Benjamin. "The Name Connection." *New Era,* June 1983, www.lds.org/new-era/1983/06/the-name-connection?lang=eng
[207] Lamb, David. "The Meaning of the Name Mormon." *Recent Book of Mormon Developments, Volume 2* (Independence: Zarahemla Research Foundation, 1992), 45.
[208] ibid.
[209] Snaith, Norman D. "Chesed." *A Theological Word Book of the Bible* (New York: MacMillan, 1951), 136-137. Cited in Michael D. Marlow, "Chesed," *Bible Research.* www.bible-researcher.com/chesed.html
[210] Dulles S.J., Avery. *Models of Revelation* (New York: Doubleday, 1983), 27-28. Cited in Givens, *By the Hand of Mormon,* 210.
[211] Thompson, Charles B. *Evidences in Proof of the Book of Mormon* (Batavia: D.D. Waite, 1841), 149-167. Cited in Givens, *By the Hand of Mormon,* 213.
[212] Thompson, *Evidences,* 86. Cited in Givens, *By the Hand of Mormon,* 149-167.
[213] Gee, Edward. *A Treatise on Prayer* (London: J.M., 1653), 187. Cited in: Givens, *By the Hand of Mormon,* 216; Edward Bickersteth, *A Treatise on Prayer* (American Tract Society), 187.
[214] Givens, Terryl. *By the Hand of Mormon* (Oxford University Press: 2002), 218-219.
[215] Cross, F.L.; Livingstone, E.A. "Prophecy." *Oxford Dictionary of the Christian Church* (Oxford: Oxford University Press, 1997), 1336. Cited in Givens, *By the Hand of Mormon,* 220.
[216] Givens, *By the Hand of Mormon,* 221.
[217] Givens, Terryl. *The Book of Mormon: A Very Short Introduction* (New York: Oxford University Press, Inc., 2009), 17.
[218] Givens. A Very Short Introduction, 18.
[219] ibid., 20.
[220] Givens, *By the Hand of Mormon,* 235.
[221] O'Dea, Thomas F. *The Mormons* (Chicago: University of Chicago Press, 1957), 28, 33. Cited in Grant Hardy, *Understanding the Book of Mormon* (New York: New York, 2010), 5.
[222] Ridenhour, Lynn. Email to author dated December 29, 2018.
[223] Bushman, Richard L. *Joseph Smith and the Beginnings of Mormonism* (University of Illinois Press, 1987), 141. Cited in Patrick McKay, *Witnessing with the Book of Mormon* (self-published, May 2017), 7.
[224] Young, Zina D.H. "How I Gained My Testimony of the Truth." *Young Woman's Journal 4* (April 1983), 318. Cited in McKay, *Witnessing,* 10.

[225] Grow, Matthew J. "The Extraordinary Life of Parley P. Pratt." *Ensign*, April 2007, //www.lds.org/ensign/2007/04/.
[226] Pratt, Parley P. *Autobiography of Parley P. Pratt* (Salt Lake City: Deseret Book Co., 1985), 20. Cited in Givens, *A Very Short Introduction*, 107.
[227] Moody, Theresa Armstrong. *Finding My Way Home* (self-published, 2018), 33-34.
[228] ibid., 34.
[229] ibid., 82.
[230] ibid., 97.
[231] Shaw, Faye. Email to author dated 1/17/2019.
[232] "The Evening and Morning Star," Volume 1.3, 22. Church of Christ, August 1832. www.centerplace.org/history/ems/
[233] Oakman. *The Call of Christ in an Age of Dilemma*, 25.

SELECTED BIBLIOGRAPHY

Times and Seasons. Nauvoo, n.d. 26 January 2019. <http://www.centerplace.org/history/ts/default.htm>.

The Magnificent Grace of God. The Urban Alternative, n.d. CD-ROM.

The Evening and Morning Star August 1832.

"A Moment of Grace." *The New York Times* 17 August 2005.

Against All Odds Israel Survives. Questar Video. Amazon Instant Video, 2006. 5 February 2018. <https://www.amazon.com/>.

Alcorn, Randy. *Heaven*. Wheaton: Tyndale House Publishers, Inc., 2004.

Altrogge, Mark. *The Glorious Life Altering Difference Between Grace and Mercy*. n.d. 27 January 2019. <https://www.biblestudytools.com/blogs/mark-altrogge/the-glorious-life-altering-difference-between-grace-and-mercy.html>.

Artson, Bradley. *The Jewish Covenant of Love*. 27 February 2012. 28 January 2019. <https://www.huffingtonpost.com/rabbi-bradley-shavit-artson/jewish-love-covenant_b_1130513.html>.

Balter, Ariel. *What is Astrophysics?* n.d. 31 January 2019. <https://www.space.com/26218-astrophysics.html>.

Barclay, Robert. *An Apology for the True Christian Divinity*. Farmington: Quaker Heritage Press, 2002 (originally published in 1678).

—. *An Apology for the True Christian Divinity: Being an Explanation and Vindication of the Principles and Doctrines of the People Called Quakers*. n.d. 30 January 2019. <http://lawlibrary.wm.edu/wythepedia/index.php/Apology_for_the_True_Christian_Divinity>.

Barclay, William. "Bible Commentaries: William Barclay's Daily Study Bible." n.d. *StudyLight.org*. 26 January 2019. <https://www.studylight.org/commentaries/dsb.html>.

—. *The Gospel of John Volume 2 (Chapters 8 to 21)*. Revised. Philadelphia: The Westminster Press, 1975.

—. *The Letters to the Galatians and Ephesians*. Ed. Gibson C. L. John. Revised. Westminster John Knox Press, 1976.

—. *The Mind of Jesus*. HarperSanFrancisco (A Division of HarperCollins Publishers), 1961.

Barth, Karl. *The Word of God and The Word of Man*. Trans. Douglas Horton. Harper & Row, 1957.

Bickersteth, Edward. *A Treatise on Prayer; Designed to Assist the Devout in the Discharge of that Duty*. New York: American Tract Society, n.d.

Bishop, John. *1041 Sermon Illustrations, Ideas and Expositions*. Ed. A. Gordon Nasby. Grand Rapids: Baker Book House, 1952.

Black Elk. "The Great Vision." n.d. *First People of America and Canada - Turtle Island*. Ed. John G. Neihardt. 28 January 2019. <https://firstpeople.us/articles/Black-Elk-Speaks/Black-Elk-Speaks-The-Great-Vision.html>.

Bloch, Abraham P. *The Biblical and Historical Background of the Jewish Holy Days*. New York: Ktav Pub House, 1978.

Bolton, Andrew. *SERMON ON THE MOUNT: Foundations for an International Peace Church*. Independence, MO: Herald Publishing House, 1999.

Bringing Every Thought Captive. By Hugh Ross. Dir. Dr. Richard Land. Perf. Hugh Ross. 18 January 2018.

Bruce, John. *Abide in Me - Sermon 2, Lessons from the Vineyard, John 15:4-5*. 25 September 2016. 27 January 2019. <https://vimeo.com/184283720>.

Burford, Dwight. *Prayers of Blessing for the Healing and the Gathering of the House of Israel*. Self-published, 2017.

—. *Why the Book of Mormon is the New Covenant Part 4: The Melchizedek Priesthood*. Self-published, 2018.

Bushman, Richard L. *Joseph Smith and The Beginnings of Mormonism*. University of Illinois Press, 1987.

Cahn, Jonathan. *The Book of Mysteries*. Lake Mary: FrontLine, 2018.

Chesed (חֶסֶד). Ed. Michael D. Marlowe. n.d. 28 January 2019. <www.bible-researcher.com/chesed.html>.

Cole, Stephen J. *Lesson 10: Judged by Your Deeds (Rom. 2:6-11)*. 2013. 26 January 2019. <https://bible.org/seriespage/lesson-10-judged-your-deeds-romans-26-11>.

"Constantine: First Christian Emperor." *Christianity Today* n.d. 26 January 2019. <http://www.christianitytoday.com/history/people/rulers/constantine.html>.

Davey, Stephen. "The Song of Zacharias: Prelude to Bethlehem - Part II." 15 December 2002. *Wisdom for the Heart.* 26 January 2019. <wisdomonline.org>.

Dickinson, Emily. *The Poems of Emily Dickinson*. Ed. R. W. Franklin. Harvard University Press, 1999. 6 February 2019.

Drummond, Henry. *I SAW THE CITY OF GOD*. n.d. 30 January 2019. <//henrydrummond.wwwhubs.com/city.htm>.

—. *The Founding of The Society*. n.d. 26 January 2019. <http://henrydrummond.wwwhubs.com/programme.htm#founding>.

Dulles, S. J., Avery. *Models of Revelation*. New York: Doubleday, 1983.

Easton, Susan Ward. "Names of Christ in the Book of Mormon." *Ensign* July 1978. 6 February 2019.

Edwards, F. Henry. *A New Commentary on the Doctrine and Covenants*. Independence, MO: Herald Publishing House, 1977.

Edwards, Jonathan. *Precious Grace*. n.d. 30 January 2019. <www.tentmaker.org/Quotes/grace_quotes.html>.

Edwards, Jonathan. "The End for which God Created the World." Edwards, Jonathan. *The Works of Jonathan Edwards*. Ed. Edward Hickman. Edinburgh: Banner of Truth, 1974. 976.

"Encyclopedia of Mormonism." n.d. *BYU Library*. Brigham Young University Harold B. Lee Library. 27 January 2019. <https://lib.byu.edu/collections/encyclopedia-of-mormonism/>.

Evans, Tony. *The Magnificent Grace of God*. Dallas, Texas: Urban Alternative, n.d. CD.

—. *The Grace of God*. Chicago: Moody Publishers, 2004.

Faber, Frederick W. *My God How Wonderful Thou Art*. 1849. 28 January 2019. <https://hymnary.org>.

Fenske, Jeff. *The Meaning of Grace*. n.d. 20 September 2018. <(site no longer available)>.

Fowler, James W. *Becoming Adult, Becoming Christian*. San Francisco: Harper & Row, 1984.

Frostenson, Anders. *The Love of God is Broad Like Beach and Meadow*. 1968. 28 January 2019. <https://hymnary.org>.

Gardner, Marilyn. *Scratched on the Walls of an Insane Asylum: The Love of God*. 9 September 2012. 28 January 2019. <https://communicatingacrossboundariesblog.com/2012/09/09/scratched-on-the-walls-of-an-insane-asylum-the-love-of-god/>.

Gee, Edward. *A Treatise on Prayer*. London: J.M., 1653.

Givens, Terryl L. *By the Hand of Mormon*. Oxford University Press, 2002.

Givens, Terryl L. *The Book of Mormon: A Very Short Introduction*. New York: Oxford University Press, Inc., 2009.

Glanzer, Ben. *MUSIC OF THE MESSAGE: The Story of "The Love of God"*. September 1950. 28 January 2019. <https://www.ministrymagazine.org/archive/1950/09/the-story-of-the-love-of-god>.

Grow, Matthew J. "The Extraordinary Life of Parley P. Pratt." *Ensign* April 2007. 29 January 2019. <https://www.lds.org/ensign/2007/04/the-extraordinary-life-of-parley-p-pratt?lang=eng>.

Halter, Ariel. *What is Astrophysics?* 21 December 2017. 28 January 2019. <https://www.space.com/26218-astrophysics.html>.

Hardy, Grant. "Book of Mormon Plates and Records." Ludlow, Daniel H. *Encyclopedia of Mormonism*. Macmillan Publishing Company, 1992. 26 January 2019. <http://eom.byu.edu/index.php/Book_of_Mormon_Plates_and_Records>.

—. *Understanding the Book of Mormon*. New York: Oxford University Press, 2010.

"Hebrew Roots/The Law and the Covenants/Covenants: The Everlasting Covenant." 9 July 2009. *Wikibooks.* 26 January 2019. <https://en.wikibooks.org/wiki/Hebrew_Roots/The_Law_and_the_Covenants/Covenants:The_Everlasting_Covenant>.

Hedges, Brian. *What Does It Mean to Abide in Christ?* 3 March 2014. 27 January 2019. <https://www.christianity.com/bible/bible-study/what-does-it-mean-to-abide-in-christ.html>.

History Of The Church of Jesus Christ of Latter-day Saints. n.d. 25 January 2019. <https://byustudies.byu.edu/history-of-the-church>.

Holland, Jeffrey R. "Be Ye Therefore Perfect - Eventually." October 2017. *General Conference.* The Church of Jesus Christ of Latter-day Saints. 26 January 2019. <https://www.lds.org/general-conference/2017/10/be-ye-therefore-perfect-eventually?lang=eng>.

Jacobs, Joseph, M. Seligsohn and Wilhelm Bacher. *Sinai, Mount.* 1906. 26 January 2019. <http://www.jewishencyclopedia.com/articles/13766-sinai-mount>.

Jeremiah, David. *A Life Beyond Amazing.* Nashville: W Publishing Group, 2017.

—. *Captured by Grace.* Brentwood: Integrity Publishers, 2006. Print.

Joni, Eareckson Tada. *Diamonds in the Dust – 366 Sparkling Devotions.* Zondervan, 1993.

Joseph Smith History, Chapter 1. n.d. 26 January 2019. <https://www.lds.org/scriptures/pgp/js-h/1?lang=eng>.

Judaism. n.d. 26 January 2019. <https://www.britannica.com/topic/Judaism>.

Kynes, William L. "Discipleship or Grace: Must it be One or the Other?" *Knowing & Doing* n.d. 27 January 2019. <http://www.cslewisinstitute.org/Discipleship_or_Grace_Kynes_Single-Page_Full_Article>.

Lamb, David. "The Meaning of the Name Mormon." *Recent Book of Mormon Developments.* Vol. 2. Independence: Zarahemla Research Foundation, 1992. 228.

Lewis, C. S. *Mere Christianity.* Macmillan Publishing Company, 1952.

Lucado, Max. *It's Not About Me*. Nashville: Integrity Publishers, 2004. Print.

Luff, Joseph. "Concerning Our Whereabouts: Watchman, What of the Night." 10 February 1930. 26 January 2019. <http://www.latterdaytruth.org/pdf/100036.pdf>.

MacArthur, John. *Zachariah's Song of Salvation: Introduction*. 18 April 1999. 7 February 2019. <www.gty.org/library/sermons-library/42-16/zachariahs-song-of-salvation-introduction>.

—. *Zachariah's Song of Salvation: The Abrahamic Covenant*. 2 May 1999. 26 January 2019. <https://gty.org/library/sermons-library/42-18/zachariahs-song-of-salvation-the-abrahamic-covenant>.

—. *Zachariah's Song of Salvation: The New Covenant, Part 2*. 23 May 1999. 26 January 2019. <https://www.gty.org/library/sermons-library/42-20/zachariahs-song-of-salvation-the-new-covenant-part-2>.

—. *Zachariah's Song of Salvation: The New Covenant, Part I*. 16 May 1999. 26 January 2019. <https://www.gty.org/library/sermons-library/42-19/zachariahs-song-of-salvation-the-new-covenant-part-1>.

MacDonald, Caroline. *A Gentleman in Prison, The Story of Tokichi Ishii*. 1922. George H. Doran Company. 28 January 2019. <http://www.archive.org/stream/gentlemaninpriso00ishiuoft/gentlemaninpriso00ishiuoft_djvu.txt>.

Mairs, Nancy. *Ordinary Times*. Boston: Beacon Press, 1993.

McKay, Sr., Patrick S. *Healing the Breach*. Lulu Publishing Services, 2018. Print.

—. *Witnessing With The Book of Mormon*. Second. Self-published, 2017.

Medinger, Alan P. "Be Ye Perfect: What Does That Mean?" 1992. *Exodus Global alliance*. 20 March 2018. <https://www.exodusglobalalliance.org/beyeperfectwhatdoesthatmeanp43.php>.

Merriam-Webster.com Dictionary. n.d. 26 January 2019. <https://www.merriam-webster.com/dictionary/>.

Merrill, William Pierson. "Rise up, O Men of God." 1911. 5 February 2018. <https://hymnary.org/text/rise_up_o_men_of_god>.

Meservy, Keith. "Ezekiel's Sticks and the Gathering of Israel." *Ensign* February 1987. 26 January 2019. <https://www.lds.org/ensign/1987/02?lang=eng>.

Millett, Robert L. "The Plates of Brass." *Ensign* January 1988. <https://www.lds.org/ensign/1988/01/the-plates-of-brass-a-witness-of-christ?lang=eng#>.

Moody, John. *Priesthood in the Book of Mormon*. 31 January 2011. Email. 26 March 2018.

—. *Search for the Sacred Record*. Self-published, 2013.

—. *The Failure of the Gentiles and the Restoration of Israel*. Self-published (contact John Moody at heartbeat816@aol.com), 2006.

—. *The Inspired Version - Stick of Judah*. Self-published, 2012.

Moody, Theresa Armstrong. *Finding My Way Home*. Ed. John Moody. Self-published (contact John Moody at heartbeat816@aol.com), 2018.

Muehlenberg, Bill. *Modern-Day Marcionism*. 27 February 2012. 28 January 2019. <https://billmuehlenberg.com/?s=modern-day+marcionism>.

Muggeridge, Malcolm. *Quote by Malcolm Muggeridge*. n.d. 27 January 2019. <http://www.quoty.org/quote/5688>.

Murray, Andrew. *The Two Covenants and The Second Blessing*. New York: Fleming H. Revell Company, 1898. Web. <https://archive.org/details/twocovenantsseco00murr>.

Nunn, T. Royal. *Covenants of the Lord: Bonded in Blood*. Independence: Self-published, 2006 Revised 2013.

Oakman, Arthur A. *The Call of Christ in an Age of Dilemma*. Independence: Herald Publishing House, 1964.

O'Dea, Thomas F. *The Mormons*. Chicago: University of Chicago Press, 1957.

Ortberg, John. *FLOW*. Carol Stream, 2005. CD-ROM. 20 September 2018.

Pierson, A. T. *Ephesians 3:8-9 Commentary*. 15 May 2018. 27 January 2019. <http://www.preceptaustin.org/ephesians_38-9>.

Piper, John. *Grace is Pardon - And Power*. n.d. 26 January 2019. <https://www.desiringgod.org/articles/grace-is-pardon-and-power>.

Pratt, Parley P. *Autobiography of Parley P. Pratt*. Ed. Parley P. Pratt. Salt Lake City: Deseret Book Company, 1985.

"Prophecy." *Oxford Dictionary of the Christian Church*. Ed. F. L. Cross and E. A. Livingstone. New York, 1997.

Pumphrey, Clint. "How the Greatest Generation Works." n.d. *howstuffworks*. 26 January 2019. <https://people.howstuffworks.com/culture-traditions/generation-gaps/greatest-generation2.htm>.

Read, Lenet Hadley. "The Golden Plates and the Feast of Trumpets." *Ensign* January 2000. <www.lds.org/ensign/>.

Religion: Three Religions, One God. n.d. 26 January 2019. <https://www.pbs.org/wgbh/globalconnections/mideast/themes/religion/index.html>.

Reynolds, Noel B. *Understanding the Abrahamic Covenant through the Book of Mormon*. 01 March 2017. 26 January 2019. <http://hdl.lib.byu.edu/1877/3771>.

Ross, Hugh. *Beyond the Cosmos: The Transdimensionality of God, Third Edition*. Covina: RTB Press, 2017. Print.

Ruffin, Mike. *Verse of Favorite Hymn Found on Wall In Insane Asylum*. 22 February 2003. 22 February 2019. <http://www.devotions.com/2003/02>.

Rupe, Richard E. *Book of Mormon Insights: God's Plan of Salvation*. Self-published, 2016. Print.

Sayers, Dorothy L. *Christian Letters to a Post-Christian World*. Grand Rapids: Erdmans, 1969.

Shoemaker, H. Stephen. *Finding Jesus in His Prayers*. Nashville: Abingdon Press, 2004.

Smith, Heman C. *History of the Reorganized Church of Jesus Christ of Latter Day Saints*. 4 (first four volumes) vols. Independence: Herald Publishing House, 1896. 26 January 2019. <RestoredGospel.com>.

Smith, Jr., Joseph. "An Epitome of Faith and Doctrine." *Times and Seasons* 1 March 1842. 26 January 2019. <http://www.centerplace.org/history/ts/v3n09.htm>.

Snaith, Norman D. "Chesed." *A Theological Word Book of the Bible*. Ed. Alan Richardson. New York: MacMillan, 1951.

Sperling, Harry, Maurice Simon and Paul P. Levertoff, *The Zohar*. 5 vols. New York: Benet, 1958.

Sperry, Sidney B. *Answers to Book of Mormon Questions*. Salt Lake City: Bookcraft, 1967.

Spielberg, Nancy. *Precious Grace*. n.d. 30 January 2019. <http://www.tentmaker.org/Quotes/grace_quotes.html>.

Sproul, R.C. *The Promises of God*. Colorado Springs, CO: David C. Cook, 2013.

—. "What is the Covenant of Redemption?" 5 March 2018. *Ligonier Ministries.* 26 January 2019. <https://ligonier.org/blog/what-covenant-redemption/>.

Storms, Sam. *Joy's Eternal Increase: Edwards on the Beauty of Heaven*. n.d. 31 January 2019. <https://www.desiringgod.org/messages/joys-eternal-increase-edwards-on-the-beauty-of-heaven>.

"The Mediator of the Covenant." *Present Truth Magazine* 4 November 2016. <http://www.presenttruthmag.com/archive/XXVIII/28p1-9.htm>.

There's a Certain Slant of Light, (320). Ed. Michael Slosek. n.d. 6 February 2019. <www.poetryfoundation.org>.

Thompson, Charles B. *Evidences in Proof of the Book of Mormon Being a Divinely Inspired Record*. Batavia: D. D. Waite, 1841.

THOUGHTS FROM GOD, BIBLICAL GRACE. n.d. 10 December 2018. <(website no longer valid as of 1/27/19)>.

Treat, Ray. "The Hidden Principle: Come Unto Christ." n.d. *Zarahemla Research Foundation.* <http://restoredcovenant.org/Default.asp?CAT=Covenant>.

Treat, Ray. "What is in the Book of Mormon is There for a Purpose." *Recent Book of Mormon Developments, Volume 2*. Zarahemla Research Foundation, 1992.

Tripp, Leo. *The Complete Book of Jewish Observance*. Behrman House Publishing/Summit Books, 1980.

Turner, Tina. "What's Love Got to Do with It?" *Private Dancer*. By Terry Britten and Lyle Graham. Prod. Terry Britten. 1984. 31 January 2019. <https://genius.com/Tina-turner-whats-love-got-to-do-with-it-lyrics>.

Tvedtnes, John A. "The Higher and Lesser Laws." *Revelation, Reason and Faith, Essays in Honor of Truman Madsen*. Ed. Donald W. Parry, Daniel C. Peterson and Stephen D. Ricks. Neal A. Maxwell Institute for Religious Scholarship (FARMS), 2002. 808. 26 January 2019. <https://publications.mi.byu.edu/fullscreen/?pub=1122&index=16>.

Urrutia, Benjamin. "The Name Connection." *New Era* June 1983. 28 January 2019. <https://www.lds.org/new-era/1983/06/the-name-connection?lang=eng>.

Yancey, Philip. *What's So Amazing About Grace*. Grand Rapids, MI: Zondervan Publishing House, 1997.

Young, Zina D. H. "How I Gained My Testimony of the Truth." *Young Woman's Journal* 4 (1893).

Zacharias, Ravi. *Jesus Among Other Gods*. W Publishing Group, 2002.

About the Author

Richard (Rich) Rupe is a life-long member of the Reorganized Church of Jesus Christ of Latter Day Saints (now known as the Community of Christ) and has a church heritage dating back to the early days of the Reorganization. Richard has a Bachelor of Arts degree with a major in Business Administration from Park University. He has authored two previous books: ***The Book of Mormon: An Inconvenient Truth*** and ***Book of Mormon Insights: God's Plan of Salvation***. He has served the church in many capacities over the years and currently is a member of the First People Congregation of the Community of Christ, non-geographic congregation involved in Native American ministries.

Rich had been a computer analyst/programmer for most of his working career. When he retired in 2004, his plan was to relax, play golf and travel. It was about that time that he began pondering the changes that had occurred in the RLDS institutional church and the very foundations of his beliefs. Rich felt motivated to examine the pros and cons of the Book of Mormon, as he realized that this book was the heart of the truthfulness of the latter day work. That search produced an affirmation of his faith and his first book: ***An Inconvenient Truth.*** A few years later he wrote his second book, ***God's Plan of Salvation.***

During his retirement years, Rich has managed to play golf once, for nine holes. He likes to say that he had plans for his life, but God had other plans. Rich's testimony is that his ministry of writing is what God had in mind for his life all along, and it is the fulfillment of his grandmother's dream. When he was only a very small child she dreamt that one day when standing in the pulpit, he would hold up the Three Books of the church and say, **"These three books are true, especially the red letters."**

Contact Information

The author may be contacted via email at:
bomplaninsights@gmail.com

Made in the USA
Coppell, TX
21 December 2019